California Politics

Fifth Edition

California Politics

A Primer

Fifth Edition

Renée B. Van Vechten
University of Redlands

Los Angeles | London | New Delhi
Singapore | Washington DC | Melbourne

FOR INFORMATION:

CQ Press

An Imprint of SAGE Publications, Inc.

2455 Teller Road

Thousand Oaks, California 91320

E-mail: order@sagepub.com

SAGE Publications Ltd.

1 Oliver's Yard

55 City Road

London, EC1Y 1SP

United Kingdom

SAGE Publications India Pvt. Ltd.

B 1/I 1 Mohan Cooperative Industrial Area

Mathura Road, New Delhi 110 044

India

SAGE Publications Asia-Pacific Pte. Ltd.

3 Church Street

#10-04 Samsung Hub

Singapore 049483

Acquisitions Editor: Monica Eckman

Editorial Assistant: Zachary Hoskins

Content Development Editor: Anna Villarruel

Production Editor: Karen Wiley

Copy Editor: Michelle Ponce

Typesetter: Hurix Digital

Proofreader: Laura Webb

Indexer: Kathy Paparchontis

Cover Designer: Michael Dubowe

Marketing Manager: Erica DeLuca

Library of Congress Cataloging-in-Publication Data

Names: Van Vechten, Renee, author.

Title: California politics : a primer / Renee B. Van Vechten.

Description: Fifth edition. | Thousand Oaks, California : CQ Press, 2018. | Includes bibliographical references and index.

Identifiers: LCCN 2017042444 | ISBN 9781506380353 (pbk. : alk. paper)

Subjects: LCCH: California—Politics and government.

Classification: LCC JK8716 .V36 2018 | DDC 320.4794—dc23

LC record available at https://lccn.loc.gov/2017042444

This book is printed on acid-free paper.

18 19 20 21 22 10 9 8 7 6 5 4 3 2 1

Contents

About the Author

Renée Bukovchik Van Vechten is a professor of political science at the University of Redlands. She earned a B.A. in political science from the University of San Diego and a Ph.D. from the University of California, Irvine. Van Vechten's political science research examines legislative processes and behavior, including the impacts of political reforms such as term limits. She teaches courses on American institutions such as Congress, reform politics, and California politics. Her expertise on state-level politics and policy is evident in her textbook, *California Politics: A Primer*, and she has a chapter in *Civic Engagement in Political Science*. Her scholarship on pedagogy and instructional practices has extended to research methods, online discussion forums, simulations, and internships. Van Vechten is serving a three-year term as a member of the APSA Council and Executive Board, as chair of the Teaching and Learning Policy Committee. She served as chair of the APSA Political Science Education organized member section from 2013 to 2015. She was the section's program chair for the 2013 annual meeting, and has been a track moderator for the APSA Teaching and Learning Conference (2014–2016). Service to the association includes membership on awards committees and the Presidential Task Force on Technology (2015–2016), and helping to facilitate the transfer of sponsorship of the *Journal of Political Science Education* to APSA. Van Vechten is also active in the Western Political Science Association, having co-chaired a conference-within-a-conference on teaching and learning (2015, 2016, 2018). She has received several teaching awards, including the Rowman and Littlefield Award for Innovative Teaching in Political Science (via APSA) in 2008, APSA's only national teaching award at that time. She is frequently consulted by local media for commentary about state and national politics.

Preface

California is a seductress. She coaxes the optimistic to rebuild after wildfires ravage their neighborhoods, and she entices struggling immigrants, middle class families, college students, and "Dreamers" to imagine a better life. The golden sun may not shine brightly for all, but the allure of undiscovered riches still arouses hopes, dreams, and plans.

California's elected leaders are also dazzled by her alchemy. The state's economy has continued to improve and buoy the nation's fortunes, and legislators continue to pass laws that enrich its reputation as an extraordinary, exceptional state where "big things happen." Legislators are attempting to outshine the federal government in areas such as climate change policy and clean energy production; they have partnered with Governor Jerry Brown to make California a global leader in the fight against climate change by extending the state's cap-and-trade program to 2030, tightening greenhouse gas emissions, and imposing a range of measures on businesses and consumers to help "green" the state. Recreational use of marijuana became legal in 2018, and lawmakers have provided the legal framework for implementing the ballot initiative that voters approved in 2016. More boldly, Democratic leaders of the Assembly and Senate have joined executive branch officials in subverting federal policies that they view as inhumane and detrimental, declaring the state a sanctuary for non-violent undocumented immigrants. With the election of Donald Trump to the U.S. presidency, California elected officials have burnished the state's reputation for resistance.

Exceptionalism seems to run in California's political blood, and these political developments reinforce the view that California occupies a class of its own. However, the daily challenges of running what is effectively one of the world's largest countries are enough to take the shine off the Golden State's reputation for being a land where dreams come true. The grinding work of government is nowhere more apparent than in the struggle to fund California's crumbling system of roads and highways with a gas tax that is resented by citizens and business owners alike. Even as lawmakers reach consensus about how to best address a persistent problem, the people do not always trust the decisions of their full-time representatives.

Are Californians exceptional in their distrust of government? Do Californians use political power differently than citizens of other states? How extraordinary is California politics, really? This short text, *California Politics: A Primer*, attempts to outline the puzzle that is California politics, providing readers with analytical tools to piece together an answer to these broad questions. By emphasizing how history, political culture, rules, and institutions influence choices that lie at the heart of governing, the text moves beyond mere recitation of facts, pressing the reader to think about how these forces conspire to shape politics today and how they will determine the state of affairs tomorrow. It asks the reader to consider what exceptional politics is and isn't, and what can be accomplished within the context of state politics.

Because this book is intended to provide the essentials of California politics, brevity and breadth eclipse detail and depth. The following pages form a tidy snapshot of how the state is governed and how its politics work. Timely examples succinctly clarify trends and concepts, but to limit the book's length, some developments are given only brief attention or a passing mention. Instructors may seize on these mentions as cues for further elaboration in class. Strong visuals in the form of figures, charts, graphs, maps, and photos also allow readers to discern the basics quickly, but readers should also take time to uncover the clues to understanding politics and tease out the rich patterns contained in these illustrations and in the accompanying captions. Some of these graphics, such as the cartograms, suggest to the reader novel ways of perceiving current trends.

What's New to the Fifth Edition

The thoroughly updated text covers recent policy developments and is informed by scholarly research on comparative state politics and the most current government reports available. Focus has shifted onto California's place in a federal system and state leaders' pointed resistance to the policies endorsed by President Donald Trump and his appointees. Particular attention has been paid to immigration and the environment, including California's sanctuary state status, greenhouse gas emissions regulations stemming from AB 32, and water and drought-related issues and fixes. These policies—and also those relating to prison reform and housing, among others—have become increasingly salient as measures of California's perceived exceptionalism, a status reinforced by bold measures that sometimes render the state a leader, and at other times, an outlier. It should be noted that to conserve space, these policy discussions have been woven into relevant chapters instead of having been sliced off into a standalone chapter dedicated to policy issues. Electoral innovations that have taken root are also described in several chapters (principally Chapter 9); some of these include the Top Two Primary; a series of changes to encourage higher voter registration and participation, including all vote-by-mail elections; the emerging impacts of restructured term limits; and expanded coverage of the citizen-led decennial redistricting process.

With a nod to the importance of political geography, a new section in Chapter 10 briefly explores how distinct segments of the population are primed for political engagement or disaffection. The "Five Californias" schema (a product of the Measure of America program series produced by the Social Science Research Council and developed by researchers Sarah Burd-Sharps and Kristen Lewis in *A Portrait of California*) helps the reader understand how human development is related to opportunity and political participation. Further, informative maps have been refreshed and a map of the state's proposed high-speed rail project has been added, and graphics have been updated for this edition wherever possible, incorporating data releases by the U.S. Census Bureau, state agencies, and public affairs research organizations.

Many of the current graphics are incorporated into PowerPoint lecture slides that are designed to provide instructors with helpful guidance and guideposts for classroom instruction. Instructors should go to http://study.sagepub.com/california5e to register and download materials, including:

- A test bank, available in Respondus, offers a diverse set of test questions for every chapter to help effectively assess students' progress and understanding.
- Editable, chapter-specific Microsoft® PowerPoint® slides offer you complete flexibility in easily creating a multimedia presentation for your course.
- All graphics from the book, in PowerPoint, PDF, and JPG, are available for use while lecturing, in discussion groups, or for importing into test material.

Finally, for the first time, key terms are indicated with bold lettering in the text and are listed, with definitions, at the end of each chapter. Terms that may be considered secondary in importance are italicized.

Acknowledgments

The clean and vigorous style in which this book is written is meant to prime the reader for engaged discussions about California politics now and hereafter. An expert (and exceedingly patient) crew at CQ Press initiated this ongoing conversation about California politics, namely Charisse Kiino, executive director extraordinaire; Nancy Matuszak, who shepherded this book carefully and skillfully for the last three editions and is hereby honored as an Adventurous Gastronome; Elise Frasier, who has earned my undying admiration for her expertise and incisiveness, synergetic spirit, and can-do attitude; and a masterful production, marketing, and content development team that includes Michelle Ponce, Elise Frasier, Zachary Hoskins, Karen Wiley, and Anna Villarruel. The book's continued success is testament to their professional prowess. I also extend sincere thanks to those colleagues who have taken the time to provide essential feedback on previous editions, as well as numerous reviewers whose insights and advice provided the thrust for improvements: David Fisk, UC-San Diego; Herbert E. Gooch III, California Lutheran University; Richard Groper, CSULA; Robert P. Hager, Jr., Los Angeles Mission College; Maria Sampanis, CSU Sacramento; Ronnee Schreiber, San Diego State University; and James Starkey, Long Beach City College. My boundless thanks also goes to the many extraordinary public employees of California who helped provide critical source material for the book, from the staff of the Legislative Analyst's Office to the Senate and Assembly standing committee staff and many in between. I salute Darren Chesin, Randy Chinn, and Brian Ebbert for their inexhaustible "institutional memory," which they have been willing to share with me; the insights and friendship of Patrick Johnston, Rick Battson, Alison Dinmore, and Mark Stivers continue to help clarify my thoughts, research, theorizing, and writing about California politics immeasurably, and make my visits to Sacramento feel familiar and welcoming. Many thanks as well to Cheryl Schmidt, and also Dean Bonner and his colleagues at the Public Policy Institute of California for their first-rate research and assistance. The inimitable Bill Stokes remains a peerless Sacramento host, jazz virtuoso, and holy reverend Irishman who has made every Sacramento adventure well worth the trip. I cherish my community of teacher-scholars at the University of Redlands, and I am blessed with a supportive community of friends and a loving family, foremost among them my awe-inspiring husband, Charlie, who has been my sunlight in shadowy times, an inspirational parent, a brilliant businessman, caring confidant, and the person to whom this effort is dedicated. I also thank my late mom, Ann, and dad, Joe, beautiful, faithful, and giving exemplars who taught me to find happiness in living each day to its fullest; my mother-in-law, Ruth, whose generosity and sense of style are as yet unmatched and who is still too young to have three great-grandchildren; my natural sorority sisters, Elise, Natasha, Juleann, and Magdalena; and my Ava and Zachary, whose astounding artwork, design sense, ecology efforts, trick shot videos, and political awareness bring smiles to my soul, and who make this state a richer, more golden place.

Introduction

As if the State of California weren't exceptional enough, it could be considered one of the largest countries in the world. Only five other nations had a larger gross domestic product than California in 2016, and its $2.6 trillion economy rivals those of France and India.[1] With a population nearing 40 million, the state boasts 4 million more people than Canada.[2] California houses more billionaires than in Hong Kong and Moscow combined.[3] Its territorial spread includes breathtaking coastlines, fertile farmland both natural and human made, one of the globe's hottest deserts, the highest and lowest points in the continental United States, dense urban zones, twenty-one mountain ranges, and ancient redwood forests—a resource-rich expanse with 1,100 miles of coastline and an area that could accommodate a dozen east coast states.

California's reputation for being the "great exception" among the American states has intensified since the political journalist Carey McWilliams characterized it that way in 1949. The state is an exaggeration; it sparks global trends, and national and world issues permeate the state's politics. Immigration, climate change, civil rights, terrorism, pandemics, economic tides, and waves of social issues push and pull on those who make policy decisions for one of the world's most diverse political communities. Unlike most democratic governments, however, elected officials share responsibility for policymaking with ordinary Californians who make laws through the initiative process at the state and local levels. This **hybrid political system** (a combination of direct and representative democracy) provides an outlet for voters' general distrust of politicians and dissatisfaction with representative government and enables the electorate to reshape it over time. If **politics** is a process through which people with differing goals and ideals try to manage their conflicts by working together to allocate values for society—which requires bargaining and compromise—then California's system is especially vulnerable to repeated attempts to fix what's perceived as broken, and parts of it may be periodically upended. For more than 100 years, the initiative process has permitted voters, wealthy corporations, and interest groups to perform a series of historical experiments on the state's political system, from rebooting elections to retuning taxation rates to refashioning the legislature through term limits. Some of these reforms, which are discussed throughout this book, are celebrated as triumphs. Proposition 13 in 1978, for example, deflated ballooning property tax rates for homeowners (now limited to 1 percent of the property's sale price) and arrested rate increases, an arrangement that voters guard watchfully to this day. On the other hand, direct democracy tends to promote all-or-nothing solutions that have been fashioned through a process devoid of bargaining and compromise, two hallmarks of democratic lawmaking.

Reforms also tend to produce unanticipated consequences that demand further repairs. Property owners may covet the low property tax rates that Prop 13 guarantees, but it has led to chronic underfunding of education and heavy reliance on user fees for public services, as well as unequal tax bills across every neighborhood. Local governments still face a backlog of critical infrastructure projects that continues to swell along with the population. Meanwhile, citizens' general disdain for taxes and politicians persists.

California's bulging population ensures that public policy issues exist on a massive scale. More than one of every eight U.S. residents lives in California, and one of every four Californians is foreign-born—the largest percentage among the states. Among them are approximately 2.5 million undocumented immigrants.[4] Prisons have shrunk by tens of thousands over the last few years as, under federal court order, many nonviolent criminals have been shifted to county jails and paroled, but California's criminal population is second only to that of Texas in size, with over 130,000 in custody and another 50,000 under some form of correctional control. In 2010, just over 10 percent of the population was over age 65; that percentage will double by 2030.[5]

Extreme weather events merely reinforce California's distinctiveness. After five long years of drought, during which time California confronted the driest winter in 500 years with desperate conservation efforts, storms in 2017 replenished the Sierra snowpack, filling those reservoirs to 190% of normal in one of the wettest winters on record. Ski season in the Sierra Nevada mountains extended into August. The lasting effects of drought, however, can be seen in the state's stricken forests, where more than 100 million dead trees have elevated the risk of both erosion and wildfires that can transform whole regions into catastrophic infernos.[6] It's also visible in the continued overpumping of groundwater that has caused land to sink faster than ever, a phenomenon called *subsidence* that buckles roads, irrigation canals, bridges, and pipes, costing state and local governments millions to fix. The detrimental effects of flooding are also painfully apparent in infrastructure failures such as the Oroville Dam, whose spillways buckled under torrential rains in 2017 and ultimately will cost about $500 million to restore.[7]

The drought may have ended, but the fights over water that continue to rage are unlike those anywhere in the United States. Farmers in the Central Valley are jockeying for the same water that helps feed Southern California, and they are pitted against environmentalists over how much flow should be diverted to replenish the failing Delta ecosystem, the complex Sacramento–San Joaquin River Delta estuary located east of San Francisco. Meanwhile, Governor Brown has endorsed the building of 35-mile-long, four-story high "twin tunnels" to send Sacramento River water underneath the imperiled Delta to the South and inland farms, at a cost of an estimated $16 billion (to be covered by water users, not the state).[8] This controversial project, named California WaterFix, whose price tag is three times the size of many states' entire annual budgets, demonstrates the magnitude of issues in

FIGURE 1.1 Gross Domestic Product, 2016 (in millions)

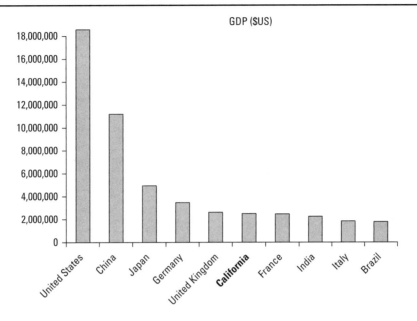

GDP ($US)

Sources: Legislative Analyst's Office, "California's Economy: One of the Largest in the World," http://www.lao.ca.gov/Publications/Report/3511; The World Bank, "Gross Domestic Product, 2016," http://databank.worldbank.org/data/download/GDP.pdf.

California. WaterFix has absorbed decades of planning, would require at least a decade of construction, and involves government agencies at all levels. It directly affects major sectors of the state, from industries such as agribusiness to the environment to 25 million residents, among them powerful stakeholders who want either to kill, reshape, or advance this project in ways that will maximize their own interests. In fall 2017, water agencies responsible for financing the project began to pull out of the deal, possibly dooming it to failure. The project demonstrates the hazards of shifting from the status quo when big money and high-powered interests are at stake.

The availability, cost, distribution, storage, and cleanliness of freshwater represent a fraction of the complex, interrelated issues that state and local elected officials deal with year round, a pile of "to-do's" that grows unceasingly. Water-related concerns are merely one dimension of climate change, a large-scale phenomenon that also intensifies wildfires, alters delicate ecosystems, spawns invasive pests that carry infectious diseases, and affects whether California can produce the craft beer, wines, and food that the world enjoys. Californians also face a daunting list of sustainability challenges brought about by natural population growth and immigration, while deteriorating roads, bridges, storm drains, water storage, sewage treatment facilities, schools, and jails compete for the public's limited attention and money. Developing new affordable housing, expanding broadband access, and installing infrastructure for zero-emissions vehicles are also on the state's wish list. Current infrastructure needs are estimated to exceed $500 billion, and waiting to make repairs merely increases the bills as problems worsen

THE FOUR SEASONS iN CALiFORNiA

EARTHQUAKE

BRUSHFiRE

MUDSLiDE

BUT HEY, THE HARMONIC KARMA IN THIS PLACE AND THE SUNSETS? WOW, AWESOME!

DENiAL

over time.[9] (Formidable public policy issues such as these are catalogued in the concluding chapter.)

Whether the goal is reducing college fees for students or restricting offshore oil drilling, different interests compete through the political process to get what they want. Governing officials weigh private against public interests, and generally they work hard to fix problems experienced by their constituents—a job that also requires them to balance the needs of their own districts against those of their city, county, or the entire state. This grand balancing act is but one reason politics often appears irrational and complex, but, like the U.S. government, California's system was designed that way, mostly through deliberate choice but also through the unintended consequences of prior decisions. California's puzzle of governing institutions reflects repeated attempts to manage conflicts that result from millions of people putting demands on a system that creates both winners and losers—not all of whom give up quietly when they lose. As happens at the federal level, state officials tend to respond to the most persistent, organized, and well-funded members of society; on the other hand, losers in California can reverse their fortunes by skillfully employing the tools of direct democracy to sidestep elected officials altogether.

Principles for Understanding California Politics

It may seem counterintuitive given the complexity of its problems, but California politics can be explained and understood logically—although political outcomes are just as often frustrating and irresponsible as they are praiseworthy and necessary. In short, six fundamental concepts—choice, political culture, institutions, collective action, rules, and history—can help us understand state politics just as they help us understand national or even local democratic politics. These concepts are employed throughout this book to explain how Californians and their representatives make governing decisions and to provide a starting point for evaluating California's political system: does it work as intended? Do citizens have realistic expectations about what problems government can solve, the services or values it provides, and how efficiently or cheaply it can do so? How do we measure "successful" politics, and how does California's political system compare to others?

Choices: At the Heart of Politics. Our starting point is the premise that *choices* are at the heart of politics. Citizens make *explicit* political choices when they decide not to participate in an election or when they cast a vote, but they also make *implicit* political choices when they send their children to private schools or refill a water bottle instead of buying a new one. Legislators' jobs consist of a series

BOX 1.1 Comparative FAST FACTS on California

	California	Texas	United States
Capital:	Sacramento	Austin	Washington, DC
Statehood:	September 9, 1850 (31st state)	December 29, 1845 (28th state)	Declared independence from Great Britain July 4, 1776
Number of U.S. House members:	53	36	435
Number of counties:	58	254	50 states
Largest city by population:**	Los Angeles, 4,042,000*	Houston, 2,100,000	New York, 8,175,000
Total population:	39,542,000*	27,862,596	323,127,513
Percentage of foreign-born persons:***	27.3%	16.8%	13.4%
Median annual household income:**	$61,818	$53,207	$53,889
Percentage of persons living below poverty level:**	16.3%	17.3%	15.5%

*California Department of Finance, "California Grew by 335,000 Residents in 2016," press release (May 1, 2017), http://www.dof.ca.gov/research/demographic/reports/estimates/e-1/documents/E-1_2017PressRelease.pdf. The U.S. Census Bureau estimated the figure to be 39,250,017 as of July 1, 2016.

**Current U.S. and Texas demographic and population figures based on U.S. 2010 census, monthly population estimates as of July 1, 2016. U.S. Census Bureau, American FactFinder, "Community Facts: Population Estimates of the Resident Population: 2016 Population Estimates (July 1, 2016)."

***For percentage of foreign-born persons, Source: Pew Research Center, "Characteristics of the U.S. Foreign-Born Population: 2015; Table 45, Nativity, by State," http://www.pewhispanic.org/2017/05/03/statistical-portrait-of-the-foreign-born-population-in-the-united-states-2015.

Ethnic Makeup of California:

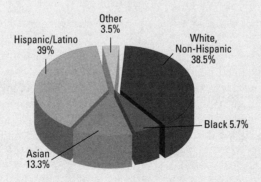

California, 2015

- Other 3.5%
- White, Non-Hispanic 38.5%
- Black 5.7%
- Asian 13.3%
- Hispanic/Latino 39%

Sources: California Department of Finance, http://www.dof.ca.gov/Reports/Demographic_Reports/documents/2011ACS_1year_Rpt_CA.pdf, p. 3. Based on American Community Survey, 2011 one-year report.

of choices that involve choosing what to say, which issues to ignore, whose recommendations to take, which phone calls to return, and how to word a law or cast a vote.

Political Culture: Collective Attitudes and Beliefs about the Role of Government. In large and diverse societies that are crammed with people who are motivated by different goals, interests, and values, a successful political system provides a process for narrowing choices to a manageable number and allows many participants to reconcile their differences as they make choices together. The decisions and customs that emerge from this process generally express the attitudes, beliefs, norms, and values about government that a political majority holds and give their governing system a distinct culture—a **political culture** that varies from state to state. As compared to Texans or Nevadans, Californians tend to be more willing to regulate businesses in favor of workers and the environment and to offer public programs that include those at the margins of society. Three other features that define California's political culture are a historical fondness for reforming government through ballot measures, a preference for Democratic officials but general detachment from political parties, and a willingness to use state regulatory power—themes that will resurface throughout this book as we examine California's exceptionalism.

Institutions: Organizations and Systems that Help People Solve Collective Action Problems. Political systems also facilitate compromises, trade-offs, and bargains that lead to acceptable solutions or alternatives. Institutions help organize this kind of action. Political **institutions** are organizations built to manage conflict by defining particular roles and rules for those who participate in them. In short, they bring people together to solve problems on behalf of society, enabling the official use of power and authority. Election systems are a good example: there are rules about who can vote and who can run for office, how the process will be controlled, and how disputes resulting from them will be resolved. Through institutions like elections, **collective action**—working together for mutual benefit—can take place. The same can be said of other institutions such as traffic courts and political parties; in each setting, people work together to solve their problems and allocate goods for a society. It should be noted, however, that the use of power and authority through political institutions can benefit some and harm others; fair and equal outcomes are not automatically ensured through democratic institutions.

Rules: Codes or Regulations Defining How Governing Power May Be Used. Rules also matter. Rules are authoritative statements, codes, or regulations that define who possesses the power to help govern and how they may legitimately use it, and rules create incentives for action or inaction. Rules are framed in constitutions; they may be expressed as laws or in administrative rules, executive orders, or court opinions, for example. Unwritten rules, also known as **norms**, also guide behavior, and daily interactions help enforce what is expected and acceptable, as reflected in the degree of civility among politicians. For instance, in the legislature, if one party reaches supermajority status (as was the case in 2016 when Democrats controlled both houses), the minority party is rendered virtually powerless because their votes are not needed to pass special bills or taxes that require approval by two-thirds of the membership.

History: The Past Helps Set the Terms of the Present. Rules are also the results of choices made throughout history, and over time a body of rules will change and grow in response to cultural shifts, influential leaders, natural disasters, scandals, economic trends, and other forces—some gradual, some sudden—creating further opportunities and incentives for political action. Enormous economic tides that define eras (think "The Great Recession" or "The Great Depression") exert especially disruptive forces in politics because behemoth governments are not designed to respond nimbly to rapid and unanticipated changes; budgets and programs are planned months and years in advance, with history providing clues to decision makers about probable developments. Sudden readjustments, particularly those made in hard times, will reverberate far into the future.

Thus, recognizing that both choices and the rules that condition them are made within a given historical context goes a long way toward explaining each state's distinctive political system. A state's political culture also contributes to that distinctiveness. These are the elements that make New York's state government so different from the governments of Oregon, Georgia, and every other state, and we should keep them in mind as we consider how California's governing institutions developed, and whether California belongs in a class of its own. In essence, a unique set of rules, its culture, and its history are key to understanding California politics. They help explain the relationship between Californians and their government, how competing expectations about "successful" politics propel change, and why elected officials can have a hard time running the state.

For years, online bloggers to *New York Times* editors opined that California was on the brink of collapse, that it was "ungovernable," but those critiques faded as the economy improved, bond debt was reduced through accelerated repayments, and balanced, on-time budgets materialized on Governor Jerry Brown's watch. Through mid-2017, state government had regained some of the people's trust, with about half of adult Californians approving of the legislature's job (51 percent) and about 55 percent believing that the state was going in the right direction.[10] Approval ratings are always subject to change, however, and loathsome tax increases—such as the 12-cent per gallon increase in the state gas tax enacted by SB1 in 2017—pose direct threats to legislators' popularity.

Californians resemble most Americans in their general aversion to politics and feeling over-taxed,[11] and yet they have found new ways to distinguish themselves from the rest of the country. More than 61.7 percent of Californians voted for Democratic presidential candidate Hillary Clinton in 2016, repudiating candidate Trump (only Hawaii was higher, at 62.2 percent).[12] California is among the first states to legally recognize a third gender option, enabling persons who identify as intersex to mark "X" instead of male or female on official documents. California was the first state to legalize marijuana use for medical purposes in 1996 but behind several states in 2016 when voters approved its recreational use. In defiance of Trump administration policies that are perceived to be anti-environment, state lawmakers and city leaders have fortified carbon emissions standards, invested more in "green" energy, and recommitted to combating climate change through subnational agreements such as Under2MOU, an agreement forged by a group of regional leaders who are committed to keeping climate change under 2 degrees Celsius. Dissenting with the Trump administration on immigration, they have denounced a proposed border wall, filed lawsuits on behalf of "Dreamers" (children who were brought to the United States illegally and grew up in the country without formal legal status), provided state funds to defend undocumented immigrants in federal deportation proceedings, and barred state and local governments from using personal information to create religious registries of any kind. Most controversially, they declared the state a "sanctuary" for nonviolent, noncriminal undocumented immigrants. As a sanctuary state, local and state law enforcement officials are prohibited from expending their resources to help federal agents enforce deportations with certain exceptions. Public safety considerations were built into the sanctuary state law signed by Jerry Brown in 2017, such that local police have discretion to hold violent felons

Renée B. Van Vechten

The California state capitol building in Sacramento

for federal authorities, immigration agents may interview jailed individuals, and certain database information may be shared with immigration agents. Otherwise, state officials will not aid the Department of Homeland Security in targeting undocumented persons—such as parents, students, and children—for removal from the United States. In response, federal officials have vowed to withhold federal funds from California should it continue to resist national arrest and deportation policies—a penalty that became less likely when a federal judge in late 2017 blocked President Trump's executive order to deny funding to sanctuary cities.[13]

These livewire issues demonstrate that federal versus state power is once again on the table, foretelling continued clashes that will test constitutional principles and citizens' understanding of good government. Californians' abiding hope that things can and should be better also motivates them to keep testing the limits of their political machinery through the initiative process—even if their general discontent with politics tends to handicap government's capacity to solve the state's pressing problems. They, like Carey McWilliams who wrote nearly 70 years ago, believe that "nothing is quite yet what it should be in California."[14]

The Golden State remains a land of mythical proportions, set apart from the rest by its commanding economy, geography, and population. Yet, the question begs to be answered: how extraordinary are California's *politics*? This book explores the reasons for the contemporary state of affairs and evaluates how history, culture, institutions, and rules contribute to the sense that California is exceptional. Generations have reimagined and brought its distinctiveness to life through their choices and actions, and collectively they have created a political system that at first glance seems incomparable in all its complexity, experimentation, and breadth. In this book we ask whether California is a justifiable outlier, a state whose politics defy simple categorization. Along the way, we also consider what it will take to enable California's several forms of government to achieve the foundational aim of a democratic government: to serve the public's welfare and interests effectively, comprehensively, and sensibly over the long term.

Key Terms

collective action: working together for mutual benefit. (p. 6)

hybrid political system: a political system that combines elements of direct and representative democracy. (p. 1)

institutions: systems and organizations that help people solve their collective action problems by defining particular roles and rules for those who participate in them and by managing conflict. (p. 6)

norms: unwritten rules that guide acceptable or expected behavior, enforced through daily interactions. (p. 6)

political culture: the attitudes, beliefs, and values about government that a majority in a state hold, as expressed in their customs and the political choices its citizens and leaders make. (p. 6)

politics: a process of bargaining and compromise through which people with differing goals and ideals try to manage their conflicts by working together to allocate values for society. (p. 1)

CHAPTER 2

Critical Junctures

California's Political History in Brief

Early California

The contours of California's contemporary political landscape began to take shape in 1542, when Spanish explorer Juan Cabrillo claimed the Native American lands now known as San Diego for a distant monarchy, thereby paving the way for European settlements along the West Coast. Assisted by Spanish troops, colonization accompanied the founding of Catholic missions throughout Baja (lower) and then Alta (northern) California. These missions, as well as military presidios (army posts), were constructed along what became known as El Camino Real, or the King's Highway, a path that roughly followed a line of major tribal establishments. Over the next two hundred years, native peoples were either subordinated or decimated by foreign diseases, soldiers, and ways of life that were unnatural to them, and the huge mission complexes and ranches, or rancheros, that replaced these groups and their settlements became the focal points for social activity and economic industry in the region.

The western lands containing California became part of Mexico when that country gained independence from Spain in 1821, and for more than two decades, Mexicans governed the region, constructing presidios and installing military leaders to protect the towns taking shape up and down the coast. In 1846, a rebellious band of American settlers, declaring California a republic, raised the hastily patched Grizzly Bear Flag at Sonoma. Within weeks, the U.S. Navy lay claim to California, and for the next two years an uncomfortable mix of American military rule and locally elected "alcaldes" (mayors who acted both as lawmakers and judges) prevailed.

Following the Mexican-American War of 1848 that ended with the Treaty of Guadalupe Hidalgo, California became the new U.S. frontier

MAP 2.1 California's Missions

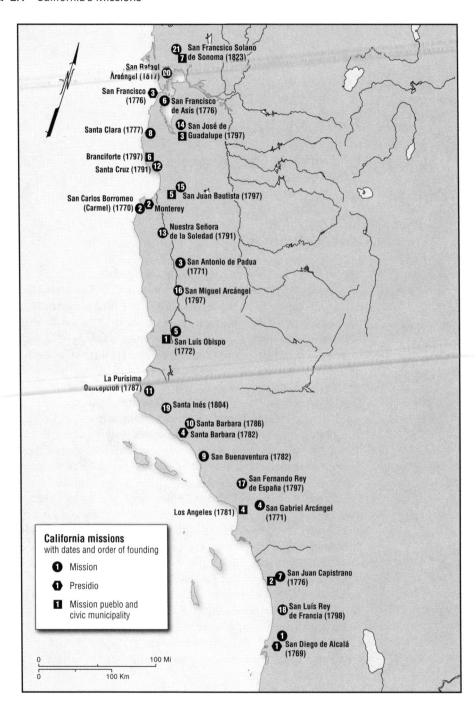

San Franscico Solano
de Sonoma (1823)

San Rafael
Aroángel (1817)

San Francisco
(1776)

San Francisco
de Asís (1776)

Santa Clara (1777)

San José de
Guadalupe (1797)

Branciforte (1797)
Santa Cruz (1791)

San Juan Bautista (1797)

San Carlos Borromeo
(Carmel) (1770)   Monterey

Nuestra Señora
de la Soledad (1791)

San Antonio de Padua
(1771)

San Miguel Arcángel
(1797)

San Luís Obispo
(1772)

La Purísima
Concepción (1787)

Santa Inés (1804)

Santa Barbara (1786)
Santa Barbara (1782)

San Buenaventura (1782)

San Fernando Rey
de España (1797)

Los Angeles (1781)   San Gabriel Arcángel
(1771)

California missions
with dates and order of founding

● Mission

● Presidio

■ Mission pueblo and
civic municipality

San Juan Capistrano
(1776)

San Luís Rey
de Francia (1798)

San Diego de Alcalá
(1769)

0   100 Mi

0   100 Km

astride a new international border. The simultaneous discovery of gold near Sacramento provoked an onslaught of settlers in what would be the first of several significant population waves to flood the West Coast during the next 125 years. The rush to the Golden State was on.

The Rise of the Southern Pacific Railroad

The tumult that lawless gold-seekers stirred up convinced many that civil government was needed. Spurning slavery and embracing self-governance, a group of mostly pre-gold-rush settlers and Mexican-American war veterans convened to write a state constitution in 1849; a year later, the U.S. Congress granted statehood, bypassing the usual compulsory territorial stage, and shortly thereafter Sacramento became the state's permanent capital. Although gold had already lured nearly 100,000 adventurers to the state in less than two years, the region remained a mostly untamed and distant outpost, separated from the East Coast by treacherous terrain and thousands of miles of ocean travel. Growing demand for more reliable linkages to the rest of the country led to the building of the transcontinental railroad in 1869, an undertaking that resulted in the importation of thousands of Chinese laborers and millions of acres of federal land grants to a few railroad companies. Eleven million acres in California were granted to the Southern Pacific Railroad alone.[1]

The wildly successful rail enterprise not only opened the West to rapid development but also consolidated economic and political power in the Central Pacific Railroad, later renamed the Southern Pacific Railroad. Owned by barons Collis Huntington, Mark Hopkins, Leland Stanford, and Charles Crocker—the **Big Four**—through the early 1900s, the Southern Pacific extended its reach to virtually all forms of shipping and transportation. Their monopoly had direct impacts on all major commercial activity within the state, from wheat prices to land values and from bank lending to the availability of lumber. The railroad barons' landholdings enabled them to control the prosperity or demise of entire towns that depended on rail stops throughout the West. Power didn't come cheap, however, and they fostered "friendships" in the White House, Congress, the state court system, and of course in local and state governments by finding every influential person's

Enduring persistent racial discrimination, punishing conditions, and a lack of labor and safety protections, Chinese immigrants laid thousands of miles of railroad tracks during the late 1800s and early 1900s.

"price." As famously depicted in Edward Keller's illustration, "The Curse of California," which appeared in San Francisco's *The Wasp* on August 19, 1882, the "S.P." (Southern Pacific Railroad) dominated every major sector of the state's economy—and politics—like a determined octopus.

Progressivism

The Southern Pacific's hold over California government during the late 1800s cannot be overestimated. One historian describes the situation in this way:

> For at least a generation after the new constitution went into effect [in 1879] the great majority of Californians believed that the influence of the railroad extended from the governor's mansion in Sacramento to the lowest ward heeler in San Francisco, and that the machine determined who should sit in city councils and on boards of supervisors; who should be sent to the House of Representatives and to the Senate in Washington; what laws should be enacted by the legislature, and what decisions should be rendered from the bench.[2]

The Southern Pacific's grip over California industry and politics was smashed, bit by bit, by muckraking journalists whose stories were pivotal in the creation of new federal regulations aimed at breaking monopolies; by the prosecution of San Francisco's corrupt political boss, Abe Ruef; and by the rise of a national political movement known as "Progressivism" that quickly took root in California. Governor Hiram Johnson (1911–1917) personified the idealistic **Progressive** spirit through his focus on eliminating every private interest from government and restoring power to the people.

Governor Johnson spearheaded an ambitious reform agenda that addressed a wide range of social, political, and economic issues that were attracting the attention of Progressives in other U.S. states. His agenda was not only grounded in a fundamental distrust of political parties, which had been hijacked by the Southern Pacific in California, but also built on an emerging philosophy that government could be run like a business, with efficiency as a clear objective. Workers' rights, municipal ownership of utility companies, universal education, conservation, morals laws, and the assurance of fair political representation topped the list of items Johnson tackled with the help of the California legislature after he entered office in 1911.

Changes in electoral laws directly targeted the ties political parties had to both the railroads and potential voters. Although *secret voting* had become state law in 1896, the practice was reinforced as a means to control elections and ensure fairness. The ability of party bosses to "select and elect" the candidates for political offices was undercut with the establishment of *direct primary elections*, in which any party member could become a candidate for office and gain the nomination of his fellow party members through a regular party election. The legislature also reclassified local elected offices as "**nonpartisan**," meaning that the political party affiliations of candidates did not appear on the ballot if they were running for municipal offices, including city councils, local school boards, and judgeships. Efficiency, the Progressives believed, demanded that voters and officials be blind to partisanship, because petty divisions wasted valuable time and resources, and the important concern was who was the best person for a position, not his political party affiliation.

A more ingenious method of controlling political parties was accomplished through **cross-filing**, which meant that any candidate's name could appear on any party's primary election ballot without

THE CURSE OF CALIFORNIA.

The Wasp, August 19, 1882, vol. 9. No. 316, pp. 520–521. Image taken from http://nationalhumanitiescenter.org/pds/gilded/power/text1/octopusimages.pdf

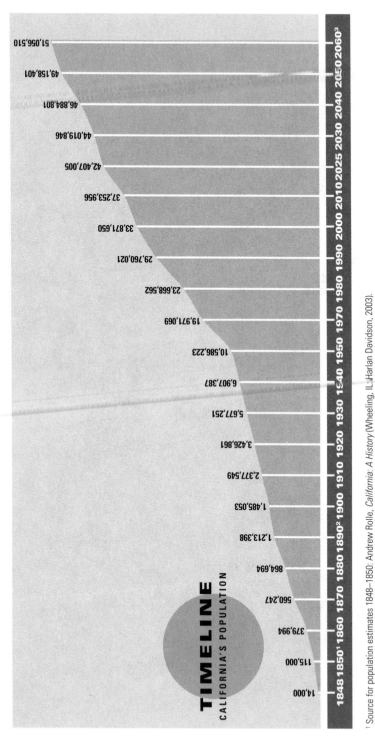

TIMELINE
CALIFORNIA'S POPULATION

Year	Population
1848[1]	14,000
1850	115,000
1860	379,994
1870	560,247
1880	864,694
1890[2]	1,213,398
1900	1,485,053
1910	2,377,549
1920	3,426,861
1930	5,677,251
1940	6,907,387
1950	10,586,223
1960	19,971,069
1970	23,668,562
1980	29,760,021
1990	33,871,650
2000	37,253,956
2010	42,407,005
2025	44,019,846
2030	46,884,801
2040	49,158,401
2050 2060[3]	51,056,510

[1] Source for population estimates 1848–1850: Andrew Rolle, *California: A History* (Wheeling, IL: Harlan Davidson, 2003).

[2] Population estimates from 1848–1880 are for nonnative populations. Native populations were not included in the U.S. census prior to 1890. Source for population estimates 1860–2010: U.S. Census Bureau.

[3] Source for population estimates 2025–2060: California Department of Finance, Demographic Research Unit, February 2017.

the candidate's party affiliation being indicated. In effect, Republicans could seek the Democrats' nomination and vice versa, thereby allowing candidates to be nominated by more than one party. This rule, which remained on the books until 1959, initially helped Progressives but later allowed Republicans to dominate the legislature despite state party registration that favored the Democrats after 1934.

Civil service exams were also instituted, which changed the hiring of local and state government employees from a system based on **patronage** (*who* one knew) to one based on merit (*what* one knew about a position and *how well* one knew it). But perhaps the most important political reform the Progressives instituted was a transformation of the relationship citizens had to California government. They accomplished this first by *guaranteeing women the right to vote* and then by adopting the tools of *direct democracy*: the *recall*, the *referendum*, and the *initiative* process (discussed in Chapter 3). By vesting the people with the power to make laws directly—even new laws that could override those already in place—Progressives redistributed political power and essentially redesigned the basic structure of government. No longer was California a purely representative democracy; it now had a *hybrid government* that combined direct and representative forms of democracy. Elected officials would now compete with the people and special interests for power through the initiative process. The Progressives had triggered the state's first giant political earthquake.

It should be noted that the Progressives' efforts to widen access to political power did not extend to every group in California, and some of the laws they passed were specifically designed to exclude certain people from decision making and restrict their political power. The most egregious examples reflected the White majority's racial hostility toward Chinese-born and other Asian-born residents, which took the form of "Alien Land Laws" that denied landownership, full property rights, citizenship, and basic civil rights to anyone of Asian descent—laws that would not be removed from the state's books for another half century.

The Power of Organized Interests

Ironically, the Progressives' attacks on political parties and the Southern Pacific created new opportunities for other kinds of special interests to influence state government. Cross-filing produced legislators with minimal party allegiances, and by the 1940s, these individuals had come to depend heavily on lobbyists for information and other "diversions" to supplement their meager $3,000 annual salary. The legendary Artie Samish, head of the liquor and racetrack lobbies from the 1920s to the 1950s, personified the power of the "third house" (organized interests represented in the lobbying corps) in his ability to control election outcomes and tax rates for industries he represented. "I am the governor of the legislature," he brazenly boasted in the 1940s. "To hell with the governor of California."[3] He was convicted and jailed for corruption not long after making this statement, but his personal downfall hardly disturbed the thriving, cozy relationships between lobbyists and legislators that continued to taint California state politics.

Growth and Industrialization in the Golden State

To outsiders, the image of California as a land of mythical possibility and untold wealth persisted even as the Great Depression took hold in the 1930s. As depicted in John Steinbeck's *The Grapes of*

Wrath, hundreds of thousands of unskilled American migrants from the mid- and southwestern Dust Bowl ("Okies" as they were pejoratively called by Californians) flooded the state, provoking a stinging social backlash that lasted at least until war production created new labor demands. The Depression also helped breathe life into what was neither the first nor the last unconventional political movement: in 1934, outspoken writer and socialist Upton Sinclair easily won the Democratic nomination for governor by waging an "End Poverty in California" (EPIC) campaign, which promised relief for lower- and middle-class Californians through a radical tax plan. His near-win mobilized conservatives, inspired left-wing Democrats to fortify social programs, and propelled the first modern attack ads—the media-driven smear campaign—into being.

Rapid urban and industrial development during the first decades of the twentieth century accompanied the invention of the automobile and the step-up in oil production preceding World War II. Ribbons of roads and highways wrapped new towns and tied them to swelling cities, and people kept arriving in California at spectacular rates. Industrialization during World War II restored the state's golden image, bringing defense-related jobs, federal funds, manufacturing, construction, and dazzling prosperity that only accelerated postwar. The building sector boomed while orange trees blossomed. To address labor shortages, the federal "Bracero" program created a new agricultural labor force by facilitating the entry of Mexican laborers into the United States, beckoning millions of men and their families to the country. Their efforts laid the foundations for California's thriving modern agribusiness sector.

Tract-housing developments materialized at an unprecedented rate, spawning demands for roads, water, schools, and other critical infrastructure. In 1947, the state fanned the spread of "car culture" with an ambitious ten-year highway plan that cost $1 million per working day. Flood control and colossal irrigation projects begun in the 1860s had transformed the San Francisco Bay and the Sacramento–San Joaquin River Delta region from wetlands filled with wildlife into a labyrinth of levees, tunnels, canals, and dams that allowed midcentury farmers to feed expanding populations. Los Angeles continued to invent itself by sprawling across floodplains with manufacturing plants and neighborhoods that depended on water imported from the north, triggering "water wars" that continue to this day. Infrastructure spending centered on moving water to the thirsty south via the State Water Project (SWP), the building of schools, establishing a first-class university system, and keeping freeways flowing—priorities that governors Earl Warren and Edmund "Pat" Brown (Jerry Brown's father) advanced through the early 1960s.

The Initiative Process Takes Hold

The political landscape was also changing dramatically midcentury. Cross-filing, which had severely disadvantaged the Democrats for forty years, was effectively eliminated through a 1952 initiative that required candidates' party affiliations to be printed on primary election ballots. With this important change, Democrats finally realized majority status in 1958 with Pat Brown in the governor's office and control of both legislative houses.

Several U.S. Supreme Court cases also necessitated fundamental changes in the way that Californians were represented in both the state and national legislatures. Between 1928 and 1965, the state employed the "federal plan," modeling its legislature on the U.S. Congress, with an upper house based on geographic areas (counties rather than states) and a lower house based on population.

Although many attempts had been made to dismantle the plan because it produced gross over-representation of northern and inland rural interests and severe underrepresentation of southern metropolitan residents in the state Senate (three-fourths of sitting senators represented low-density rural areas), it remained in place until a federal court struck it down; per the U.S. Supreme Court ruling in *Reynolds v. Sims* (1964), the California system was found to violate the "one person–one vote" principle.[4] After 1965, political influence passed from legislators representing the north to those representing the south and also from rural "cow counties" to urban interests. Moreover, putting legislators in charge of redrawing their own districts reopened the possibility for gerrymandering, the practice of manipulating district boundaries to virtually ensure the reelection of incumbents and the continuation of the majority party in power.

The revival of parties in the legislature during the 1960s was greatly assisted by the Democratic Speaker of the California State Assembly, "Big Daddy" Jesse Unruh, who understood how to influence the reelection of loyal partisans by controlling the flow of campaign donations, what he referred to as the "mother's milk of politics."[5] Unruh also helped orchestrate an overhaul of the legislature through Proposition 1A, a measure designed to "Update the State!" via constitutional cleanup in 1966. Prop 1A *professionalized* the lawmaking body by endowing it with the "three S's": higher *salary*, many more *staff*, and year-round *session*. The intent was to create a legislative body that could separate itself from the enticements of lobbyists by giving it the necessary resources to compete on more equal footing with the executive branch, and 73.5 percent of California voters welcomed the political shake-up. Lawmakers' annual pay doubled to $16,000 to reflect their new full-time status, and staff members were hired to write and analyze bills.

Professionalization transformed the legislature into a highly paid, well-staffed institution that quickly gained a reputation as a policy and political reform leader among the states. In 1971, the legislature was described as possessing "all the characteristics that a legislature should have," having "proved itself capable of leading the nation in the development of legislation to deal with some of our most critical problems."[6] It didn't take long for the shine to fade, however, as the legislature appeared to let certain taxation policies fly out of control in the mid-1970s.

Propelled by anger over the legislature's inability to reconcile skyrocketing property taxes and a multibillion-dollar state budget surplus, voters revolted against "spendthrift politicians" who "will not act to reduce . . . property taxes."[7] Fully realizing the energizing power of a grassroots political movement through the initiative process, citizens overwhelmingly approved **Proposition 13**, which limited annual property tax to 1 percent of a property's assessed value.[8] Prop 13 forever changed the rules regarding taxation and state budgeting by imposing a two-thirds vote requirement to raise either state or local taxes, a **supermajority** rule that both empowers a minority determined to forestall any tax increases and can significantly jeopardize the legislature's ability to pass balanced budgets on time. Prop 13 sparked the dramatic use of the initiative process that continues today.

The faith in self-governance and mistrust of politicians that spurred Progressives into action and citizens to approve Prop 13 continued to cause political tremors in California politics. The view that citizens were more trustworthy than their representatives only intensified during the 1980s after three legislators were convicted of bribery in an FBI sting labeled "Shrimpscam" (a fictitious shrimp company "paid" legislators to introduce bills favoring the company), reinforcing the perception that Sacramento was full of corrupt, self-indulgent politicians. State lawmakers' reputation for being "arrogant and unresponsive" only grew as the power of incumbency (being an elected official) and membership turnover in the legislature stagnated. In 1990 they were targeted again, this time by

The passage of Proposition 13 in June 1978 opened a new chapter in California history, demonstrating the power of the initiative and the strength of antitax forces. The initiative's authors, Howard Jarvis and Paul Gann (not pictured here), led the antitaxation effort. Prop 13's strict limits on property taxes sparked similar "taxpayer revolts" across the United States.

Proposition 140 (discussed in Chapter 4), which imposed term limits on all state elected officials, eliminating the chance to develop long careers in a single office. By 2004, lifelong legislative careers were over.

Parties and elections have also been targeted through ballot initiatives. In the tradition of cross-filing, the "blanket primary" created by Proposition 198 (approved in 1996) briefly allowed all persons to vote in any political party's primary election regardless of party membership before it was declared unconstitutional by the U.S. Supreme Court. This idea finally succeeded as a "voter preference primary" law in 2010, or what is better known as the "Top-Two primary" (Prop 14; more will be said about this later). Importantly, in that same year, voters transferred the authority to draw electoral district lines (boundaries defining the geographic areas that legislators represent) from lawmakers to a citizen commission (Prop 11).

Voters have also altered policymaking processes by controlling decision-making rules. Proposition 98, enacted in 1988, significantly constrains the legislature by mandating that public schools (grades K–12) and community colleges receive an amount equal to roughly 40 percent of the state's general fund budget each year. Proposition 39, approved in 2000, affects the voters' ability to approve school bonds by lowering the supermajority requirement to 55 percent (from two-thirds). Proposition 26 recategorizes most "fees" as taxes, subjecting them to a two-thirds supermajority approval, and Proposition 25 allows legislators to pass the state budget with a simple majority vote (lowered from a two-thirds supermajority) but denies legislators a paycheck if they fail to pass the budget on time. Voters recently approved Proposition 54, mandating that all bills must be in print at least 72 hours before a legislative vote, and requiring audiovisual recordings of all public proceedings be posted online within 24 hours. This sampling of initiatives reveals a firmly established reform tradition that will continue to reshape California's government and how it operates.

Hyperdiversity in a Modern State

Hybrid government reinforces California's distinctiveness, but probably no condition defines politics in California more than the state's great human diversity, which is as much a source of rich heritage and culture as it is a divisive force that drives political competition. Differences stemming from ethnicity, race, gender, religion, age, sexuality, ideology, socioeconomic class, and street address (to name but a few sources) do not inevitably breed conflict; however, these differences often are the source of intense political clashes in the state. The political realm is where these differences are expressed as divergent goals and ideals in the search for group recognition, power, or public goods, and the vital challenge for California's political representatives and institutions is to aggregate interests rather than aggravate them.

A post–World War II baby boom inflated the state's population while waves of immigration and migration throughout the mid- to late twentieth century produced minor political tremors. A marked national population shift from the Rust Belt to the Sun Belt boosted California's economy, as well as its population, over the latter half of the twentieth century. Another wave of people from Southeast Asia arrived during the late 1960s to the mid-1970s, following the Vietnam War, and the most recent influx of immigrants occurred during the 1980s and 1990s, when the state's economic prosperity encouraged large-scale migration from Mexico and other Latin and Central American countries.

Immigration, legal and illegal, as well as natural population growth, have therefore produced a hyperdiverse state in which many groups vie for political legitimacy and attention, for public services and goods, and for power and influence. California is home to the largest Asian population in the United States, including Southeast Asians, who are among the fastest-growing ethnic groups in the state.[9] Having displaced Whites in 2015 as the state's largest ethnic group, Latinos now constitute 40 percent of the state's population.[10] Still underrepresented at the polls, Latinos have yet to realize the fullness of political power in California.

Continually changing demographic patterns help drive public policy debates, as they often raise questions about what it means to be a citizen. Undocumented immigrants continue to arrive (or overstay legal visas, the most common way one becomes "unauthorized"), raising their numbers in California to almost 2.5 million.[11] Impassioned campaigns have been waged over how to treat this shadow population who, despite state and some city officials' efforts to offer sanctuary, live in fear of federal deportation. Immigration-related issues that have surfaced in ballot measures include whether to make English the state's official language (approved by 73.2 percent of voters in 1986), whether to teach children only in English (passed by 60.9 percent of voters in 1998 as Proposition 227), whether to deny citizenship to children born in the state to undocumented workers (a federal constitutional issue), and whether to allow undocumented immigrants the ability to obtain in-state tuition rates or Cal Grants (the California Development, Relief, and Education for Alien Minors Act, known as the DREAM Act, signed into law in 2011). AB 60, a law passed in 2013, allows undocumented immigrants to obtain noncommercial driver's licenses, something many Californians have opposed for symbolic and practical reasons, though this right has already been enabled in the District of Columbia and twelve other states, including Colorado and Illinois (Oregon voters rescinded their law in 2014).[12] Less than three years into the program the Department of Motor Vehicles (DMV) had issued more than 900,000 of these specially designated licenses, and at least one study shows that they help reduce hit-and-run accidents.[13]

Residential patterns also raise questions about cultural assimilation versus cultural preservation. Some subpopulations tend to concentrate geographically, forming "Little Saigons," "Chinatowns," or barrios. Also known to representatives as "communities of interest," these communities have performed the historical role of absorbing foreign laborers and refugees, including the approximately fifty thousand Vietnamese who arrived after the Vietnam War and the approximately three million Latinos who joined family members in the United States as part of a 1986 federal amnesty program. Chinatown in San Francisco remains the largest enclave of its kind, home to the largest concentration of ethnic Chinese outside China. The trends of "balkanization" (communities separated by race or ethnicity) and **gentrification** (the movement of affluent residents into renovated city zones from

Children at Jefferson Elementary School in Sanger, a city near Fresno, are among the state's plurality (40 percent) Latino population. In 2015–16 they represented more than half (54 percent) of all students enrolled in California K–12 schools, whereas non-Hispanic Whites were 24 percent, Asian and Pacific Islanders were 12 percent, and African Americans were 6 percent.

which poorer residents have been displaced) have become more pronounced during recent decades, reflecting widening income inequality. These patterns are also manifest in five radically different community types that political geographers have identified: they call them the "Five Californias."[14] Indicated mainly by income and education levels, health, and the opportunities these afford, the realities that these five different social classes experience translate into wildly different sociopolitical needs and demands. Even though the largest population sector is struggling financially, the top One Percent both disproportionately fund state government and also influence policy (see Chapter 9).

The sheer volume of basic human and special needs created by this hyperdiversity has tended to outstrip government capacity in the areas of health care, housing, public education, legal and correctional services, infrastructure development, environmental protection, and public welfare. Population growth will continue to animate taxation, budget, and policy debates, providing plenty of fissures that will test the foundations of state government.

Recalling a Governor

The constant energy of gradual population change contrasts sharply with the sudden jolts that unexpected events can send through a political system. The most significant political earthquake of the new millennium in California hit in 2003 with the recall of Governor Gray Davis, a dizzying, circus-like event that solidified the state's image as a national outlier. The mild-mannered, uncharismatic Governor Davis had gained a reputation as a "pay-to-play" politician who rewarded friendly public employee unions with generous contracts and was blamed for skyrocketing electricity bills, tripling the car tax, and overdue budgets that contained accounting gimmicks.[15] After Republican U.S. Representative Darrell Issa infused the recall effort with more than $1 million, enough signatures were gathered to trigger a special recall election.

For the first time ever, Californians would be asked if they wanted to keep or replace their governor and simultaneously choose a successor if enough voted for the recall. Hundreds of potential candidates jostled for attention, including actor Arnold Schwarzenegger, who surprised *The Tonight Show* audience by announcing his candidacy during the show.

The spectacular election season lasted only seventy-six days (a normal cycle is about twice as long), during which time the candidates spent $80 million, captivated the mainstream media, and participated in televised debates. On October 7, 2003, 55.4 percent of voters selected "yes" on the recall question, and 48.7 percent chose Schwarzenegger from among 135 candidates on the ballot to replace Davis. With 61.2 percent of registered voters having participated in the election, a high turnout historically speaking, Californians demonstrated that they'd had enough "politics as usual" by exploiting the tools of direct democracy to shake up their government once again.

Pushing Ahead With More Reforms

Arnold Schwarzenegger's "outsider" approach to governing involved centrist appeals to Californians on common themes such as the environment and government reform, and he will probably be best remembered for signing AB 32, the nation's first law to regulate greenhouse gas emissions. Today AB 32 is being enacted through a carbon emissions cap-and-trade system and other greenhouse gas-related mandates, and it survived a public referendum to dismantle it.[16] He may also be remembered for a jaw-dropping $27 billion budget deficit that mushroomed near the end of his term.

Elections remained at the epicenter of political change throughout Schwarzenegger's two terms. The people adopted new rules for redistricting with the Voters FIRST Act (Proposition 11), stripping lawmakers of the responsibility for redrawing their own districts and mandating that a new nonpartisan citizens' commission assume the job; a later initiative added congressional redistricting to the commission's duties. Voters also approved the "Top-Two primary" (Prop 14 in 2010), an adaptation of the open primary, or "jungle primary" as some call it. In a Top-Two election, *all* registered voters, including independents, may choose among all candidates running for different offices, not just their own party's candidates. The new rules force the top two vote-getters for every seat into a runoff in the November general election. Thus, in November 2012, a total of 28 U.S. House, state Senate, and Assembly contests—some extremely aggressive—pitted Democrats against fellow Democrats or set Republicans against fellow Republicans.[17] Similar scenarios have played out in 2014, with twenty-five same-party match-ups, and in 2016, with twenty-seven. Advocates of Prop 14 hoped that more moderates would replace strident ideologues who tend to resist compromise, but so far there is little evidence that the electoral changes have greatly reduced polarization (which is the inclination for members of both parties to occupy the far right or left ends of the ideological spectrum) or have significantly moderated legislative politics.[18] However, observers point to specific cases in which the more moderate candidates were selected over their competitors in the general election, and more members of the state legislature now associate with the "moderate caucus."[19] Additionally, the new system allows independents, or "no party preference" voters, to participate fully in primary elections. Although moderation hasn't flourished as proponents had hoped, citizens appear satisfied with the new system.[20]

The Return of Jerry Brown

Adding to the seismic proportions of the 2010 election was the reelection of Jerry Brown as governor after almost thirty years, the only person to hold that office for four terms.

One of the most striking facts about Edmund G. "Jerry" Brown is that he was one of the youngest governors in California history when he assumed office in 1975 at age thirty-six, and he became the oldest governor when he retook the oath of office in 2011 at age seventy-two—overtaking his own record with his final reelection at age seventy-six. An experienced statesman whose résumé includes having been a candidate for the U.S. presidency three times, secretary of state in the 1970s, Oakland mayor, and state attorney general immediately before retaking the governorship, Brown spent the first years of his new tenure wrangling the state's deficit-plagued budget into balance by slicing spending and seeking a voter-approved tax measure to fund public education (Prop 30). By sharply reducing public services that fellow Democrats considered sacred, including health care and education, and by using the initiative process to help enact his agenda, he showed that he would govern with calculated moderation. Brown's governing approach has been to "think big," getting behind gigantic infrastructure projects such as the Delta twin tunnels (see Chapter 1) and endorsing a state high-speed rail project that could eventually connect Sacramento to San Diego—a project whose stupefying costs have drawn fire, currently estimated to be between $70 and $100 billion.[21]

An intellectual motivated by a strong sense of social justice, Governor Brown has shown little patience for those who would place politics above science, and he has staunchly defended the state's aggressive climate change policies. As national EPA director, Mike Pruitt, questioned climate science and signaled a rollback of environmental protections, Brown swore resistance. Calling the Trump administration's approach "a miasma of nonsense," he pledged: "We've got the scientists, we've got the lawyers, and we're ready to fight."[22]

The 2017-18 state budget, the most significant economic statement of state leaders' political priorities, anticipated federal-state showdowns on several fronts and also a possible economic downturn. The governor's key priorities—maintaining fiscal prudence, investing in education, counteracting the effects of poverty, and improving the state's transportation infrastructure—were evident in set-asides for the "Rainy Day Fund," more money for education, tax credits for the working poor and self-employed, and implementation of a higher gas tax.[23]

Criminal justice reform also remains near the top of Brown's political agenda. Through shifting nonserious, nonviolent, nonsexual inmates (known as "triple-nons") to county jails and parole, the incarcerated population has been reduced to levels at or below federal court mandates in a process called "**realignment**," yet corrections absorb over 11 percent of the state budget. To keep these populations from exploding further, Brown has tended to veto bills that create new crimes, cautioning, "we should pause and reflect how our system . . . could be made more human, more just, and more cost-effective."[24] The legislature has done so by looking for ways to loosen automatic sentencing enhancements, and the people voted to make parole easier for nonviolent felons and to empower judges (not district attorneys) to decide whether juveniles can be tried as adults (Prop 57).

Brown has skirmished occasionally with Democratic legislators, who attained supermajority status in both the Assembly and Senate in 2012 and again in 2016, a feat that enables them to approve tax and fee hikes without the minority party's say-so and also override the governor's vetoes (yet they haven't tried to do so as of 2017). For instance, although Brown has signed between 85 and 90 percent of bills sent to his desk, he "deeply disappointed" the Democratic Speaker by vetoing a bill that would have created tax breaks for developers who built low-income housing[25] and rejected sales tax exemptions for diapers and tampons. In another veto message, he noted that doubling the penalty to $490 for drivers who fail to slow or move away from a stopped emergency vehicle seemed "more punitive than deterrent."[26] In fact, he has made a point of saying that "not every human problem deserves a law," although his Republican opponents may feel as if that has become standard practice in California.

With drought in the rear-view mirror, California is headed into a future that is clouded by proposed policy changes at the federal level. Yet predicting oncoming developments and making provisions to change course mid-year is as easy as forecasting the next tsunami. If Congress slashes health care funding to states, coverage will be jeopardized for millions of Californians of all ages. Federal immigration enforcement has put California on a collision course with the national government as city and state officials prioritize keeping immigrant families intact, regardless of citizenship status. Legislators have also been creating the regulatory framework to control the cultivation, distribution, and use of recreational marijuana, a move that antagonizes the anti-drug-oriented federal Department of Justice, which has the ability to enforce national law that lists marijuana as a Schedule I illegal substance. Even state wages contrast sharply with federal priorities: California's minimum wage rose to $11 per hour on January 1, 2018, increasing by one dollar yearly until it reaches $15 per hour in 2022; meanwhile, the federal minimum wage has remained at $7.25 per hour since 2009.[27] Each of these issues puts California at odds with the federal administration, which has vowed to cut state funding for health care and other programs. By virtue of its leaders' defiance, California is once again "out in front," this time poised to bring further clarity to federal-state relations.

Conclusion: Political Earthquakes and Evolving Institutions

Like real seismic events, political earthquakes are difficult to predict. Some of the tensions that produce them are ever-present, such as in the demographic fault lines that define neighborhoods and the uneasy alliance between representative and direct democracy. Periodic ruptures that take the form of ballot measures, recalls, or landmark legislation release some of that tension. Although political earthquakes may be triggered by conditions or events that can't be controlled—such as a weak global economy, a new federal administration, Supreme Court decisions, or wars—the shock waves that these events produce have the potential to bring about transformations both large and small. Throughout California's history, political earthquakes have reconfigured relationships between the elected and the governed, between citizens and their governing institutions, and among citizens. Each of these upheavals has involved choices about who may use power and how they may do so legitimately. Rules have also mattered: in some cases, the shake-ups were about whether to change the rules themselves, whereas in other cases the rules shaped the alternatives available and determined who could choose among them, be they voters, legislators, or other leaders such as governors. Often, policy decisions provoke supercharged emotional reactions because they raise questions about shared values and have the potential to shape the social, economic, and political culture in which people will live. Finally, history also plays a role in creating opportunities for action or in creating conditions that shape alternatives. As this historical review demonstrates, California's past pulses in the political institutions, culture, rules, and choices of today, which in turn will provide keys to unlocking the Golden State's political future.

Key Terms

Big Four: Collis Huntington, Mark Hopkins, Leland Stanford, and Charles Crocker, four railroad tycoons who wielded disproportionate influence over California politics, having owned the Central (later Southern) Pacific Railroad that constructed the western length of the transcontinental railroad (1863–1869). (p. 11)

civil service: government employment that is not based on political party loyalty alone, but rather, on merit that is usually earned through professional training and experience. Endorsed by Progressives. (p. 15)

cross-filing: an early form of an open primary election, in which the name of any candidate (minus political party affiliation) could appear on any political party's primary election ballot. Officially in effect in California from 1913 to 1959. (p. 12)

gentrification: the movement of affluent residents into renovated city zones from which poorer residents have been displaced. (p. 19)

nonpartisan elections: elections in which names of candidates (usually for local offices) appear on ballots without reference to their partisan identification. Established by Progressives. (p. 12)

patronage: the awarding of government jobs to political party loyalists. (p. 15)

professionalization: Proposition 1A in 1966, made the state legislature a full-time operation resembling the U.S. Congress; professional legislators have high salaries, many full-time staff members, and year-round sessions. (p. 17)

Progressives: members of a national political movement that took root in state-based political parties of that name; they tried to reform government to rid it of special interests and return it to "the people." Influential actions in California included establishing direct democracy, among other important electoral reforms. (p. 12)

Proposition 13: landmark proposition in 1978 that limited property taxes to 1% of the purchase price of a property and imposed a two-thirds vote threshold for raising taxes. Rekindled Californians' usage of the initiative process. (p. 17)

realignment: the process of shifting state prison inmates to county jails and parole in order to reduce prison overcrowding. (p. 22)

supermajority: a majority rule that requires reaching a threshold above 50% plus one. The threshold is commonly two-thirds in California for raising taxes and passing urgency measures. (p. 17)

CHAPTER 3

Direct Democracy

San Franciscans had to be wondering whether "enough was enough" when the 319-page voter guide arrived ahead of the 2016 general election. The bloated pamphlet contained over 350 arguments relating to 25 local **ballot measures**, a bewildering blend of proposed changes to housing policy, tree maintenance, taxes, bonds, mayoral powers, elections, lobbying, and police accountability—not to mention a tax on soda. Next came the 224-page California voter information guide issued by the secretary of state, covering 17 initiatives relating to marijuana legalization, gun control, the death penalty, prescription drug pricing, a plastic bag ban, and more: forty-two ballot measures in all.

Direct democracy was intended to supplement the regular lawmaking process, to be, a safeguard for when the legislature "either viciously or negligently fails or refuses" to act.[1] Yet, on mundane and complex matters alike, whether they have considered them on the merits or not, and being accountable to no one but themselves, "on election day every voting Californian is a lawmaker."[2] Indeed, the U.S. Supreme Court confirmed in 2015 that the people are in fact a legislature when they exercise their power to make laws.[3] For more than one hundred years, California has had a *hybrid government* that is part representative, part direct democracy, a design that the nation's founders carefully avoided.[4]

At first, California's government reflected the U.S. founders' belief that elected representatives working in separate branches—executive and legislative, namely—would check each other with overlapping powers, filter the passions of their constituents through a deliberative process, find compromises, and create good public policy. Lawmakers and presidents would compete for power, and these arrangements would safely allow ambition to counteract ambition, as James Madison noted in the *Federalist Papers*. Spurning this logic, in 1911 California Progressive reformers removed those checks by establishing the initiative, referendum, and recall, thereby creating a hybrid government in which the people can make laws without their representatives' involvement. What we might call the first branch of California government is the people's power to govern themselves through the instruments of direct democracy. Article II of the state constitution affirms this view: "All political power is inherent in the people . . . and they have the right to alter or reform it when the public good may require."

The Statewide Initiative Process

At the state level, the **direct initiative** gives Californians the power to propose constitutional amendments and laws that fellow citizens will vote on without the participation of either the legislature or the governor. The initiative process exists in 23 other states, although specific requirements vary, and many states permit the **indirect initiative**, which allows legislatures to consider and sometimes amend citizen-initiated measures before they are presented to the public for a vote. The California legislature is barred from making changes of any kind to citizens' ballot **propositions**, either before or after an election (see Box 3.1), and it retains the power to propose constitutional amendments, bond measures, and changes to laws, all of which can appear as propositions in primary and general elections that are subject to popular vote—so-called **"legislatively referred" measures**.

Prior to the "Prop 13 revolution" that emboldened Californians to use the initiative process, Oregon led the states with the most initiatives. Since then, Californians have produced more propositions: from 1979 to 2016, voters considered 210 separate initiatives put forward by fellow citizens, compared to 157 in Oregon and 115 in Colorado.[5] Considering all types of measures, including bonds, referenda, and legislatively referred initiatives, California still leads the states with more than 444 measures having been put to voters between 1979 and 2016.[6] Voters reject most citizen initiatives, however. From 1912 to 2016, they only approved 35.1 percent of them.[7] Proposed laws typically fail even before they make it to the ballot because their sponsors fail to gather enough signatures in time or too many submitted signatures are invalidated; in fact, 75 percent of proposed initiatives fail to qualify.[8]

Initiatives cover all manner of subjects at the state level. Issues that surface frequently include taxation, welfare, public morality, immigration, education, criminal justice, and civil rights. Most prevalent are measures that focus on government and the political process—reforms intended to change the rules for political participation or to control the behavior of elected officials—and it's no coincidence that term limits for statewide officials exist almost exclusively in states with the initiative process (Louisiana is the only exception). Requiring that two-thirds of all lawmakers agree to raise a tax or fee is another example of how Californians have played a vital role in manipulating the institutional context for political decision making by imposing rules on legislators. Without a doubt, initiatives have fundamentally altered California government and politics (see Table 3.1 and Figure 3.1).

Unfortunately, reforms are forced on government incoherently and are not based on a process that involves compromise. They also cannot be amended or changed once approved, except through the initiative process. For example, voters approved changes to the juvenile justice system in 2000, requiring that minors aged 14 to 18 who committed certain violent offenses be tried as adults, among other intricate provisions relating to gangs and parole. Unable to address some of

TABLE 3.1   Selected Landmark Initiatives in California, 1966–2016

Number	Description	Year
Proposition 1A	Constitutional reform, legislative professionalization	1966
Proposition 9	"Political Reform Act" (campaign finance reform)	1974
Proposition 13	Property tax limitation	1978
Proposition 98	Minimum annual funding levels for education	1988
Propositions 140, 28	Term limits for state officeholders; 12 years total in either house	1990; 2012
Proposition 184	Three-strikes law	1994
Proposition 187	Ineligibility of illegal aliens for public services	1994
Proposition 215	Medical use of marijuana	1996
Proposition 5	Tribal state gaming compacts, tribal casinos	1998
Proposition 227	Elimination of bilingual education	1998
Propositions 11, 20	Citizens redistricting commission to redraw state and congressional districts	2008; 2010
Proposition 8	Definition of marriage (invalidated by U.S. Supreme Court in 2015)	2009
Proposition 14	Open primary elections (Top-Two Primary)	2010
Proposition 67	Recreational use of marijuana	2016

the injustices that arose from the law, and desiring to reduce costs and promote rehabilitation, Governor Brown pushed Proposition 57 to the voters in 2016 and they ultimately agreed that the law should require judges—not district attorneys—to determine whether minors should be tried as adults under certain circumstances.

The initiative process both directly and indirectly conditions the actions of all California elected officials, as intended. Some initiative measures can, however, exacerbate divisions, eroding their ability to act collectively for the common good. For instance, Proposition 26 reclassifies almost all regulatory fees and charges as taxes so that they are subject to the same two-thirds vote threshold that Prop 13 imposed. While this change may seem fairer because it requires both sides to come together in agreement, in fact it privileges the "super-minority" (a few people) over the simple majority (that is, the most people) because absolutely no revenue-raising measures can succeed without the minority's consent (unless one party represents a supermajority, as the Democrats did after the elections of 2012 and 2016). Historically in the state legislature, supermajority rules like these have driven majority political party Democrats and minority political party Republicans into long standoffs over how to balance the state budget, regulate businesses, address public health issues, and clean up the environment. In other words, direct democracy conditions the way representative democracy works.

Citizens can propose laws at the city, county, and state levels in California. Any registered voter may propose a law (an *initiative statute*) or a change to the state constitution (a *constitutional amendment*),

FIGURE 3.1 Number of Statewide Initiatives that Qualified and Voters Approved in California, 1912–2016

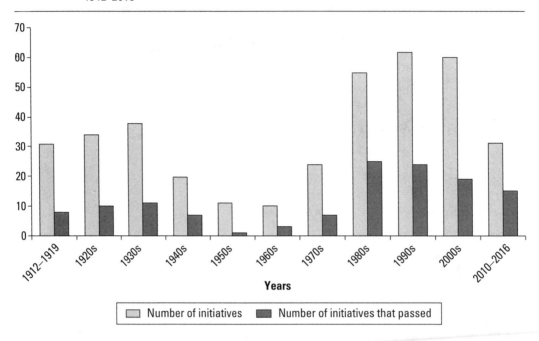

Sources. California Secretary of State, "Initiative Totals by Summary Year, 1912–November 2016," http://www.sos.ca.gov/elections/ballot-measures/pdf/initiative-totals-summary-year.pdf; Legislative Analyst's Office, "Ballot Measures by Type, 1974 to Present," accessed July 1, 2017, http://www.lao.ca.gov/BallotAnalysis/BallotByType.

Note: Excludes measures referred by legislature and referenda. Two initiatives in the 1980s and one initiative in 1999 qualified for the ballot but were removed from the ballot by court order.

and both types pass with simple majority approval. However, because the average person lacks the money and time to gather hundreds of thousands of valid voter signatures for statewide proposi-tions, well-funded interest groups now dominate a system that was intended to *reduce* their influence. In practice, nearly anyone who can spend at least $1.5 million ($3 million on average, ranging past $6 million) to hire a signature-gathering firm can qualify a measure for the ballot.[9] Special interest groups, corporations, wealthy individuals, political parties, and even elected officials (playing the role of "concerned citizens") use the state's initiative process to circumvent regular lawmaking channels because it "is the only way for [them] to get the policy they want."[10] Large donors practically monopo-lize the system: a mere forty-eight entities, from businesses to individuals to unions, contributed half of the approximately $2.3 billion spent on initiative campaigns from 2000 to mid-2012, while "small donors" who gave $1,000 or less accounted for just over *2 percent* of that total.[11] Although the process remains primarily a check against government unresponsiveness and corruption, Hiram Johnson's Progressives would probably be surprised at how the process works today.

Preparation Stage: Drafting, Public Review, and Titling

The first step in bringing an idea to the ballot is drafting, or writing, the text of the proposed law. Measures are worded carefully to fit the needs and goals of their sponsors, and it is their responsibility to correct errors or ambiguities that may later provide opponents with a convenient excuse to challenge them in court. A proposed initiative must be submitted with $2,000 to the attorney general's office, where it will be posted online for a 30-day public review period. Up to five days after the review period concludes, authors may change the wording before the attorney general assigns a title and summary of 100 words or fewer.[12] From that point on, the wording of the proposed law cannot be changed. The state also prepares a fiscal analysis of the proposed law if the attorney general requests one.

Qualification Stage: Circulating Petitions, Gathering Signatures, and Signature Verification

During the qualification stage, the initiative's proponents must circulate strictly formatted petitions containing the official title and summary and gather enough valid voter signatures to qualify the measure for the ballot. Signatures can come from anywhere in California because there are no specific quotas that must be met in each county, as some states require, but everyone who signs must be a registered voter in the county where the petition was signed. Signature requirements are based on a percentage of all votes cast for governor during the previous election: from 2014 to 2018 the requirement is 5 percent for an initiative (365,880 signatures) and 8 percent for a constitutional amendment (585,407 signatures). These totals dropped significantly in 2014 based on low voter turnout, a reduction that was expected to ease the burden of signature collection. (The number of petitions in circulation did increase immediately [to 94 in 2015], but this was not historically unusual.)

Proponents have 180 days (6 months) to collect signatures on their formal petitions. Usually a signature collection firm is hired to run the statewide effort, and the rule of thumb is to gather almost twice as many signatures as required because up to 40 percent or so will likely be invalidated later.[13] In practice this means collecting about 700,000 signatures with costs ranging from $2.75 to over $11 per valid signature, depending on deadlines and company fees.[14] Means of collecting signatures include *in person* in public places, such as in front of grocery stores or at churches using the "clipboard method" (by one person) or "table method" (one person sits at a table while a companion approaches passersby); *direct mail* (generally not cost-effective); and *door-to-door* (rare). Electronic signature gathering is not allowed.

After 25 percent of the required number of signatures have been gathered, the initiative's proponents must notify the secretary of state, who will then relay the measure to the legislature. Although the language cannot be changed at this point, both houses must hold public hearings that are meant to heighten awareness and enhance the public record about them.

Completed petitions must be submitted to the appropriate elections official (typically the county clerk or registrar of voters) in the county where each petition was filled out. There they will count and verify the signatures by using a random sampling technique to determine how many signatures qualify. If, at least 131 days before the next general election, the secretary of state concludes that enough registered voters signed the filed petitions, the measure is certified, given a number, and becomes known as "Proposition [number]."

MAP 3.1   States with the Initiative Process, 2017

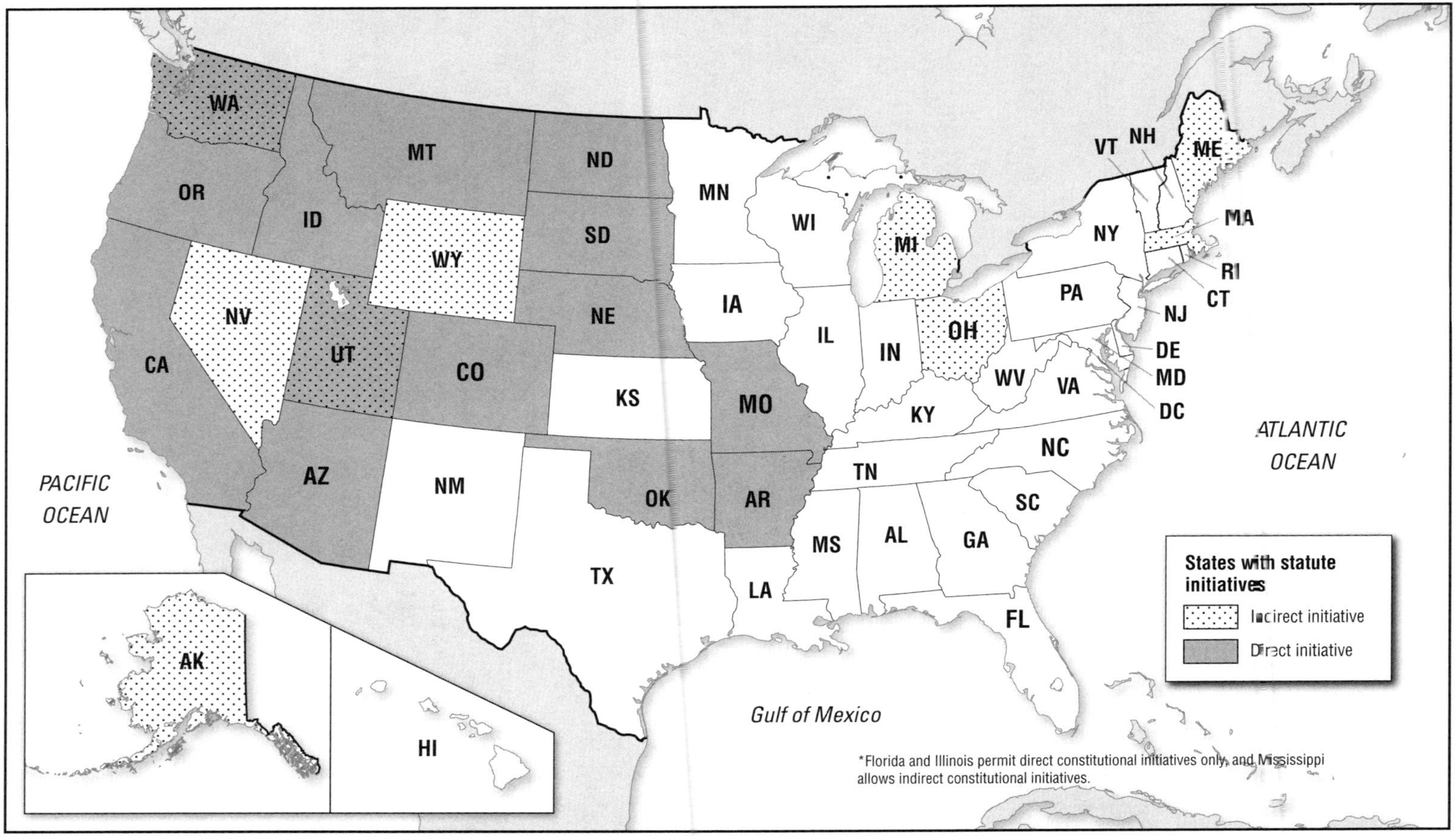

States with statute initiatives

- Indirect initiative
- Direct initiative

*Florida and Illinois permit direct constitutional initiatives only, and Mississippi allows indirect constitutional initiatives.

ATLANTIC OCEAN

Gulf of Mexico

PACIFIC OCEAN

Source: National Conference of State Legislatures, "Initiative and Referendum States," http://www.ncsl.org/legislatures-elections/elections/chart-of-the-initiative-states.aspx.

Campaign Stage: Persuading Potential Voters

Most initiative attempts fail during the qualification stage because insufficient signatures were gathered or because too many were found to be invalid, but for successful proponents, the campaigning stage begins the moment the secretary of state certifies their measure. In the coming months, they will usually raise and spend millions of dollars to mobilize or sway voters. A thriving political consulting industry has grown around the need to manage fund-raising, television and radio advertising, social media messaging, and mass mailings. The price of initiative campaigns has become supersized, and the most expensive in U.S. history have taken place in California (see Table 3.2). Unlimited donations to ballot measure campaigns are permissible, and it is not uncommon for supporters and opponents to spend $100 million combined on highly controversial measures, a benchmark easily surpassed in 2016 with Prop 61, a proposal to tie state drug costs to the prices paid by the U.S. Department of Veterans Affairs. The pharmaceutical industry spent over $109 million to defeat it; opponents, $19 million (it failed). Their cash represented a big chunk of the $447.7 million spent on ballot measures in 2016, a figure almost sure to be topped in 2018 or 2020.[15] Not surprisingly, more money tends to be spent when big industries are directly affected in some way, whereas uncontroversial measures tend to attract little or no spending. Aside from campaign finance considerations, the secretary of state meanwhile prepares the official ballot guide that will be sent to all registered voters (available online in 2018), which includes an analysis of every measure's purpose, effect, and fiscal impacts, along with arguments and rebuttals.

Postelection Stage: Court Challenges and Implementation

Only a *simple majority* is needed to pass an initiative or to recall an elected official, but a *supermajority* (two-thirds vote) is required for any general obligation bond and most school bonds (55 percent). Initiative laws generally take effect the day after they are approved, unlike bills, which normally go into effect on January 1 the following year. Election results don't always settle issues, however. Opponents often file lawsuits as soon as the votes are counted, triggering expensive court battles over a measure's constitutionality, meaning, or validity. These battles can last years and may result in partial or total invalidation of the measure. A legal challenge to Proposition 8, a constitutional amendment defining marriage as between a man and a woman, was initiated shortly after the proposition's passage in 2008. The case twisted through the state courts, where it was eventually upheld by the California Supreme Court. It was then pushed into the federal court system, where it was struck down by a district court as unconstitutional. The U.S. Supreme Court declined to hear the case in 2013, allowing the appellate court's ruling to stand, so same-sex marriages in California became legal that year. In June 2015, the U.S. Supreme Court settled the issue by ruling that the Fourteenth Amendment requires all states to issue marriage licenses to same-sex couples and to recognize same-sex marriages performed in other states.

   Public officials may also search for ways to get around laws they find objectionable, and there is always the likelihood that a contentious issue will be revisited in a future proposition, because new laws often have unintended consequences and because losers always have another chance to prevail.

The Power of the Initiative Process

Initiative use is robust for other reasons. Corporations and special interest groups find initiatives appealing because they know that successful measures can translate into financial gain or

FIGURE 3.2 Sample Ballot with Initiatives

OFFICIAL BALLOT
PRESIDENTIAL GENERAL ELECTION
SANTA BARBARA COUNTY, CALIFORNIA
NOVEMBER 8, 2016

BT 001

INSTRUCTIONS TO VOTERS: To vote for a candidate whose name appears on the ballot, **FILL IN THE OVAL** to the left of your choice using pencil or blue/black ink. **DO NOT** vote for more than the number of candidates allowed. To vote for a qualified write-in candidate, write the person's name in the blank space provided and **FILL IN THE OVAL** to the left. To vote on any measure, **FILL IN THE OVAL** to the left of the word "YES" or the word "NO." <u>All distinguishing marks or erasures are forbidden.</u> If you tear, deface, or wrongly mark your ballot, return it to the Elections Official and obtain another.

VOTE LIKE THIS: ⬤

TURN BALLOT OVER -- VOTE BOTH SIDES

PARTY-NOMINATED OFFICES

The party label accompanying the name of a candidate for party-nominated office on the general election ballot means that the candidate is the official nominee of the party shown.

PRESIDENT AND VICE PRESIDENT
Vote for One Party

- HILLARY CLINTON — *Democratic*
  for President
  TIM KAINE
  for Vice President
- GLORIA ESTELA LA RIVA — *Peace and Freedom*
  for President
  DENNIS J. BANKS
  for Vice President
- DONALD J. TRUMP — *Republican, American Independent*
  for President
  MICHAEL R. PENCE
  for Vice President
- GARY JOHNSON — *Libertarian*
  for President
  BILL WELD
  for Vice President
- JILL STEIN — *Green*
  for President
  AJAMU BARAKA
  for Vice President
- _____

VOTER-NOMINATED AND NONPARTISAN OFFICES

All voters, regardless of the party preference they disclose upon registration, or refusal to disclose a party preference, may vote for any candidate for a voter-nominated or nonpartisan office. The party preference, if any, designated by a candidate for a voter-nominated office is selected by the candidate and is shown for the information of the voters only. It does not imply that the candidate is nominated or endorsed by the party or that the party approves of the candidate. The party preference, if any, of a candidate for a nonpartisan office does not appear on the ballot.

UNITED STATES SENATOR
Vote for One

- LORETTA L. SANCHEZ
  Party Preference: Democratic
  United States Congresswoman
- KAMALA D. HARRIS
  Party Preference: Democratic
  Attorney General of California

UNITED STATES REPRESENTATIVE 24TH DISTRICT
Vote for One

- JUSTIN DONALD FAREED
  Party Preference: Republican
  Small Businessman/Rancher
- SALUD CARBAJAL
  Party Preference: Democratic
  Santa Barbara County Supervisor

STATE SENATOR 19TH DISTRICT
Vote for One

- HANNAH-BETH JACKSON
  Party Preference: Democratic
  State Senator
- COLIN PATRICK WALCH
  Party Preference: Republican
  Entrepreneur/Hospitality Restaurateur

MEMBER OF THE STATE ASSEMBLY 37TH DISTRICT
Vote for One

- S. MONIQUE LIMON
  Party Preference: Democratic
  Educator/School Boardmember
- EDWARD FULLER
  Party Preference: None
  Planning Commissioner/Businessman

SCHOOL

CARPINTERIA UNIFIED SCHOOL DISTRICT
Governing Board Member
Trustee Area No. 1
Vote for no more than Two

- ROGELIO DELGADO
  Businessman/Parent
- MAUREEN "FOLEY" CLAFFEY
  Parent/Educator/Entrepreneur
- GARY BLAIR
  Retired Court CEO

CARPINTERIA VALLEY WATER DISTRICT
Director
Vote for no more than Two

- CASE J. VAN WINGERDEN
  Greenhouse Agricain Grower
- POLLY HOLCOMBE
  Incumbent
- STEVE BUNTING
  Independent Financial Advisor

MEASURES SUBMITTED TO THE VOTERS

STATE

PROPOSITION 51
SCHOOL BONDS. FUNDING FOR K-12 SCHOOL AND COMMUNITY COLLEGE FACILITIES. INITIATIVE STATUTE. Authorizes $9 billion in general obligation bonds for new construction and modernization of K-12 public school facilities, charter schools and vocational education facilities, and California Community Colleges facilities. Fiscal Impact: State costs of about $17.6 billion to pay off both the principal ($9 billion) and interest ($8.6 billion) on the bonds. Payments of about $500 million per year for 35 years.

○ YES   ○ NO

PROPOSITION 52
MEDI-CAL HOSPITAL FEE PROGRAM. INITIATIVE CONSTITUTIONAL AMENDMENT AND STATUTE. Extends indefinitely an existing statute that imposes fees on hospitals to fund Medi-Cal health care services, care for uninsured patients, and children's health coverage. Fiscal Impact: Uncertain fiscal effect, ranging from relatively little impact to annual state General Fund savings of around $1 billion and increased funding for public hospitals in the low hundreds of millions of dollars annually.

○ YES   ○ NO

PROPOSITION 53
REVENUE BONDS. STATEWIDE VOTER APPROVAL. INITIATIVE CONSTITUTIONAL AMENDMENT. Requires statewide voter approval before any revenue bonds can be issued or sold by the state for certain projects if the bond amount exceeds $2 billion. Fiscal Impact: State and local fiscal effects are unknown and would depend on which projects are affected by the measure and what actions government agencies and voters take in response to the measure's voting requirement.

○ YES   ○ NO

PROPOSITION 54
LEGISLATURE. LEGISLATION AND PROCEEDINGS. INITIATIVE CONSTITUTIONAL AMENDMENT AND STATUTE. Prohibits Legislature from passing any bill unless published on Internet for 72 hours before vote. Requires Legislature to record its proceedings and post on Internet. Authorizes use of recordings. Fiscal Impact: One-time costs of $1 million to $2 million and ongoing costs of about $1 million annually to record legislative meetings and make videos of those meetings available on the Internet.

○ YES   ○ NO

PROPOSITION 55
TAX EXTENSION TO FUND EDUCATION AND HEALTHCARE. INITIATIVE CONSTITUTIONAL AMENDMENT. Extends by twelve years the temporary personal income tax increases enacted in 2012 on earnings over $250,000, with revenues allocated to K-12 schools, California Community Colleges, and, in certain years, healthcare. Fiscal Impact: Increased state revenues—$4 billion to $9 billion annually from 2019–2030—depending on economy and stock market. Increased funding for schools, community colleges, health care for low-income people, budget reserves, and debt payments.

○ YES   ○ NO

PROPOSITION 56
CIGARETTE TAX TO FUND HEALTHCARE, TOBACCO USE PREVENTION, RESEARCH, AND LAW ENFORCEMENT. INITIATIVE CONSTITUTIONAL AMENDMENT AND STATUTE. Increases cigarette tax by $2.00 per pack, with equivalent increase on other tobacco products and electronic cigarettes containing nicotine. Fiscal Impact: Additional net state revenue of $1 billion to $1.4 billion in 2017-18, with potentially lower revenues in future years. Revenues would be used primarily to augment spending on health care for low-income Californians.

○ YES   ○ NO

PROPOSITION 57
CRIMINAL SENTENCES. PAROLE. JUVENILE CRIMINAL PROCEEDINGS AND SENTENCING. INITIATIVE CONSTITUTIONAL AMENDMENT AND STATUTE. Allows parole consideration for nonviolent felons. Authorizes sentence credits for rehabilitation, good behavior, and education. Provides juvenile court judge decides whether juvenile will be prosecuted as adult. Fiscal Impact: Net state savings likely in the tens of millions of dollars annually, depending on implementation. Net county costs of likely a few million dollars annually.

○ YES   ○ NO

PROPOSITION 58
ENGLISH PROFICIENCY. MULTILINGUAL EDUCATION. INITIATIVE STATUTE. Preserves requirement that public schools ensure students obtain English language proficiency. Requires school districts to solicit parent/community input in developing language acquisition programs. Requires instruction to ensure English acquisition as rapidly and effectively as possible. Authorizes school districts to establish dual-language immersion programs for both native and non-native English speakers. Fiscal Impact: No notable fiscal effect on school districts or state government.

○ YES   ○ NO

PROPOSITION 64
MARIJUANA LEGALIZATION. INITIATIVE STATUTE.
Legalizes marijuana under state law, for use by adults 21 or older. Imposes state taxes on sales and cultivation. Provides for industry licensing and establishes standards for marijuana products. Allows local regulation and taxation. Fiscal Impact: Additional tax revenues ranging from high hundreds of millions of dollars to over $1 billion annually, mostly dedicated to specific purposes. Reduced criminal justice costs of tens of millions of dollars annually.

○ YES   ○ NO

PROPOSITION 65
CARRYOUT BAGS. CHARGES. INITIATIVE STATUTE.
Redirects money collected by grocery and certain other retail stores through mandated sale of carryout bags. Requires stores to deposit bag sale proceeds into a special fund to support specified environmental projects. Fiscal Impact: Potential state revenue of several tens of millions of dollars annually under certain circumstances, with the monies used to support certain environmental programs.

○ YES   ○ NO

TABLE 3.2 Five Most Expensive Ballot Measure Campaigns (adjusted figures*)

Proposition	Election year	Subject	Total spent	Spent by proponents	Spent by opponents	Pass/fail (% margin)
87	2006	Oil taxes	$184,340,000	$71,461,000	$112,879,000	F (45/55)
32	2012	Union dues	$145,109,000	$64,174,000	$80,935,000	F (43/57)
30	2012	Taxes for education	$141,350,000	$73,124,000	$68,226,000	P (55/45)
5	1998	Indian gaming	$136,563,000	$97,400,000	$39,163,000	P (62/38)
61	2016	Drug pricing	$128,258,000	$19,152,000	$109,106,000	F (47/53)

Sources: California Secretary of State, Powersearch: http://powersearch.sos.ca.gov/. Figures for Prop 5 from Center for Governmental Studies, *Democracy by Initiative: Shaping California's Fourth Branch of Government*, 2nd ed. (Los Angeles, CA: Center for Governmental Studies, 2008).

*Note: All figures have been adjusted to **2016 dollars** and rounded. Figures do not include independent expenditures.

MARK RALSTON/AFP/Getty Images

After other states banned transgender youth from using the locker room or bathroom of their choice, California's Fair Employment and Housing law (FEHA) was changed in 2017, creating an individual right to use bathrooms and locker rooms corresponding to one's preferred gender identity or expression. All single-user bathrooms must be also designated as "gender-neutral," and employers must honor the wishes of employees to be identified by their preferred gender pronoun.

friendlier regulations. Aspiring politicians and lawmakers build their reputations by sponsoring propositions that can't get traction in the legislature. Competition also plays a role: adversaries can take their fights to the ballot with dueling, "rival" measures that propose very different solutions to a problem. If *both* rival measures receive enough votes to pass, the one attracting *more* votes goes into effect. (On a side note, in a move only the savviest of politicians might attempt, Brown signed a bill into law requiring that constitutional amendments be listed on the ballot first, thus ensuring that his measure, Prop 30, would appear at the top of the ballot, well ahead of his rival's measure, Prop 38.[16])

Today, the power of the average voter has been eclipsed by industry initiative activity and special interest group imperatives. Millionaires and billionaires, not average citizens, can afford to qualify their pet projects or big ideas. There are no limits on contributions to ballot campaigns, and two-thirds of all donations are in amounts of $1 million or more.[17] The result: voters endure fanatical campaigns waged by organizations and corporations with deep pockets, their strategies packaged in media barrages containing oversimplified messages. Usually armed only with these biased accounts, voters must decide on complex policies frequently crafted without the benefit of compromise, and these policies may set rules that are difficult to amend later. Not surprisingly, voters confronted with thick ballot guides often look for shortcuts such as endorsements on which to base their decisions, and confused voters tend to vote no, especially when the ramifications of voting yes are unclear. Still, residents and voters of all types (about 72 percent) like the system and think it's a "good thing that a majority of voters can make laws and change public policies."[18] That said, fewer than 20 percent of adults think that the system is fine the way it is; three out of four people (76 percent) feel that major or minor changes are needed, from reducing the number of propositions to making the system less complicated and confusing.[19] Given California's history, it is only a matter of time before citizens further reform the process (see Box 3.1). Representatives may also introduce reforms through regular lawmaking channels, as they did recently with SB 202, a law that ended the practice of voting on initiatives in primary elections. Now citizen-generated propositions appear only in general elections or special elections called by the governor; the legislature may place initiatives, constitutional amendments, or bonds on any state election ballot.

Referendum

Citizens may also repeal recently signed laws, parts of laws, or redistricting maps. To prompt a **referendum**, petitioners must collect the same number of valid signatures required for an initiative (365,880, from 2014 to 2018) within 90 days after the scorned law goes into effect. If the referendum qualifies for the ballot—since 2011, referenda may only appear on general election ballots—voters must choose to vote "yes" if they want to retain the law in question or "no" if they want to nullify it. Prompting referenda through petitions happens rarely: only forty-nine have qualified for the ballot since 1912, and voters have historically been more likely to repeal existing laws than to retain them (58.3 percent of laws were rejected through referenda; 41.7 percent were retained).[20] Gaming compacts negotiated between Native American tribes and the governor usually surface as referenda, and the people have approved all but one (rejected in 2014). Recently, plastic bag manufacturers recoiled from a new state law banning single-use plastic grocery bags and gathered enough signatures to trigger a referendum through Prop 67; in 2016 the people voted to keep the law.

Cartoon labels: CALIFORNIA CIVICS 101 — HOW THE INITIATIVE PROCESS HAS REINED IN THE SPECIAL INTERESTS: SPECIAL INTERESTS — INITIATIVE PROCESS

A far more common type of referendum is a *bond measure*, first approved by the legislature and then passed along to voters for approval. The constitution requires that voters approve state borrowing above $300,000. Bond measures authorize the state treasurer to sell bonds on the open market, which essentially are promises to pay back with interest any amounts loaned to the state. Bonds are typically used to finance multimillion- or multibillion-dollar infrastructure projects ranging from water restoration to library renovation, and since 2000, the average bond has cost more than $5 billion (see Chapter 8). After drought laid bare some of the state water system's flaws, in 2014 voters ratified Proposition 1, a $7,545,000,000 water bond intended to improve water reliability. Most bond measures generate little controversy and around 60 percent pass, although some bond-funded ventures continue to generate conflict as they're implemented, such as a high-speed rail project that voters approved in 2008, now continually under fire as projected costs mount and plans are continually modified. Notably, financing state government projects with billion-dollar bonds involves substantial financial penalties and hidden costs: a sizable share of the state's annual budget each year is dedicated to paying interest, or "servicing the debt," and *taxpayers end up paying about twice the face amount of what is borrowed* after the interest and capital are repaid. Few voters are aware that a $10 billion bond will actually cost around $20 billion to pay off (the final price tag depends on interest rates, and inflation brings the actual costs closer to $1.40 per dollar borrowed).

Recall

California is one of nineteen states allowing voters to remove and replace *state* elected officials between regular elections, meaning that they can "**recall**" lawmakers, justices, and anyone serving in an elected executive capacity such as the governor or attorney general. It is one of at least 29 states permitting the recall of *local* officials, including any person elected in a city or county, or to a court, school or community college board, or special district board.[21] It should be noted that citizens do *not* have the right to recall federal representatives, meaning U.S. House and Senate members.

A California recall election contains two parts: one, voters answer "yes" or "no" as to whether the representative in question should be removed from office; two, they may choose a replacement from anyone listed on the ballot, regardless of whether they voted to remove the official. This method of removing a politician before his or her term ends differs categorically from impeachment, whereby charges of misconduct in office are leveled, a trial is held by the state Senate with a two-thirds vote required to convict, and the Assembly votes to impeach (a deed that hasn't occurred in California since the mid-1800s).[22] Nationwide, the majority of recall attempts are aimed at local officials such as judges, city council members, or school board members; recalls of state officials rarely triumph— although two state legislators in Colorado who had voted for stricter gun control legislation were singled out by the National Rifle Association and were successfully recalled by voters in September 2013.

Low recall success rates are partly ensured through fairly high signature requirements and relatively short deadlines. Signature thresholds vary with the office and size of the jurisdiction, or the area represented by the targeted official. For lawmakers and appeals court judges in California, for instance, petitioners have 160 days to meet the signature threshold, which is equal to 20 percent of the votes cast in the last election for the official being recalled. For mayors and other local officials, the number is based on registered voters: 30 percent if fewer than 1,000 people are registered, declining to 10 percent if over 100,000 are registered.[23] For statewide officials, signatures must be obtained from voters in at least five different counties, with minimums in each jurisdiction tied to the prior election results. These rules also apply to recalling the governor, and proponents have just over five months to submit valid signatures equal to 12 percent of the votes cast during the previous gubernatorial election (just over 878,000 signatures). In some states, the signature threshold to recall a governor looms as high as 40 percent of eligible voters.

No specific grounds for removal are needed to launch a recall in California—officials can be recalled for any reason or cause—but proponents must state their reasons on the petitions they circulate. Since 1913, 162 recalls have been launched against state elected officials in California, but a mere *nine* of these qualified for the ballot, and only five ultimately succeeded.[24] By far, the most dramatic example was the 2003 recall of Governor Gray Davis, discussed in Chapter 2. Freshman Democratic Senator Josh Newman found himself in the crosshairs in 2017 for voting to support higher gas taxes. Signature gathering was robust in his district, which he won by a razor-thin margin. Recall advocates' chances for success narrowed after Democrats revised the law to require that every signature be verified (a full check), signators be allowed to withdraw their names up to 30 days later, and cost estimates for a special election be gathered and publicized (changes that apply to all future recalls). These mandates pushed the possible recall election into 2018, when it could be held during the state's June primaries. Ironically, it takes a simple majority to recall an incumbent, but the replacement wins by plurality vote (the most votes of all cast), so Arnold Schwarzenegger could have won with far less than the 48.7 percent he received in an election that featured 135 candidates.

Direct Democracy at the Local Level

It shouldn't be surprising that the three forms of direct democracy—the initiative, referendum, and recall—are available in every California county, city, and school district and are used more frequently at the local level than at the state level. Voters are regularly invited to weigh in on changes to their city constitutions (charter amendments), local laws, bonds, citizen initiatives, and recalls of local officials. Local measures are adopted more often than state propositions, but seldom sparks a sensation unless they stem from a scandal commanding local headlines, or the fortunes of deep-pocketed interests are at stake (such as land use changes or pension reforms affecting unionized employees), or public morality is at issue (sex and drugs).

Controversial decisions on school boards lead to the most recalls—about 75 percent of all recalls are against elected school board members—yet they remain relatively rare events, and the same is true of local referenda. On the other hand, citizens have the power to generate ordinances through the local initiative process, and they do so with local flair and variable success historically. In 2015–16, local ballot measures found receptive audiences in voters, who approved 78.8 percent of them.[25] The majority of local initiatives relate to matters of growth and development, also known as land use; governance, or political reform; taxation; and local funding for education.[26] Recent initiatives have concerned whether to shut marijuana dispensaries out of cities or regulate them; allow new housing developments or protect open space; impose term limits on city council members and/or county supervisors; conduct elections differently (San Francisco now allows Saturday voting); or alter public employees' benefits (eliminate pensions, for example). Ballot measures have touched on every manner of civil rights, liberties, and public morals; for instance, pornographic film actors in Los Angeles County must wear condoms during filming thanks to Measure B, a county initiative. **Parcel tax** proposals are appearing more frequently on local ballots as well; these are additional taxes or assessments based on square footage of a property, number of units, or a house's or building's value that voters can impose on themselves to pay for local infrastructure projects, such as renovating local schools or hospitals. Typically these "piggyback" taxes are attached to a property tax bill.

When well-funded interests have a stake in the outcome, especially large corporations or unions, campaign spending can quickly accelerate far beyond the reach of local citizens. The American Beverage Association, whose members include Dr Pepper Snapple Group, Pepsi-Cola, and Coca-Cola, spent $22.5 million to defeat a one-cent-per-ounce tax on sugary drinks in San Francisco; proponents, including billionaire Michael Bloomberg, spent $15.3 million. The industry had succeeded in defeating a similar two-cent-per-ounce proposal in 2014, but voters approved the 2016 measure.[27] Usually when the spending disparity stretches past 10-to-1, "The voters are hearing from only one side. Your voice is drowned out."[28]

With two exceptions, the procedures for circulating a petition for a city or county initiative are similar to those at the state level and are spelled out in the state's election codes: signature requirements, strict circulation guidelines, signature verification carried out by the county registrar of voters, and certification either by the registrar or the city clerk. One exception is that signature requirements vary among cities because they are based on prior turnout (for local laws) or voter registration (for charter amendments); thus, it takes 9,485 signatures to qualify an initiative ordinance in San Francisco but 21,494 in the City of San Diego.[29]

The second glaring difference lies in local use of the *indirect initiative*. Unlike the state process, citizens must first file a notice of intent to circulate a petition, and, depending on the number of valid

BOX 3.1 **Reforming the Initiative Process**

Is the initiative process ripe for reform? Californians overwhelmingly support their right to make laws alongside the state legislature, but many acknowledge the process isn't perfect. Its built-in biases have long been recognized, and resource-rich special interests have advantages over average citizens at every stage, a situation that contradicts the original intent of empowering the many at the expense of the few. Fixing these problems and others will require balancing individual power and free-speech rights. Opinion is sharply divided over whether and how to address these complex issues and how effective any solutions would be.

Problems and Suggested Remedies

Problem: It is far easier for paid circulators to collect enough valid signatures than it is for volunteer-based groups; virtually anyone can qualify an initiative by paying a professional signature-gathering firm about $1 to $3 million (depending on number of signatures needed and proximity to deadlines).

Remedy: Ban paid signature gathering or require that a certain percentage of signatures be gathered by volunteers. Extend the deadline to a year, enabling grassroots volunteer movements more time to organize.

Problem: Big money dominates the initiative process.

Remedy: Because capping campaign donations violates free speech protections, improve disclosure laws instead: immediately and prominently displaying that donor information on initiative petitions and campaign advertisements.

Problem: It is difficult to trace donors to ballot campaigns.

Remedy: Require in-ad disclosure of top donors to campaign committees; make online state government resources easier to discover and navigate.

Problem: Ballot measures are confusing and complex.

Remedy: Publicize legislative hearings to generate more substantive discussion about a measure's probable impacts. Use more diverse media to help voters find reliable, comprehensive election resources and information. If two conflicting measures are being considered in the same election, place them together in the ballot pamphlet and explain which will prevail if both pass.

Problem: There are too many initiatives.

Remedy: Require the legislature to vote on proposed laws first. After a public hearing on a measure, the legislature could vote on passing it, with or without any changes that the initiative's authors may approve or reject. Courts could be given a role in verifying that the legislature's version respects the authors' intent. Also, if a measure requires a supermajority vote of the legislature, require the same threshold for the ballot measure.

Problem: It is too difficult to revise initiatives once they become law. They cannot be changed except through future ballot measures, even if flaws are discovered.

Remedy: Allow the legislature to amend measures after a certain amount of time, holding lawmakers to strict guidelines, special conditions (such as a supermajority vote), or further review.

Problem: The process clutters the state constitution with redundant and contradictory amendments.

Remedy: Enable more frequent, comprehensive reviews of the state constitution to weed out obsolete, unnecessary, or contradictory language. Alternatively, require a constitutional revision commission to meet periodically and make recommendations that voters or lawmakers may act upon.

Problem: Too many initiatives are declared unconstitutional.

Remedy: Hold legislative hearings before measures qualify, and publicize conflicts. Empower the attorney general or a panel of active or retired judges to review proposed measures and assess whether they are consistent with the California state constitution. Inform voters of any discrepancies, and give authors the option to withdraw their measures.

For further reading, see Center for Governmental Studies, *Democracy by Initiative: Shaping California's Fourth Branch of Government*, 2nd ed. (Los Angeles, CA: Center for Governmental Studies, 2008), http://policyarchive.org/handle/10207/bitstreams/5800.pdf.

FIGURE 3.3 Local Ballot Measures in California: Subject Matter and Approval Rates, 2015–2016*

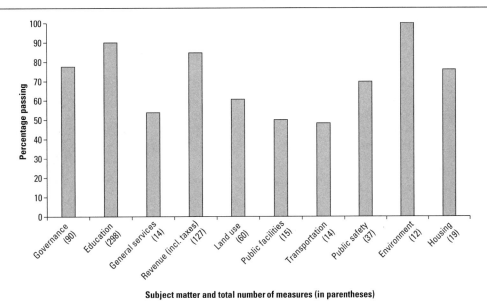

Subject matter and total number of measures (in parentheses)

Source: California Elections Data Archive, "Table B, Summary of Outcomes for All County, City, and School District Ballot Measures by Topic of Measure and County, 2016," Institute for Social Research (Sacramento, CA) and Office of the California Secretary of State (Sacramento, CA), n.d., http://www.csus.edu/isr/projects/ceda%20reports/2016/table-b-2016.pdf.

Note: Of 872 total measures, 687 passed and 185 failed (1 "other" was omitted).

*"Local" refers to county, municipal, and school board. Numbers in parentheses represent the total number of local ballot measures.

signatures gathered, the local governing board (either the city council or county supervisors) may first consider and adopt a proposed measure without alteration before it is submitted to voters. If the local governing body approves the measure, then it becomes a local law.

Los Angeles requires nearly 300,000 valid signatures (not less than 20 percent of registered voters) for the Board of Supervisors either to adopt the ordinance at their next regular meeting or to call a special election for voters to consider it. Local initiatives are placed on ballots as "Measure [letter]," such as "Measure U," as distinct from state propositions, which are assigned numbers. In 2015–16, citizens of 206 California cities considered one or more local ballot measures, 872 in all.[30]

Conclusion: The Perils and Promises of Hybrid Democracy

The tools of direct democracy—the initiative, referendum, and recall—render California's government a hybrid type in which citizens possess the power to make or reject laws and elect or eject representatives, one of only 11 states that permit all three.[31] Yet even among this minority, California's uncommon brand of direct citizen empowerment sets it apart. From being the first state to legalize medical marijuana to having staged the only modern recall of a governor, California politics is distinctively different not only because of its hybrid form but also because of the policies and outcomes it has produced.

California's blend of representative and direct democracy gives the people tremendous power to govern themselves, but, ironically, citizens generally do not feel as if they are in control. In an outsized state with a sprawling population, money is a megaphone, and the initiative process favors the well funded. Whether it's because of the money they can spend to spread their messages across major media markets, the blocs of voters they can mobilize, or the time they can dedicate to campaigning, resource-rich special interests overshadow a process that was established to give voice to the powerless.

The initiative process creates winners who use public authority to establish their version of reform and their vision of "better" policy that reflects their values and interests. It also produces losers who have the right to overcome their opponents by imposing their vision of good government through future ballots, should enough voters agree with them. This give-and-take over time is the essence of political struggle, but in a purely representative democracy, conflicts are harnessed by elected officials and saddled to a lawmaking institution where they are tamed through deliberation and compromise. Because initiatives offer one-size-fits-all solutions and are not open to amendment, direct democracy precludes bargaining and compromise. Unlike bills, which pass through many hands and multiple points where they can be challenged, tweaked, reconsidered, or adjusted to accommodate concerns, the referendum, recall, and initiative take *one* unchanging form that demands merely a yes or no response from voters at *one* point in time. The initiative process in California also unleashes political conflicts to a diverse population where deafening, one-sided arguments are promulgated through social media and paid political advertising. Simple messages and emotional appeals are easier to broadcast across the expanse of California than the nuances and complexities normally associated with lawmaking and policycraft.

Furthermore, neither the initiative nor the referendum lends itself to an integrated set of laws or institutional rules. Thus, new reforms are layered upon prior reforms in California, and newer laws are imperfectly fitted to existing statutes, an incremental process that tends to breed a disordered system of governing. This is a key reason the Golden State's government appears illogical. In fact, state building through the ballot box has proceeded incoherently for decades, often in response to scandals and crises, but often because of voters' hopeful desire for better government.

Even though voters make far fewer decisions at the ballot box than legislators make in a typical morning in the Capitol, the political, fiscal, and social impacts of initiatives and referenda can profoundly upset the status quo—frequently with unintended consequences. Yet direct democracy is sacred in California. Despite the systemic flaws that people see in the initiative process, at least six in ten citizens believe they make better public policy decisions than elected officials do,[32] and voters continually reshape their government with the goal of "making things work." California's hybrid democracy doesn't ensure that things will get better or that government will work more efficiently, but direct democracy feeds citizens' hopes that it will. For better or worse, Californians will continue to use direct democracy to restructure their relationships with their government and with each other.

Key Terms

ballot measure: a proposed law or amendment to the state constitution or local charter that appears on an election ballot for the voters' consideration, usually labeled as "Proposition #" or "Measure [letter]." (p. 25)

direct initiative: a citizen-proposed law that requires a vote of the people instead of the legislature to become law. (p. 26)

indirect initiative: a citizen-proposed law that must be first considered by the legislature, which then may adopt it; if not adopted, it will appear on the next election ballot. In California, only *local* initiatives may be enacted through this method. (p. 26)

legislatively referred measure: a proposed state law (statute), constitutional amendment, or bond (ballot measure) that the legislature has passed and that requires voter approval to take effect. (p. 26)

parcel tax: a method of raising local revenues by assessing a characteristic of a property, such as square footage or number of units. (p. 37)

proposition: a proposed state law or constitutional amendment that appears on an election ballot for the voters' consideration; another word for "ballot measure." (p. 26)

recall: an election in which the people may decide to force a sitting elected official from office and replace him or her with a new representative. (p. 36)

referendum: a law passed by a legislature that is subject to the vote of the people and will be invalidated if rejected. (p. 34)

CHAPTER 4

The State Legislature

Should individuals be allowed to bring their guns onto any school campus? Should unvaccinated children be prohibited from enrolling in public schools? Should the importation and sale of shark fins be banned? Should all Californians have access to affordable health, mental, and dental care, regardless of citizenship status? Legislators answer just such questions. Throughout the lawmaking process, they are obligated to express the will of the citizens they represent, and they make decisions that touch almost every aspect of people's lives.

Design, Purpose, and Function of the Legislature

In California's system of separated powers, the legislature makes law or policy, the executive branch enforces or implements it, and the judicial branch interprets the other branches' actions and the laws they make. Chapters 2 and 3 discussed how the people also dabble in lawmaking through the initiative process, but primarily legislators are responsible for solving the state's problems. California's full-time lawmakers are far better suited to the task than are average citizens. They grapple with complex issues year-round and are assisted by professional staff members who help anticipate outcomes of the bills they create, research the history of similar attempts, evaluate alternatives, and analyze costs of proposed laws.

California's legislature resembles the U.S. Congress in both structure and function. Like its federal counterpart, it is bicameral, meaning that it is divided into two houses that check each other. Legislators in both the state's eighty-member lower house, called the *Assembly*, and the forty-member upper house, the *Senate*, represent districts that are among the most populous in the nation: based on the 2010 census, Assembly districts average 465,600 people, and Senate districts are larger than U.S. House

Lower house:	Assembly, 80 members
Upper house:	Senate, 40 members
Term length:	Assembly, 2 years; Senate, 4 years
Term limits:	12 years (combined) in the Assembly and/or Senate
Majority party in Assembly and Senate:	Democratic
Leaders:	Speaker of the Assembly, president pro tem of the Senate, minority leaders of the Assembly and Senate
Leaders' salaries:	$123,326* annually plus a per diem of $183/day**
Legislators' salaries:	$107,242* annually plus a per diem of $183/day**

Source: California Citizens Compensation Commission, "Salaries of Elected Officials," effective December 4, 2017, http://www.calhr.ca.gov/cccc/pages/cccc-salaries.aspx. On June 19, 2017, commissioners voted to implement a 3 percent pay increase for all state elected officials.

*Legislators also receive a car allowance of $300 per month, which replaced the state-paid vehicle and gas card in 2011. Legislative salaries hit an all-time high in 2008 when regular members were paid $116,208 plus per diem.

**Per the Senate and Assembly rules committees, per diem amounts are tied to federal government reimbursement rates and are intended to cover daily expenses associated with working away from home. Total amounts vary annually with the number of days in session and by chamber. On average in 2016, Assembly members and senators collected a total of $35,559.

districts, averaging 931,350 residents.[1] Candidates for both institutions submit to grueling, expensive campaigns. Well-paid and heavily staffed, legislators also meet year-round like Congress members do; their "professionalized" status puts them in a small class of states that equip the legislature to counterbalance the administrative branch. Only the legislatures of New York, Pennsylvania, and Michigan are comparable to California's, and excepting six states that *approach* professionalized status, the remaining "citizen" legislatures are on a sliding scale of short sessions, low pay, and few staff.[2] Unlike members of the U.S. Congress, however, California legislators have **term limits**. In 1990, voters adopted Proposition 140, an initiative that restricted the number of terms that Assembly members and senators could hold. Prop 28 (approved in 2012) reduced the total number of years that lawmakers can serve to twelve (from fourteen), and now allows them to serve all twelve years in a single house or to split their time between the two chambers. A *lifetime ban* means that lawmakers are prohibited from serving in those offices once they've reached the twelve-year limit. Although over a quarter of all legislators were new to their seats in December 2016 (almost 30 percent were freshmen two years prior), it's likely they will stay in office and help stabilize a legislature that has been wracked by membership turnover every two years.[3] Observers already note that new legislators are waiting longer to scout their next jobs and are beginning to spend more time tackling "big picture" issues and long-term projects. Overall, term limits have profoundly influenced individual representatives' perspectives and the way the legislature operates, a point revisited later in this chapter.

Legislators are elected from districts that are redrawn once per decade based on the U.S. Census. State Senate and Assembly committees commanded the **redistricting** process until voters—weary of hearing about gerrymandering and mapping tricks to keep **incumbents** in office—passed

Proposition 11, the Voters FIRST Act (in 2008), transferring the mapmaking power to a fourteen-member, independent citizens' commission—making California one of 13 states to relocate primary redistricting power outside the legislature.[4] To be chosen once a decade through a multistage, public process, the politically balanced and demographically diverse commission is charged with drawing districts based on "strict, nonpartisan rules designed to ensure fair representation."[5] The rules mandate equal population, adherence to the federal Voting Rights Act, contiguous (all parts touching) and compact districts that respect existing communities, and they also eliminate incumbency protection and partisan districting from consideration.[6] According to the very first commission's final report, "every aspect" of the 2011 process was open; they held public hearings in 32 locations around the state and invited extensive review of their process.[7] While redistricting remains inherently political because it creates winners and losers, the commission created state district maps that reflected their mandates and voter priorities, and their blueprints survived judicial scrutiny and one statewide referendum challenge. Researchers have shown the commission's state maps did produce more compact and somewhat more competitive districts, and they argue the Democratic tilt that occurred after implementation is likely due to incumbency strength as well as party registration that favors the Democrats in most places and Republicans in relatively few.[8] Their authority to redesign California's U.S. House districts, enabled in 2010 through Prop 20, was indirectly tested in a recent federal court case against Arizona's citizen redistricting commission, and the U.S. Supreme Court upheld the principle that a citizen commission may help determine the "time, manner, and place" of Congressional elections through redistricting, just as it does for state government.[9]

Although a few high-profile criminal cases have been brought against California lawmakers over the past century, hundreds of public-spirited men and women have served and are serving resolutely and honorably as California state legislators. Yet, a fervent antipolitician, antigovernment sentiment prevails among Californians, and the individuals whose job it is to sustain representative democracy are scorned rather than appreciated for the challenging work they do. As this chapter shows, lawmakers work hard to fulfill the expectations of their constituents and to meet the relentless demands of a state with a population of 40 million and counting.

California Representatives at Work

California's legislature has come a long way from the days when allegiances to the Southern Pacific Railroad earned it the nicknames "the legislature of a thousand steals" and "the legislature of a thousand drinks." Today its full-time, professional members are the highest paid in the nation, earning more than $142,000 per year, including per diem payments intended to cover living costs. Special interests and their lobbyists still permeate Sacramento politics with their presence, favors, money, and messages, but legislators' loyalties these days are splintered by district needs, statewide demands, and partisanship. Their crammed schedules are split between their home districts and Sacramento (see Table 4.1, "A Day in the Life").

Nowadays, about 20 percent of members are climbing the steepest part of the learning curve. Term limits create large classes of freshman every two years, pushing others into campaigns for the next office and year-round fund-raising. Prop 28 has begun to slow turnover rates, but legislators' desire to stay in politics will continue to keep rates relatively high. In past years, supermajority rules and rigid ideological positioning drove Democrats and Republicans to gridlock over raising

AP Photo/Rich Pedroncell

The Assembly floor is normally a beehive of activity when the house is in session. From the Speaker's view at the polished wood desk, the Democrats are seated to the left and Republicans to the right, reflecting their traditional ideological placement (Democrats appear on the right in the photo). Members cast votes by pressing buttons on their desks, and votes are registered on digital display boards at the front of the chamber.

taxes and cutting social programs, key components of balancing the budget on time—particularly in tough economic times. Now that only a simple majority is needed to pass the budget, and healthier economic times have made tough trade-offs and cutbacks less likely, Republican representatives have fallen to new levels of irrelevance in most policy debates. However, it may be surprising that day-to-day, legislators from both political parties work closely together in committees and other meetings, socialize outside the legislature, and agree on many fixes for local and state problems. Every term, hundreds of bills pass "on consent," or unanimously. They may disagree on fundamentals, and their core differences are exacerbated during economic downturns and highlighted by starkly controversial issues such as providing health care or social services to undocumented immigrants—yet *members of the two parties work together often*, rather than rarely. **Bipartisanship** plays an essential role in California politics.

In many ways the legislature is a microcosm of California (see Figure 4.1). A wider range of ages and backgrounds are represented, and for the first time ever, over half of all Assembly members (54 percent) identify as racial or ethnic minorities, rendering it a majority-minority chamber.[10] The Senate, however, remains mostly White (78 percent). There are more women than before term limits, but their numbers dropped to under 25 percent in 2016, the lowest since 1991–92. There are eight members of the LGBT caucus—the first of its kind to be officially recognized by

FIGURE 4.1 Profile of California's Population versus California State Legislature, 2017

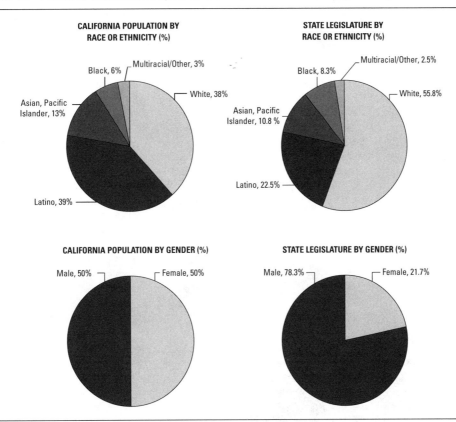

CALIFORNIA POPULATION BY
RACE OR ETHNICITY (%)

Multiracial/Other, 3%
Black, 6%
White, 38%
Asian, Pacific Islander, 13%
Latino, 39%

STATE LEGISLATURE BY
RACE OR ETHNICITY (%)

Multiracial/Other, 2.5%
Black, 8.3%
White, 55.8%
Asian, Pacific Islander, 10.8 %
Latino, 22.5%

CALIFORNIA POPULATION BY GENDER (%)

Male, 50%
Female, 50%

STATE LEGISLATURE BY GENDER (%)

Male, 78.3%
Female, 21.7%

Sources: California Department of Finance, "Report P-3: Population Projections by Race/Ethnicity, Detailed Age, and Gender, 2010–2060," December 2014, http://www.dof.ca.gov/research/demographic/reports/projections/P-3; California Research Bureau, "Demographics in the California Legislature," California State Library, December 15, 2016, www.library.ca.gov/crb/16/LegDemographicsNov16.txt.

a state legislature. The extent to which a legislature is, as U.S. founder John Adams put it, "an exact portrait, in miniature, of the people at large,"[11] is a measure of *descriptive representation*. The extent to which members translate their values, backgrounds, and preferences into meaningful policies is *substantive representation*. Their work as representatives falls into several large categories: *lawmaking and policymaking, annual budgeting, constituency service*, and *oversight* of the executive branch.

Lawmaking and Policymaking

Assembly members and senators fulfill their representative functions chiefly through performing various aspects of **lawmaking**, or codifying rules of conduct, and **policymaking**, defined loosely

BOX 4.2 **Term Limits: Political Earthquake**

Have term limits for legislators been good or bad? Both supporters and detractors can find ammunition in the findings. One thing neither side can deny, however, is that the reform has dramatically changed the rules of representation and the environment in which legislators work. Legislators elected in 2012 or after will help alter current understandings of the law's effects, because voters changed term limits (with Prop 28) to allow twelve years "in the Assembly, Senate, or both, in any combination of terms."

Prior to the passage of Prop 140 in 1990, state legislators were belittled as out-of-touch careerists who had developed cozy relationships with lobbyists and whose reelection seemed guaranteed. The legislature's reputation sank after a Federal Bureau of Investigation (FBI) sting in 1988 netted fourteen state officials who were charged with bribery, including three legislators who went to jail.

The electorate was ready for change when an initiative modeled on one passed shortly before in Oklahoma qualified for the ballot. It restricted senators to two terms (a total of eight years) and Assembly members to three terms (six years) during their lifetimes. Echoes of the early California Progressives were heard in proponents' sweeping promises to restore a "government of citizens representing their fellow citizens."* The measure quickly gained momentum and passed with just over 52 percent of the vote. Since then, support for term limits among Californians has solidified and increased, and twenty other states subsequently adopted similar measures, although these were invalidated or repealed in six states, bringing the current total number of states with term limits to fifteen. In 2012, modifications to the term limits law were approved by 61 percent of California voters, who accepted arguments that politicians were "more focused on campaigning for their next office than doing their jobs."** Lawmakers are now permitted to stay up to twelve years in one chamber so they might "develop the expertise to get things done."

AP Photo/Susan Ragan

Term limits had immediate impacts in 1990. Long-term legislators were forced to campaign for other elected offices, and staff members were driven into private lobbying firms when Prop 140 slashed legislative budgets. Within a few years, long-standing Speaker Willie Brown was mayor of San Francisco, Assembly careers were ending for good, and sitting senators were anticipating their next career moves. Overall, the wide-ranging effects of term limits have touched virtually every aspect of legislative life, and they have ranged from positive to negative.

Willie Brown, Speaker of the California state Assembly from 1980 to 1995, was an easy target of term limits supporters for his perceived abuses of power and flashy style.

Electoral Changes

- Competition has increased for political offices at all levels, from county boards of supervisors to U.S. Congress, as more termed-out legislators who want to stay in politics seek other offices.
- Intraparty competition has risen as members of the same party vie for the same seats—usually in the state Senate but also in Congress, on county boards of supervisors, and city councils, and as executive

constitutional officers. This effect is exacerbated by the "Top-Two primary," which often produces general election races in which each candidate squares off against another member of his or her own party.

- Open-seat primary elections created through term limits are ferociously competitive, attracting millions of dollars in spending; open-seat general elections in a handful of districts are highly competitive as well.
- Incumbents still have huge advantages—about 95 percent are reelected. Many cruise to victory without serious challengers, and some face no challengers at all. Because individuals may be reelected five times to the Assembly and twice to the Senate, those incumbent-dominated contests reduce electoral competitiveness overall.
- For legislators elected under Prop 140 rules (elected prior to 2012), the Senate is a logical step up for members of the lower house; nearly all senators have been former state Assembly members. A few have returned or will return to the Assembly to finish serving out a final term before reaching their lifetime limit (fourteen years; their last term would end in 2024). This pattern is changing as new legislators seek reelection to spend up to twelve years in one place, rather than risk losing their seats to run for the other chamber. The Senate already contains more new legislators who have never had Assembly experience (three of nine freshmen elected in 2016; five elected 2014).

Membership Changes

- Far higher numbers of **open seats** have encouraged the candidacies and election of racial/ethnic minority members—higher than would be expected through redistricting alone. After the 2016 elections, 44 percent of the entire body were Latino, African American, Asian American, or other racial/ethnic minority, and almost all were Democrats (46/53).
- Higher turnover has led to high numbers of female candidates for office in most years since 1990. In the 2016 general legislative elections, almost half (47/100) included a female candidate.
- The total percentage of women legislators follows a longer historical upward trend predating term limits; however, this number peaked in 2005–06 and has declined since.
- Women are occupying more leadership roles in both houses than before; these trends are more apparent among Democrats, in part because Democratic women have served as lawmakers in greater numbers than have Republican women.

Institutional Changes

- Newer legislators have recently experienced the effects of current laws in their districts and have fresh ideas about how to address problems arising from them.
- "Institutional memory" is weaker than in the preterm limits era, as career legislators and their staff have left at regular intervals; members are less expert across a range of policy areas than in the past, and their knowledge of how state systems interrelate is poorer. As more legislators accumulate experience in one chamber under Prop 28, they should build expertise and gain longer term perspectives.
- Under Prop 140, the average senator has had about two and a half times as much legislative experience as the average Assembly member. Under Prop 28, senators' and Assembly members' experience is expected to equalize.
- Senate staff members tend to be more experienced than Assembly staff members and consider the upper house to be the "watchdog" of the more turnover-prone Assembly. This attitudinal difference, shared by staff and senators alike, will probably persist because the Senate has half as many members as the Assembly, and senators enjoy four years between elections rather than two.
- Lobbyists who represent powerful groups, have experience, and are well connected can quickly establish relationships and exert undue influence over legislators. Lobbyists must work harder to get to know new legislators, however, as new members are likely to regard lobbyists with skepticism.
- Executive branch departments command informational resources and benefit from less frequent institutional turnover, rendering oversight by the legislature even more difficult than in the past.

BOX 4.2 (Continued)

Behavioral Changes

- "Lame duck" legislators (those in their last terms) lack electoral accountability to their current districts.
- Many look to their next possible constituency when considering how to vote; some feel less obligated to lobbyists in their last terms and more frequently feel free to "vote their conscience."
- Smaller district-level projects delivering immediate results are more attractive to legislators who are term-limited.
- Longer tenures under Prop 28 seem to be encouraging longer term, more comprehensive lawmaking; previously this suffered, as legislators limited to a few years in office lack the time and incentive to tackle big projects or issues that will outlast their tenures.
- Changes to the term limits law were implemented because of a pervasive sense that "everyone is running for the next office." Term-limited legislators will still run for other offices (about two-thirds of legislators will do so within two years of their term limits), and most will find work in the public sector, but institutional turnover is expected to decrease as more legislators "play it safe" by staying in the same office until their twelve-year clocks run out.

Sources: Author's data. See also Thad Kousser, Bruce Cain, and Karl Kurtz, "The Legislature: Life under Term Limits," in *Governing California: Politics, Government, and Public Policy in the Golden State*, 3rd ed., Ed. Ethan Rarick (Berkeley, CA: Public Policy Press, Institute of Governmental Studies, 2013); and Ava Alexandar, *Citizen Legislators or Political Musical Chairs? Term Limits in California* (Los Angeles, CA: Center for Governmental Studies, 2011).

*California Secretary of State, "Argument in Favor of Proposition 140," November 1990 ballot pamphlet.

**Jennifer A. Waggoner, Kathay Feng, and Hank Lacayo, "Argument in Favor of Proposition 28," in *Presidential Primary Election Ballot Pamphlet* (Sacramento California Secretary of State, 2012), http://voterguide.sos.ca.gov/past/2012/primary/propositions/28/arguments-rebuttals.htm.

as, "what government decides to do or not to do." To deal with approximately five thousand bills and measures introduced in a two-year session, they gather information through research generated by their legislative staffers, pay attention to the cues given by their colleagues, hear arguments from hundreds of people—mostly lobbyists—about proposed laws, and visit sites such as schools and interact with community leaders and citizens to get a better sense of their districts. They introduce bills addressing problems that lobbyists or constituents bring to their attention; bills that could become new **statutes**, or official laws, are variously referred to as "legislative proposals," "proposed legislation," "pieces of legislation," or simply "**legislation**" as they move through the lawmaking process. As members of committees (where the bulk of policymaking occurs), they help shape or amend legislation after fielding complaints, statements, and predictions from witnesses who will potentially be affected by proposed changes. They deliberate and vote on bills, first in committee, and later on the Assembly or Senate floor, where every member has a chance to vote on every piece of legislation. Because all bills must be passed in identical form by both houses before they can be sent to the governor for a signature or veto, members also build support for, or opposition to, measures that are moving through the other house.

As in Congress, much of a legislator's workload is derived from membership on committees, the institution's powerhouses. The Assembly boasts thirty-two standing policy committees, plus almost fifty subcommittees and "select" committees on issues ranging from the budget to craft brewing to the Olympics to cybersecurity—enough for each member of the majority party to become a chair if desired. Half as large, the Senate has twenty-one standing policy committees, ten subcommittees, and still more select, special, and joint committees (eight are shared "jointly" with the Assembly). In both chambers, committees are staffed by policy specialists whose intimate knowledge of past and present policy solutions allow them to play key roles in analyzing and shaping the bills referred to their committee.

In bygone eras, the committee chairmen would rule over their fiefdoms for decades, protecting pet projects, crushing bills at a whim, and blessing others before sending them to the Assembly or Senate floor for final consideration by all members. Power is no longer highly concentrated in a few leaders and chairs as it once was, because turnover leads to relatively less expert members and more competition for choice chairpersonships. Given that most senators are former Assembly members, they usually have about four years of legislative experience when they are appointed as committee chairs. By contrast, many freshmen with no legislative experience have chaired Assembly committees under term limits, but that is changing as Prop 28 takes effect.

Each bill bears the imprint of a unique set of players, is shaped by the rules, and is affected by timing. Throughout the bill passage process, "**stakeholders**"—individuals and groups either directly or indirectly affected by a law or policy, or those who have a stake in the outcome—voice their concerns, demanding or pleading for accommodation. Observers are often surprised at the overt influence that special interests wield in the process. When they raise objections to provisions in bills, legislators listen and respond, sometimes by killing bills entirely. Lawmakers tend to be extra sensitive to the fears and threats expressed by well-financed, vocal, influential, and large organizations that support their political party or are active in their districts—as some say, "The squeaky wheels get the grease." For instance, if a bill to address greenhouse gas (GHG) emissions is being considered, then lobbyists for big oil and gas companies will likely be arguing that it is a "job killer" in face-to-face meetings with lawmakers or their staff and will be forcefully presenting their cases in committee hearings, just as environmental lobbyists will be vigorously arguing that it will mitigate the effects of climate change. This scenario recently occurred before Governor Brown signed SB 32 (a companion bill to AB 32), which set stricter state emission reduction targets for 2030.

Relationships also matter. Partisans tend to support fellow partisans, but legislators who share a certain characteristic might be more inclined to develop political alliances, even with others "across the aisle." Apart from the all-important political **party caucuses** in both houses, which are formal groups that help like-minded legislators coordinate their work on a political agenda or a related set of issues, other legislative caucuses enable bipartisan collaboration. These include several based on demographics (Latino, Black, Women's, or LGBT, for example), a few based on mutual policy interests (Outdoor Sporting, Environmental, Technology and Innovation, etc.), and a couple formed around geography (Bay Area, Rural). There is also a "Mod Caucus," an informal association of Democratic legislators who tend to be probusiness and consider themselves to be ideologically moderate. Over time, representatives tend to develop what is commonly referred to as "social capital": a shared sense of norms, interpersonal networks, and trust among colleagues. Because, in the final analysis, compromise and bargaining are key, relationships among the players—from legislative staff to legislators to lobbyists to the governor's staff—help facilitate the necessary give-and-take to co-construct workable policy solutions.

Bills vary in scope, cost, urgency, and significance and cover every imaginable topic. Most go no further than being referred to a committee, and not bringing up a bill in committee after it has been referred is the easiest way for a chair to kill it. Of lowest significance but highly symbolic are simple *resolutions* passed to express the legislature's position on particular issues. For example, one of the

Assembly's first official acts of the 2016–17 session was to pass a resolution urging President-elect Trump to continue President Obama's program that defers deportation for undocumented immigrant children (also known as DACA).

Inexpensive *local bills*, which deal with such concerns as specific land uses, may matter a lot to the people directly affected by the legislation but usually have only minor impacts on state government. Just one example: a 2017 bill added the community of Calexico to a state gang crime and violence prevention program so that it could receive state funding.[12] Many bills relate to the administration of government and *make technical changes* or *amendments to existing state law*. These proposed statutes might impose mandates, or obligations, on local governments or agencies, such as requiring that all single-user restrooms in any public place or business be gender neutral or prohibiting public schools from using "Redskins" to name a mascot or team. New laws are also needed to authorize public agencies to take on new responsibilities or to collect fees, such as allowing cities to close streets to traffic where serious crime or illegal dumping persists. Other bills create new categories of crime, authorize studies, or set up programs. For example, it is now illegal to import or sell elephant ivory or rhinoceros horn (with certain exceptions), and it took a law to set up a recovery program for unused paint or fluorescent lightbulbs that might otherwise be illegally dumped. These types of statutes tend to signal the Democratic majority party's values—"progressive," "liberal," and leaning moderate nowadays.

Legislators also introduce bills that at first glance may appear to make modest changes, but that, when enacted into law, can have enormous effects on Californians and their local governments, especially over time. For instance, the California Environmental Quality Act, the state's environmental protection law known as CEQA (pronounced "see-kwa"), signed into law by Governor Ronald Reagan in 1970, was developed to supplement new federal regulations regarding land use and pollution. It "requires state and local agencies to identify the significant environmental impacts of their actions and to avoid or mitigate those impacts, if feasible."[13] An environmental review must be completed for any public works project or any commercial activity requiring a government permit, and if potentially damaging activities are detected in the plans, then alterations must be made. Having matured through statutes and court opinions over the years, CEQA codes have had profound impacts on infrastructure development, including the design, size, cost, and location of projects such as bridges and water storage, and the time it takes to completion. CEQA is thus partly to blame for a growing housing shortage afflicting the state, because strict regulations have caused property development costs to rise, placed some areas off-limits to development, and can be abused to delay construction projects by tying them up in court. These issues are especially acute near the coast, where workers are forced to seek housing further inland, forcing prices up in those areas, and causing traffic and pollution to escalate. Home prices and rents vary statewide, but the average homebuyer pays two-and-a-half times the national average, and even California's least expensive housing markets are more expensive than the national average.[14] Although CEQA remains a key tool for protecting the environment, lawmakers are considering how to amend it to jumpstart affordable housing markets.[15]

CEQA amendments belong in a category of bills that have multimillion- or billion-dollar impacts, tend to demand intricate knowledge of existing law, affect many different groups, and usually require years of preparation, study, and compromise. Term-limited members tend to lack the incentive to unravel knotty problems that take years to understand and for which they will receive little credit, but longer time in one house seems to be counteracting this tendency. Other examples of "big bills" could include revising workers' compensation benefits and regulating ecosystems such as the Delta and its related maze of waterways. Reshaping the state health care system to comply with federal regulations is another big-ticket item that lawmakers spent years working on, and at this writing, uncertainty surrounds the national Affordable Care Act (ACA), which may be repealed and/or replaced under the Trump administration. Health insurance for several million residents has been achieved through a state-run plan called "Covered California," or through low- or no-cost Medi-Cal, the state's version of universal health insurance for poor and disabled people, including approximately 170,000 undocumented immigrant children. The state stands to lose billions of Medicaid dollars if proposed cuts are approved (about $78 billion less over eight years under one bill proposed in Fall 2017[16]), affecting all 13.5 million people whose current Medi-Cal coverage includes primary, specialized, acute, and long-term care services.

Given the scope and complexity of policy issues, legislators need help. Knowledge is power in Sacramento, and although lobbyists are always ready and willing to share their information, legislators rely heavily on staff to help them understand problems and develop policy. Thousands of staff members work directly for legislators in the capitol, in district offices, or for committees, and only three states (New York, Pennsylvania, and Texas) employ more.[17]

Inside each legislator's capitol and district office are *personal staff*: individuals hired to prepare bills their bosses will introduce, analyze the thousands of other bills that cross a legislator's desk during a two-year term, assist with scheduling, and perform constituent relations. Professional *committee staff* members work for a specific Assembly or Senate committee, and manage all aspects of shepherding bills through the process, from scheduling witnesses who will testify at committee hearings to writing detailed analyses for each bill. The smaller Senate retained more veteran professional committee staff under the original term limits law and has tended to view itself collectively as having a stronger filter for "bad ideas," but this imbalance will likely even out as more lawmakers accumulate a dozen years of experience in a single house, fostering institutional stability that encourages staff members to stay as well. In addition, staff work for both political parties' leadership and routinely provide their own bill analyses and vote recommendations to their party members.

Legislators also heavily depend on institutional housekeepers like the Assembly chief clerk or the Senate's secretary to ensure that legislators follow standing rules and parliamentary procedures. The nonpartisan *Legislative Analyst's Office (LAO)* has been the so-called conscience and eyes and ears of the legislature since 1941, providing professional analysis of the annual budget as well as fiscal and policy advice based on continuing, in-depth research of statewide programs. With analysts divided into nine subject areas that include education, health, criminal justice, and infrastructure, the LAO remains one of the premier sources of information about state programs and the budget. Similarly, since 1913 the nonpartisan *Legislative Counsel* has acted as an in-house law firm, crafting legislators' proposals into formal bills, rendering legal opinions, and making bill information available electronically (any bill can be accessed online at http://leginfo.legislature.ca.gov).

It should also be noted that the majority party controls the fate of nearly all bills because a simple majority vote (41 in the Assembly, 21 in the Senate) is all that's needed to pass most bills, although a good number of bills are noncontroversial and pass unanimously. With a simple majority also needed to pass the annual budget, the majority party can enact its agenda without being held hostage by a minority party trying to extract concessions in exchange for votes. The bottom line: today, minority-party Republicans are at the mercy of majority-party Democrats when

Assemblywoman Lorena Gonzalez

> **Lorena** @LorenaSGonzalez · Sep 11
> Lady Legislators on the floor, getting it done! #TheFutureIsFemale
>
> L. Gonzalez Fletcher, Sharon Quirk-Silva, Sabrina Cervantes and 2 others
>
> 💬 1   🔁 20   ♡ 88   ✉

In 2017 women in the Assembly and Senate held 26 of 120 seats, representing 21.5 percent of the legislature—a departure from the highs of 31 percent in the Assembly (2004) and 32.5 percent in the Senate (2008). Slightly more women are serving in local governments, which is a traditional training ground for California state legislators.

it comes to lawmaking, and their bills rarely move out of committee—unless they are deemed "harmless" by the Democrats. Usually the majority party can safely ignore the minority unless votes are needed to pass urgency bills or fiscal measures such as new tax or fee hikes that require a two-thirds supermajority (54 in the Assembly, 27 in the Senate), a discouraging position for those

FIGURE 4.2 How a Bill Becomes a Law

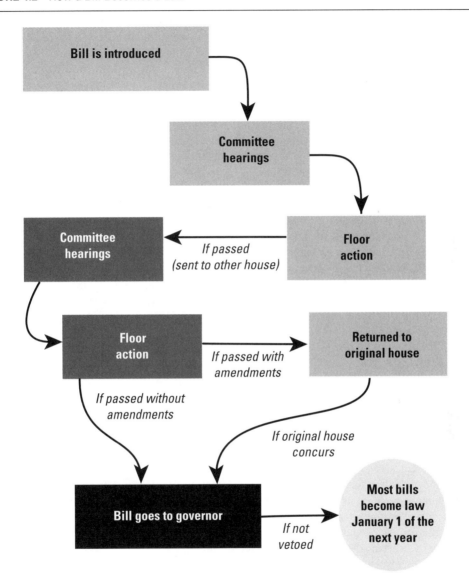

in the minority. The 2012 elections laid a new milestone when, for the first time since 1883, Democrats secured a supermajority in both houses, and they repeated the accomplishment in 2016.[18] With fifty-five Democrats in the lower house and twenty-eight in the upper house, they enjoyed a "veto-proof" majority for several months (special elections in 2013 broke the streak) and again from 2016 into 2018, meaning that they could raise taxes or override a gubernatorial veto without relying on Republican votes. As Governor Brown opined in a 2013 interview, "The Republicans appear to have no power. . . . They aren't needed for any votes."[19] To be effective, Republicans contribute to the process in other ways. For instance, they keep the majority party accountable by raising pointed questions in committee hearings and voicing concerns during floor debates, by shaping their bills to attract consensus, and by trying to amend the Democratic majority's bills to soften potential impacts on their constituents.

Annual Budgeting

It takes the legislature more than half the year to work out an annual budget for the **fiscal year** (FY) that starts July 1 and ends the following June 30, twelve months covered by the state budget. The process formally begins on or before January 10 when the governor submits his version to the legislature, and it should end by June 15, when the budget is officially due. Long-overdue budgets had been the norm for decades, but delays ceased after voters passed Prop 25 in 2010, an initiative that lowered the vote threshold needed to enact the budget to a simple majority.

During the winter and spring of a normal fiscal year, the budget committees and subcommittees in both houses divvy up the work of determining how much money is needed to keep government programs running. They use the governor's budget as a benchmark for estimating costs and potential state revenues. Big-ticket items such as education are either automatically funded or, like basic health care services and prisons, are permanent commitments, leaving a relatively smaller chunk of the budget pie for discretionary purposes; therefore, each legislator fights hard for the crumbs. The inherently partisan process becomes incendiary during tight budget years and is tempered when the economy is looking up and there is **unified government,** meaning that both houses of the legislature and the governor's office are controlled by one party, as has been the case since Jerry Brown's election in 2010.

Constituency Service and Outreach

Constituency service entails "helping constituents navigate through the government system,"[20] particularly when their troubles stem from bureaucratic "red tape." Legislators hire caseworkers to help them respond quickly to requests, and these personal staff members, who typically work in district offices, spend their days tracking down answers from administrators in state agencies like Caltrans and scheduling appointments at other state agencies for frustrated constituents, among other things. Legislators take constituency service seriously, although this part of the job is not mentioned in the state constitution. Many consider it "paramount to return every phone call, letter, and e-mail" and make government seem friendlier through personal contact.[21]

Most legislators try to communicate frequently with the residents of their districts through e-mail, Facebook, Twitter, official websites, or bulk-mail newsletters. Other activities include addressing select community groups, such as Rotary, or attending special public events (store openings, ground-breakings for public facilities, parades, and so forth). Through this kind of outreach, or public relations, as some members call it, representatives educate those in the district about issues, get to know their constituents and what they care about, and reinforce their chances for reelection by enhancing their name recognition and reputation.

TABLE 4.1 A Day in the Life of Assembly Member Shirley Weber

July 11, 2017 Tuesday	
7:45 a.m.	Leave for Capitol
8:30	Senate Public Safety Committee Hearing—Present three bills: AB 90, 1448, and 1528
9:30	Meeting with Senator Portantino, re: SB 328 (bill coming before the Assembly Education committee)
10:00	Briefing by staff for Assembly Higher Education Committee meeting
10:50	Photo with Black Capitol Staff and Members on West Steps of Capitol
11:10	Meeting with California Schools Board Association, re: AB 1220**
11:30	Meeting with Compton Unified School Board members, re: SB 765
11:45	Meet and Greet with Senator Stern, chair of Senate Elections Committee
12:00 p.m.	Noon Democratic Caucus Meeting, lunch provided
*1:30	Higher Education Committee Hearing
*1:30	Senate Human Services Committee—Present AB 1106
*1:30	Senate Natural Resources and Water Committee—Present AB 1323 and special hearing on water stakeholder group
3:30	Meeting re: Campus Climate Select Committee and Anti-Semitism on campuses
*4:00	Meeting with committee chair and stakeholders, re: AB 1220
*4:00	Meeting with committee chair and stakeholders, re: AB 1220
6:00	Phone call with AB 1220 opposition
7:00	Leave Capitol for home; dinner at home
8:00	Calls regarding bill presentations on Wednesday
9:00	Prepare for committee hearing (Assembly Elections and Education)

* Note overlaps. **AB 1220 proposes changes to employment rules for certificated school employees.

Executive Branch Oversight

Who monitors programs to ensure that a law is being carried out according to the legislature's intent? Ideally, Assembly members, senators, and their staff members should be systematically reviewing programs and questioning administrators by having them appear before committees, but term-limited legislators often lack the time and staff resources to determine if the laws they have created are being faithfully executed. In practice, they rely on investigative reports in the media, lobbyists, citizens, and administrators to sound the alarm about needed fixes. Once a problem is identified, the Assembly and Senate can rescue legislative intent in a number of ways. For example, they might address the offending administrators personally or write a bill to clear up confusion over an existing statute. On the rare occasion when an issue grabs the media's attention, lawmakers might respond more dramatically, by interrogating uncooperative administrators in a public forum and then threatening to eliminate their positions, yank authority away from them, or reduce their program funding (a governor can also fire irresponsible administrators). In addition, senators influence programs through their power to confirm hundreds of gubernatorial appointees to the major executive departments and influential state boards and commissions, such as the seventeen-member California Community Colleges Board of Governors. Leaders in both houses also have the privilege of directly appointing some members of a few select boards, such as the twelve-member California Coastal Commission. They also can initiate legislation to change the size of committees.

Renée B. Van Vechten

The Senate Rules Committee, headed by the Senate president pro tem, holds hearings to confirm the governor's appointees. Majority political party members (currently the Democrats) always outnumber those in the minority party on committees.

Leaders

Aside from the governor, the speaker of the Assembly and the president pro tem of the Senate are among the most powerful figures in Sacramento. Along with the governor and the minority leaders of each house, these individuals form the "Big Five" of California government: the leaders who speak for all their fellow party members in their respective houses and are ultimately responsible for cobbling together last-minute political bargains that clinch the budget or guarantee the signing of big bills. These days, the "**Big Three**" Democratic leaders (the top two legislative leaders plus the governor) are most visible and central to the process.

A party leader's job is to keep his or her majority in power or to regain majority status. Nonstop fund-raising, policymaking, rulemaking, and deal making all serve that overarching objective. Leaders oversee their party caucus (all the members of a party in one house) and help shape the electorate's understanding of what it means to support a Democratic or Republican agenda. Still, institutional agendas are fluid, and they emerge from commonalities among legislators' individual efforts more often than they are imposed by elites at the top. However, the general rule is, what leadership wants, leadership gets. Leaders' ability to obtain desired results rests on many factors, including their wielding credible weapons such as the power to remove members from choice committees or kill their bills. Leaders may also endorse opponents, cut off campaign funds, reduce office budgets midyear, or move members out of offices or parking spaces to new and undesirable locations. For instance, Assemblyman Evan Low was removed as chair of the Business and Professions Committee in 2017 after he cast the Assembly's only Democratic vote against the transportation bill that raised gas taxes and imposed new car registration fees.

The speaker is the most visible member of the Assembly and its spokesperson at-large. He or she negotiates budgets, bills, and policies on behalf of the entire membership; curries a high profile with the press; and cultivates a distinct culture of discipline and institutional independence through a unique and personal leadership style. The speaker actively fund-raises in a manner that rewards his or her own faithful political party members and punishes the disloyal. The Senate's president pro tem plays these same roles, and as legislative experience has pooled in the upper house in a term-limited era, the Senate leader's visibility has increased relative to that of the speaker. Under revised term limits, it is likely that the two leaders will possess roughly equal clout.

The speaker appoints chairs and members to all Assembly committees, as does the president pro tem in the Senate through his or her chairing of the all-powerful, five-member Rules Committee. The president pro tem also can use the Rules Committee's power over the governor's key administrative appointments as a bargaining chip in budget and bill negotiations—a tool the speaker lacks.

These days, neither the speaker nor the Senate president pro tem regularly leads floor sessions. Visitors catch glimpses of these leaders as they crisscross the floor to speak privately with members in an effort to find support for bills and negotiate deals while normal business proceeds. More often than not, a colleague acting as an assistant "pro tem" guides floor proceedings. Although the lieutenant governor is named the "president" of the state Senate, no executive branch official ever presides; practically speaking, it would be considered a breach of protocol and a violation of separation of powers. The "LG" can, however, cast a tie-breaking vote if needed.

Leaders never forget that they are chosen by colleagues and stay in power only as long as they can maintain high levels of trust and confidence by meeting their colleagues' political needs. This was as true for flashy former Speaker Willie Brown (1980–1995) as it is for speakers such as Anthony Rendon (2016–) today. No tyrants can survive, if only because so many potential replacements impatiently wait in the wings—and under term limits, opportunities recur with regularity. Brown presided over the Assembly for almost fifteen years. In the span of fifteen years following his exit there were *ten* speakers. Most of the speakers since 1996 have served for about two years apiece (Fabian Nuñez and John Pérez each served four years), but speakers' tenures are expected to lengthen under term limits that permit Assembly members to serve up to twelve years.

Conclusion: Of the People, for the People

California's professionalized legislature is geared to lead the largest state in the nation and has few peers. Only a handful of other state legislatures are similarly compensated, staffed, work year-round, and produce as much model legislation. Yet in most ways, California has at least some company: it is not the only state with term limits, an unpredictable initiative process, a citizens' redistricting commission, or an unusual legislative selection process that produces expensive elections (see Chapter 9). Perhaps it is both the magnitude and sum of its innovations that make it seem exceptional, including policies reflecting more liberal Democratic priorities that are diametrically opposed by majorities in other, more conservative U.S. states.

Although the legislature's basic framework has changed little since the constitutional revision of 1879, major changes in electoral law, redistricting, campaign finance rules, ethics laws, compensation levels, and terms of office have molded and remolded California's legislative environment. Propositions continue to complicate the already difficult task of condensing a multitude of competing interests into a set of effective governing principles. Californians have been quick to alter the political rules in attempts to make their representatives resistant to what is generally regarded as the poisonous influence of partisanship, money, and power, yet these forces are inescapable. Lawmaking is *supposed* to be hard, and conflict is inevitable in an institution brimming with ambitious officials who share similar powers and responsibilities. Short of creating a tyranny, no reform will change that, as it is in every state. Bills bear the imprints of competing interest groups, parties, leaders, funding sources, personal ambitions, rules, history, and a host of other factors that influence choice and impede the easy resolution of issues. The next election also exerts gravitational pull on representatives who rarely stray far from the status quo. In California, however, the policymaking process is further complicated by direct democracy and hyperdiversity, which tend to make its politics seem more exceptional.

Despite these various counterpressures, more often than not, Democrats and Republicans cooperate to enact policies that reflect the people's will and needs as they understand them. Their basic disagreements about how to govern effectively surface visibly in many areas of law and state budgeting, but representatives also deal with countless issues that are *not* divisive. The ways in which they work together and the policy solutions they produce are often hidden from view, contributing to the public's sense that lawmakers are generally ineffective and the widespread idea that citizens make better decisions.

When it comes to the scope of issues with which it deals, the California legislature comes closer to the U.S. Congress than any other state legislature in the nation. It remains the best hope for each citizen to achieve a degree of representation that would be unimaginable under an unelected bureaucracy, a dictatorial governor, or even a part-time legislature responsible for helping to govern one

Assembly Speaker Anthony Rendon (left) and Senate President Pro Tem Kevin de León are spokespersons for not only their Democratic caucus members, but also their respective legislative chambers. Senate leaders were more experienced than Speakers under the original term limits law, but now that the rules allow members to stay in one chamber for up to twelve years, the two leaders will likely attain roughly equal levels of influence and prestige.

of the largest "countries" on the globe. The lawmaking body is closer to the people than the other two branches could ever be: neither the elected executives nor judges can understand the needs and interests of California's communities as thoroughly as firmly anchored representatives can.

Key Terms

Big Three: speaker of the Assembly, president pro tem of the Senate, and the governor. These three usually confer and negotiate over big bills and the budget. (p. 59)

bipartisanship: agreement or cooperation between members of two opposing political parties. (p. 46)

caucus: an organization through which like-minded legislators coordinate their policy making efforts. (p. 51)

constituency service: actions lawmakers take to address the particular needs of individuals in their district. (p. 56)

fiscal year: the twelve months for which a budget is effective; in California, July 1—June 30 of the following year. (p. 56)

incumbent: a person who currently holds an elected seat; for example, a legislator. (p. 44)

lawmaking: codifying rules of conduct, or formalizing the rules about what practices are acceptable in a society; also called "legislating." (p. 47)

legislation: laws or proposed laws. (p. 50)

open seat: an election in which no incumbent is defending the seat. (p. 49)

Party caucus: a formal organization of all members of a political party; the Democratic Caucuses and Republican Caucuses of both the Senate and Assembly organize their members for legislative action. (p. 51)

policymaking: what government decides to do or not to do about an issue. (p. 47)

redistricting: the process of redrawing the district lines for representation; a citizens' commission completes this task in California, designing single-member districts, or one representative per district. (p. 44)

stakeholder: an entity such as an individual, group, government agency, business, or organization that has an interest (a "stake") in the outcome of a government decision because it is (or they are) either directly or indirectly affected by the outcomes. (p. 51)

statute: a formal or written law. (p. 50)

term limits: a restriction on the number of times a person can be elected to or serve in an elective office. In California, after elected officials have reached the limit of twelve years in the legislature (or eight years [two terms] in an executive office), they cannot serve in that office again (a lifetime ban). (p. 44)

unified government: one political party holds a majority in both chambers of the legislature and the governor's office. (p. 56)

CHAPTER 5

The Executive Branch

June 6, 2017, "AS TRUMP STEPS BACK, JERRY BROWN TALKS CLI-MATE CHANGE IN CHINA"

Ending a historic sit-down meeting in Beijing, *Governor Jerry Brown* and President Xi Jinping sealed their "green" alliance with a handshake. Brown had already spent a week campaigning against fossil fuels, cementing relationships with Chinese leaders, and signing agreements that would simultaneously boost economic growth and slow carbon emissions.[1]

June 30, 2017, "12 STATES JOIN CALIFORNIA IN REFUSAL TO TURN OVER VOTE DATA"

Labeling President Trump's allegation of massive voter fraud in the 2016 election as a personal "fixation" that is "deeply flawed," *Secretary of State Alex Padilla* refused to supply a presidential commission with state voter information.[2]

March 2, 2017, "CALIFORNIA ATTORNEY GENERAL OPENS DC OFFICE"

State Attorney General Xavier Becerra took the unusual step of opening a Washington, DC office in order to coordinate policy actions with the state's Congress members. "Decisions that are going to affect California are going to be played out in Washington, DC, and I think it's important for my office to have a presence here," Becerra said.[3]

California's Plural Executive

As Trump administration policies began to take shape in 2017, California leaders arrayed themselves for battle on international and national fronts. Enforcement of federal drug and immigration laws, environmental protection rollbacks, vote integrity, and U.S. federal funds were all on the map. And Governor Brown wasn't the only California official leading the charge, as the above scenarios demonstrate.

The Founders of the United States rejected the notion that more than one person could effectively lead an executive branch. They argued that only a single individual, the president, could bring energy to an office that would otherwise be fractured by competing ambitions and differences of opinion. What then are we to make of California's plural executive, which comprises a whopping eight constitutional executive officers plus a five-member board—one of the biggest sets of officers in the nation? In a state where Democrats attract the great majority of votes overall, administrative duties spread over nine separate constitutional offices—or the twelve officers who occupy those seats—is less challenging than one might expect. Executives who are ideologically compatible support each other's decisions. Still, there are reasons for concern. When offices are divided among Democrats and Republicans, as has been the case in some years, inconsistent governing decisions can cause confusion and create legal conundrums.

Term limits on each office—two four-year terms under Proposition 140—also dull executives' incentives to cooperate with one another. As ambitious colleagues, they are potential or actual rivals for each others' seats, playing a game of political musical chairs. Each must build his or her own name brand through independent actions that merit media attention. However, despite their towering list of responsibilities and leadership of the nation's most populous state, like most elected officials, they remain obscure to average residents. Relative anonymity is one reason why former Attorney General Kamala Harris announced her candidacy for U.S. Senate almost two years ahead of the 2016 election: even high-profile state executives need to create name recognition across a largely detached electorate. The story behind her candidacy also demonstrates the important dynamic of partisanship among state executives: working together—and not at cross-purposes—is easier when they represent the same party. Democrats were elected to fill ten of twelve statewide offices in 2014 (one is nonpartisan but a Democrat occupies it), and Harris's chief potential rival, Lieutenant Governor Gavin Newsom, was aiming squarely for the governorship in 2018—an arrangement that benefited both aspirants.

The duty of an *executive* is to carry out laws and policies. Whereas federal administrators direct agencies in their departments to implement a coherent presidential agenda, in California, a wide assortment of departments, agencies, and commissions serve different masters: the governor, other California executives, the legislature, the entities they are supposed to regulate, or a combination of any of the above. Years of legislative and administrative turf battles, as well as popular initiatives, have produced a thicket of offices, boards, agencies, and commissions, some of which retain independent regulatory power and many more of which follow the governor's lead. In theory, the dispersion of power across several top offices inoculates government against the worst effects of a single, inept leader, but a fragmented power structure can produce inconsistent government policy and counteract accountability.

Exactly these concerns were raised in a negative audit of the state's major tax collection agency, the Board of Equalization (BOE), in 2017. Legislators and the governor seized the opportunity to gut the state agency and, at a breakneck pace rarely reached by state government, created the new Department of Tax and Fee Administration and transferred almost all the BOE's tax-related responsibilities to it—a reorganization that streamlined tax operations and collections.

Governor Brown has reorganized and trimmed the administrative branch since taking office, yet he can only go so far. The tangled, bureaucratic nature of state government is probably nowhere more apparent than in the realm of education. Although the *governor* influences education through budgetary choices and eliminated the duplicative Secretary of Education's office, it is the elected *state superintendent of public instruction* who heads the system by constitutional mandate, overseeing the *Department of Education,* the agency through which the public school system is regulated and controlled as required by law, taking cues from the administration's powerful *State Board of Education,* also appointed by the governor but technically administered by the superintendent, who in turn implements the educational regulations of the state board . . . not to mention the *Assembly* and *Senate education committees* that steer education bills into law, or the *local school district boards* that actually operate schools day to day(!). This sort of confusion

Figure 5.1 California Executives and Musical Chairs, 2017

Under term limits that took effect in 1990, an individual may be elected to the same seat only twice. Elected officials are usually looking for their next jobs long before eight years are up, and open statewide offices are attractive options to those who have campaigned statewide and have run other aspects of state government. In a term-limited era, it's all about the "next" office.

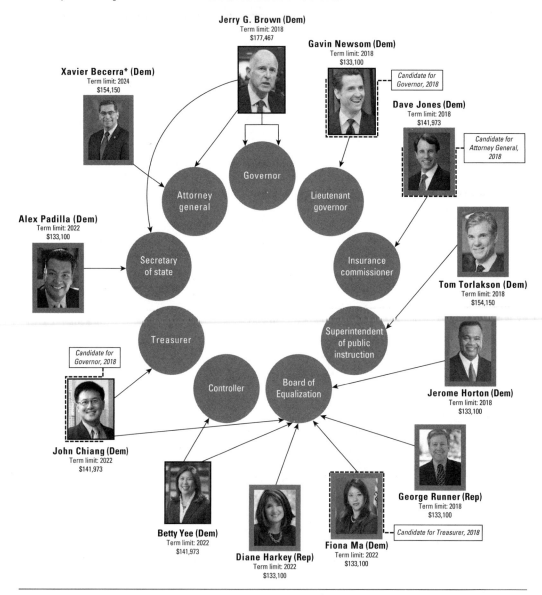

Notes: A shaded frame indicates that the executive served as an elected legislator in the Assembly, the Senate, or both.

*Twelve-term Congressman Xavier Becerra was appointed by Governor Brown to replace Kamala Harris, elected U.S. Senator in 2016. He will stand for election as Attorney General in 2018.

exists because not only are educational policy issues complex, but also because the governor, the superintendent, legislators, local officials, and the people want to influence one of the state's most important public resources.

California's Governor

According to the state constitution, "The supreme executive power of this State is vested in the Governor," which places him or her *first among equals*—for none of the elected executive officers answer directly to the governor. The most widely recognized and most powerful figure in California's state government possesses constitutional duties much like those of most other state governors; what distinguishes the office is both the size and hyperdiversity of the constituency, which is the entire state population, as well as the resulting volume of conflicts to be addressed.

The usual route to office is through a battering election that commands national headlines. Only former Governor Arnold Schwarzenegger initially escaped primary and general election contests, as well as an extended campaign, by winning office through a recall election in 2003, replacing the unpopular Governor Gray Davis, who was only one year into his second term. Those with prior elected experience, strong partisans, and prodigious fund-raisers tend to survive the regular winnowing process—qualities that boosted Jerry Brown to victory over his recent Republican opponents: eBay cofounder Meg Whitman in 2010 and Neel Kashkari (a banker) in 2014. Brown regained the seat after having served two terms as governor (1975–1983, before term limits took effect), secretary of state, mayor of Oakland, and state attorney general.

Head of State

A governor has responsibilities both formal and informal. The role of *head of state* resonates with average citizens: the governor appears at official ceremonies and public events, summarizes California's outlook and his or her agenda in an annual "State of the State" address, receives and entertains foreign dignitaries, and speaks for Californians on both national and international political stages. He or she also functions as the state's official liaison to federal officials in Washington, DC, and works with other state governors to advance causes nationally.

Chief Executive

The power to execute or carry out the law rests with the governor. Putting the law into practice is not something the governor can do alone, however. Brown employs almost 90 key "personal" staff to provide advice and assistance with research and communication

TABLE 5.1 Modern-Era California Governors by Party Affiliation

1943–1954 (12)	Earl Warren	Republican*
1955–1958 (4)	Goodwin Knight	Republican
1959–1966 (8)	Edmund "Pat" Brown	Democratic
1967–1974 (8)	Ronald Reagan	Republican
1975–1982 (8)	Edmund "Jerry" Brown Jr.	Democratic
1983–1990 (8)	George Deukmejian	Republican
1991–1998 (8)	Pete Wilson	Republican
1999–2003 (5)	Gray Davis	Democratic
2003–2010 (8)	Arnold Schwarzenegger	Republican
2011–2018 (8)	Edmund "Jerry" Brown Jr.	Democratic

*Warren also received the nomination of the Democratic Party.

(Schwarzenegger employed 202 at the end of his second term). His cabinet secretaries, who oversee major departments containing scores of agencies, help implement mandated programs throughout the state and coordinate the governor's policies. They are among the 800 top-level appointees placed throughout the administration to head state agencies and departments. Collectively, these appointees put into practice the governor's vision of good governance through the daily decisions they make about thousands of issues.

The governor also appoints members to about 320 state boards and commissions with more than 2,000 slots to be filled. Examples include boards that manage county fairs, professional licensing bureaus, and specialized councils that deal with everything from marine fisheries to the arts to sex offenders. Appointees to about one hundred administrative positions and eighty boards and commissions require Senate approval, and overall only a fraction of appointees serve at the governor's pleasure—meaning that only a few can be let go for almost any reason. For instance, civil service laws protect virtually all state employees, and roughly 99 percent are hired based on merit rather than nepotism, favoritism, or patronage.[4] Outside of this, on rare occasion the governor may name a replacement to an open U.S. Senate seat or constitutional executive office. The governor also has the power to fill vacancies throughout the judiciary (superior, appellate, and supreme courts), although his appointees to appellate and supreme courts must first be reviewed and confirmed by two different judicial commissions and are later subject to voter approval at retention elections (see Chapter 6). The governor may also issue **executive orders** instructing state employees in how to implement a law or policy, but the governor's power falls short of forcing all elected executives—constitutional partners such as the controller or attorney general—to do his or her bidding.

Legislative Powers

Legislatively, the governor plays a significant role by *setting policy priorities* for California not only through proposed laws but also through the budget. The power to *call special elections* and *legislative sessions* to deal with extraordinary matters and the expertise of long-term, *permanent employees* dedicated to research and program oversight, tend to give the governor's office significant institutional advantages over the legislature. Governor Brown called a special session in 2017 to address how California funds roads and highways, but it ended without any new laws (the issue was resolved later in regular session).

The governor and his aides monitor bills at all stages of the legislative process. They propose laws and signal to legislators what kinds of bills he would or wouldn't sign. They testify before Assembly or Senate committees about pending measures and help build coalitions of support or opposition

Steve Granitz/Wire Image

Edmund Gerald Brown, Jr., also known as Jerry Brown, is the only governor to have served four full terms (from 1975–1982 and 2011–2018). He has also served as a community college board trustee, secretary of state, mayor of Oakland, state Democratic Party chair, and state attorney general.

among legislators, interest groups, and other stakeholders, and Governor Brown himself has taken the extraordinary step of testifying before legislative committees on at least two occasions. Staff participate in critical final negotiations over a bill's wording and price tag. The governor's legislative secretary advises the governor to *veto* or *sign* legislation, because a bill submitted to the governor by the legislature becomes law after twelve days without **gubernatorial** action. In 2016, Brown signed 900 bills into law and vetoed a higher percentage of bills than in previous years: 15 percent. Like governors in four out of five states, the governor of California wields the **line-item veto**, the power to reduce or eliminate dollar amounts in bills or the budget. This is also called "blue pencil" authority, because in the 1960s, governors actually used an editor's blue pencil to cross out items in print. For the first time in 34 years (in 2016), Governor Brown did not use his veto power on the budget, in contrast to 2012 when he unleashed his power to eliminate over $195 million in spending. Overall he has used it sparingly. Veto overrides of spending items or any bill passed by the legislature are rarely attempted or successful; legislators generally regard them as a tool to embarrass the governor, and they are wary of retaliation. In fact, the last recorded successful override occurred in response to one of "young" Governor Jerry Brown's budget-related line-item vetoes in early 1980.[5]

Budgeting Power

Budgeting power arguably gives the administration a powerful advantage over the Assembly and Senate. On January 10 of each year, the governor submits to the legislature a proposed annual state budget for the upcoming fiscal year. The muscular **Department of Finance (DOF)**, a permanent clearinghouse for state financial and demographic information, works in tandem with the governor, executive departments, and agencies to specify the initial budget in January, based on projections, and revises it in May based on actual tax receipts. By law, the *director of finance* serves as the governor's chief fiscal policy advisor, overseeing nearly 450 employees who work year-round to prepare the following year's budget and enact the previous year's financial plan. They also analyze proposed laws that would have a fiscal impact on the state.[6]

Chief of Security

If the governor *calls a state of emergency* during a drought or after a natural disaster or terrorist act, he or she is authorized to suspend certain laws and use private property in the impacted area, and the locality becomes eligible for state emergency funds. The governor also promotes security as *commander in chief* of the state's National Guard, which may be called on at short notice to deliver, for example, emergency services to victims of natural disasters such as earthquakes or fires. The State Military Reserve is the defense force placed under exclusive control of the governor; the land-based California Army National Guard and the Air National Guard, dedicated to cyberspace, space, and air capabilities, provide support. The governor can authorize California emergency personnel to assist with response and recovery efforts when international disasters strike, as they did when a 7.1 magnitude earthquake hit Mexico City in fall 2017.

With few restraints, the governor also can reduce penalties associated with a crime by offering *clemency*; that is, he or she can pardon individuals or shorten sentences through commutation, even for death row inmates. Pardoning means that the offense stays on the individual's record, but no further penalties or restrictions will be imposed, and certain rights (gun ownership, professional licenses) may be restored. The governor must report all acts of clemency and the reasons for them to the legislature annually. In contrast to Governor Schwarzenegger who pardoned 16 people, as

Governor Brown headed into his last year in office, he had already pardoned nearly 1,000 persons who had earned the privilege by demonstrating "exemplary behavior following their conviction" for at least ten years following their release.[7] (Incidentally, most of those convictions were drug-related offenses.) Finally, the governor has the authority *to extradite fugitives* from other states.

Sources of Power

A state governor's powers resemble those of U.S. presidents and are spelled out formally in each state's constitution, but the structure of California's plural executive introduces a different set of constraints than those that exist at the national level. For instance, the governor may set policy priorities through the budget, but he or she shares responsibility for day-to-day administration with executive officers and career administrators who may have different agendas. To overcome this structural disadvantage, the governor must draw on other sources of power to be an effective leader.

One source of power is *institutional*, such as whether the governor's political party holds a *majority* in both the Assembly and the Senate, as well as the *numerical advantage of the majority*. Brown's own Democratic party has held the majority during all of his years as governor, and they even reached supermajority status during parts of his third and fourth terms, meaning that they possessed the votes to override his vetoes (although they never attempted to do so). Another institutional factor is the *cohesiveness of parties* in the legislature, because the presence of many moderates may make the governor's job of reaching compromises much easier, whereas rigid or extreme partisans who are unwilling to budge from their positions can potentially thwart a more moderate governor's plans by obstructing specific bill language or foiling supermajority votes.

Power can also stem from a governor's *popularity*, *personal qualities*, and *style*. The governor's image as a loyal partisan friend or possibly as an untrustworthy party turncoat affects his or her ability to gather votes for preferred bills or provisions in them. For example, Governor Arnold Schwarzenegger alienated fellow Republicans by working with Democrats and championing policies that defied the state party's official platform. Jerry Brown (2011–2018), despite having chaired the California Democratic Party at one time, has struck a "no nonsense" note of practicality and toughness in his negotiations with Democratic leaders, disappointing them repeatedly with cuts to favored programs in lean budget years but earning him high marks from citizens. Aware of Brown's popularity and generally supportive of his ideological approach, Democratic legislators have backed him, even if they can't always count on his unquestioning loyalty. Personal *charisma*, the *power to persuade*, the *perception of having a mandate*, and *strategic use of the media* can also go a long way in enhancing a governor's power base. Varied, lifelong *political experience* can also be a source of strength, as it has been for Governor Jerry Brown. No doubt Brown's stature as a statesman helped convince China's President Xi Jinping to ally with him in the global fight against climate change.

The Constitutional Executive Officers

Should the governor leave the state at any time, the *lieutenant governor* (LG) takes temporary control; should the governor resign, retire early, die, become disabled, or be impeached, the lieutenant governor takes the gubernatorial oath of office. Topping the LG's lackluster list of duties is presiding over the Senate, which in practice means exercising a rare tie-breaking vote. The "governor-in-waiting" is also a voting member of the California State University (CSU) Board of

Trustees and the University of California Board of Regents and sits on several other regulatory and advisory state boards ex officio, or "automatically" by virtue of his or her position. The LG's staff includes only six people.

Second in power to the governor is actually the *attorney general* (AG), known as the state's "top cop" or chief law enforcement officer. Through the state's Department of Justice (DOJ), the AG employs deputy attorneys general to help represent the people of California in court cases, provides legal counsel to state officials, coordinates statewide narcotics enforcement efforts, enforces state firearms and gambling laws, fights fraud, assists with criminal investigations, provides forensic science services, and supervises all sheriffs, police chiefs, and state agencies to enforce the law adequately and uniformly. All told, approximately 4,400 people work for the DOJ. The office is inherently political not only because the state's lead lawyer is elected and may use the position as a stepping-stone to bigger and better offices (AG is also said to be shorthand for "aspiring governor"), but also because he or she privileges some causes above others. Xavier Becerra, a former career Congressman and the first Latino to hold the position of AG, was appointed to the position when his predecessor, Kamala Harris, became a U.S. Senator. He has prioritized the protection of immigrant youth and students from deportation, transgender equality, and the environment (among other issues) by suing federal agencies such as the Environmental Protection Agency (EPA) and filing friend of the court (*amicus curiae*) briefs in lawsuits.

More than five hundred employees assist the *secretary of state,* who acts as the chief elections officer and oversees all aspects of federal and state elections held within California. This includes registering voters, distributing ballot pamphlets in ten languages, printing ballots, certifying the integrity of voting machines, compiling election results, and certifying and publishing election results online and in print. With a new, fully operational statewide voter database called VoteCal, the secretary of state's office is offering expanded voter registration services to make voting more "customer-friendly," including online registration (http://registertovote.ca.gov), pre-registration for 16- and 17-year olds, all mail-in ballot elections (coming soon), and same-day voter registration (on election day). As advocated by the secretary, some counties are leading the transition away from neighborhood polling places to all-purpose "vote centers" that will accept universal absentee ballots or walk-ins and will be open 30 days prior to an election. The Political Reform Division of the secretary of state's office implements rules relating to proper disclosure of lobbying and campaign finance activity and makes that information available electronically (http://cal-access.ss.ca.gov, plus a user-friendly version at powersearch.sos.ca.gov). As keeper of official historical records, the secretary of state also charters corporations and nonprofits, maintains business filings, stores complete records of official executive and legislative acts, and safeguards the state archives. All notaries public, persons authorized to formally certify signatures, are commissioned through this state office. The secretary also maintains several registries, including domestic partnerships, advanced health care directives, and "Safe at Home," a confidential address and name change program for victims of domestic violence and sexual assault, as well as reproductive health care workers and patients.

Fragmentation of authority is most evident in the three separate offices that regulate the flow of money through the state government. The prominent *controller* ("comptroller" in some states) is the chief fiscal officer who pays the state's bills and continually monitors the state's financial situation by keeping a tally of the state's accounts. State employees and vendors who sell services or goods to the state will see the controller's signature on their payment checks. As the state officer who is ultimately responsible for ensuring that certain moneys due to the state are collected fairly, the controller is the at-large member of the State Board of Equalization and sits on numerous advisory boards, including the Franchise Tax Board (which administers personal income and corporate tax laws) and more than sixty other commissions and organizations relating to state payouts for employee pensions, construction projects, and other large categories of expenses. The controller oversees a staff of almost 1,400 people.

The second money officer is the *treasurer*, the state's banker who manages the state's investments, assets, and bond debt. Every year the state borrows several billion dollars to finance huge infrastructure projects such as the rebuilding of bridges or schools, and this borrowing takes the form of bonds sold to investors. The treasurer manages the state's mountainous debt by selling and repaying bonds on an ongoing basis, trying to secure acceptable credit ratings that lead to lower loan interest rates, and maintaining the state's financial assets. About 230 employees round out the treasurer's office. The treasurer also chairs or sits on almost sixty boards that are authorized to raise and spend money on huge infrastructure plans for railways and roads, building and repairing schools, water supplies, housing, and more.

The five-member *Board of Equalization* completes the trifecta of money offices, but it is a mere shadow of its former self. Established by the state constitution in 1879 to ensure that property taxes were collected uniformly throughout the state, over time it became responsible for collecting $60.5 billion in taxes and fees every year—about 30 percent of the state's annual revenues. After a 2017 government audit exposed questionable accounting practices and shady campaign donations, the legislature and governor used the budget process to demolish the BOE by moving 90 percent of its 4,700 employees into a brand new agency: the Department of Tax and Fee Administration. A smaller slice of the workforce was reconstituted into a second, quasi-judicial entity: the Office of Tax Appeals, designed to settle disputes between taxpayers and tax collectors. The BOE itself, consisting of the state controller and four other elected regional officials (two Democrats and two Republicans after the 2014 elections), reverted to its original constitutional mandate, which is to equalize property taxes and collect alcohol excise taxes. Surely it is only a matter of time before the BOE is eliminated through constitutional amendment, a recurring recommendation from constitutional revision commissions and the Legislative Analyst's Office since 1929.

In the same anti-tax spirit that led to the passage of Proposition 13, voters rebelled against spiraling auto insurance rates and elevated the Office of *Insurance Commissioner* from a governor-appointed subagency to a full-scale executive office in 1988. To protect consumers who participate in the world's sixth largest insurance market, the elected commissioner is supported by 1,250 employees who oversee the $123 billion-a-year insurance industry by reviewing and preapproving rates for car and home owners' (property and casualty) insurance, investigating fraud, and resolving consumer complaints. The commissioner also makes sure that insurance companies are solvent, licenses agents and companies operating in California, and enforces rulings against violators. The department has taken a stronger role in reviewing health insurance rate increases as well, though the commissioner lacks authority both to force companies to reduce rates and to reject exorbitant rate increases. In 2014, health insurers and others spent $57 million to defeat a ballot measure (Prop 45) that would have empowered the commissioner to authorize health rate increases; supporters raised and spent roughly $4.4 million.[8] It failed.

As the overseer of all public schools, the *superintendent of public instruction* heads the Department of Education and chairs the State Board of Education, guiding education policy and advocating for student achievement as the state's only nonpartisan executive officer. The superintendent is the point person for statewide student testing and reporting, including implementation of the state's standardized testing system (California Assessment of Student Performance and Progress, or CAASPP) as well as high school exit exams; data collection on a range of education-related issues

Secretary of State Alex Padilla, a former state senator who has a degree in engineering from the Massachusetts Institute of Technology, knows the importance of a well-designed system. Since winning office in 2014, he has helped modernize the state's voter registration and elections processes by endorsing new laws that establish voting centers that will open a month prior to election day, institute vote-by-mail elections that should bring down the costs of elections, and enable voter pre-registration for 16- and 17-year olds.

such as dropout rates, yearly funding levels for K–12 and community college education, and student achievement levels; and implementation of education-related federal court opinions, the No Child Left Behind Act, and related U.S. education policy initiatives. Like other state constitutional officers tasked with coordinating policy among a snarl of governing bodies, the superintendent sits as an ex officio member on more than one hundred education-related boards and commissions.

Although these executive officers are free to consult each other and frequently find themselves in each other's company, at no point do they meet as a governing board, and no institutional mechanism exists to coordinate their work. Sometimes this arrangement makes for strange bedfellows, as Governor Schwarzenegger found in 2009 when he wrote an executive order closing all state offices two Fridays per month, an order also intended to cover those headed by his fellow constitutional officers. However, his mandate legally could not apply to his colleagues, who promptly ignored it. One lesson to be gleaned from this example is that an organizational structure that allows Democrats and Republicans to share **executive power** virtually guarantees that latent differences in governing philosophies and approaches exist, and it usually takes a crisis to make those differences visible and put them to the test.

FIGURE 5.2 Organization Chart of California's Executive Branch

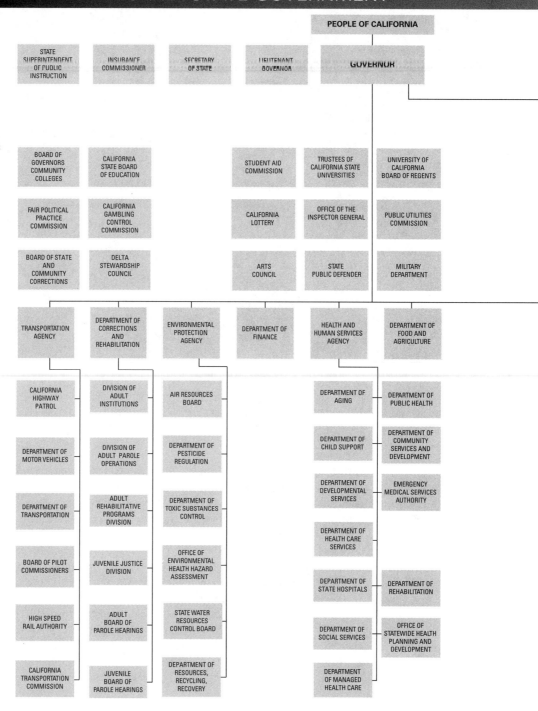

CALIFORNIA STATE GOVERNMENT

PEOPLE OF CALIFORNIA

STATE SUPERINTENDENT OF PUBLIC INSTRUCTION

INSURANCE COMMISSIONER

SECRETARY OF STATE

LIEUTENANT GOVERNOR

GOVERNOR

BOARD OF GOVERNORS COMMUNITY COLLEGES

CALIFORNIA STATE BOARD OF EDUCATION

STUDENT AID COMMISSION

TRUSTEES OF CALIFORNIA STATE UNIVERSITIES

UNIVERSITY OF CALIFORNIA BOARD OF REGENTS

FAIR POLITICAL PRACTICE COMMISSION

CALIFORNIA GAMBLING CONTROL COMMISSION

CALIFORNIA LOTTERY

OFFICE OF THE INSPECTOR GENERAL

PUBLIC UTILITIES COMMISSION

BOARD OF STATE AND COMMUNITY CORRECTIONS

DELTA STEWARDSHIP COUNCIL

ARTS COUNCIL

STATE PUBLIC DEFENDER

MILITARY DEPARTMENT

TRANSPORTATION AGENCY

DEPARTMENT OF CORRECTIONS AND REHABILITATION

ENVIRONMENTAL PROTECTION AGENCY

DEPARTMENT OF FINANCE

HEALTH AND HUMAN SERVICES AGENCY

DEPARTMENT OF FOOD AND AGRICULTURE

CALIFORNIA HIGHWAY PATROL

DIVISION OF ADULT INSTITUTIONS

AIR RESOURCES BOARD

DEPARTMENT OF AGING

DEPARTMENT OF PUBLIC HEALTH

DEPARTMENT OF MOTOR VEHICLES

DIVISION OF ADULT PAROLE OPERATIONS

DEPARTMENT OF PESTICIDE REGULATION

DEPARTMENT OF CHILD SUPPORT

DEPARTMENT OF COMMUNITY SERVICES AND DEVELOPMENT

DEPARTMENT OF TRANSPORTATION

ADULT REHABILITATIVE PROGRAMS DIVISION

DEPARTMENT OF TOXIC SUBSTANCES CONTROL

DEPARTMENT OF DEVELOPMENTAL SERVICES

EMERGENCY MEDICAL SERVICES AUTHORITY

BOARD OF PILOT COMMISSIONERS

JUVENILE JUSTICE DIVISION

OFFICE OF ENVIRONMENTAL HEALTH HAZARD ASSESSMENT

DEPARTMENT OF HEALTH CARE SERVICES

HIGH SPEED RAIL AUTHORITY

ADULT BOARD OF PAROLE HEARINGS

STATE WATER RESOURCES CONTROL BOARD

DEPARTMENT OF STATE HOSPITALS

DEPARTMENT OF REHABILITATION

DEPARTMENT OF SOCIAL SERVICES

OFFICE OF STATEWIDE HEALTH PLANNING AND DEVELOPMENT

CALIFORNIA TRANSPORTATION COMMISSION

JUVENILE BOARD OF PAROLE HEARINGS

DEPARTMENT OF RESOURCES, RECYCLING, RECOVERY

DEPARTMENT OF MANAGED HEALTH CARE

THE EXECUTIVE BRANCH

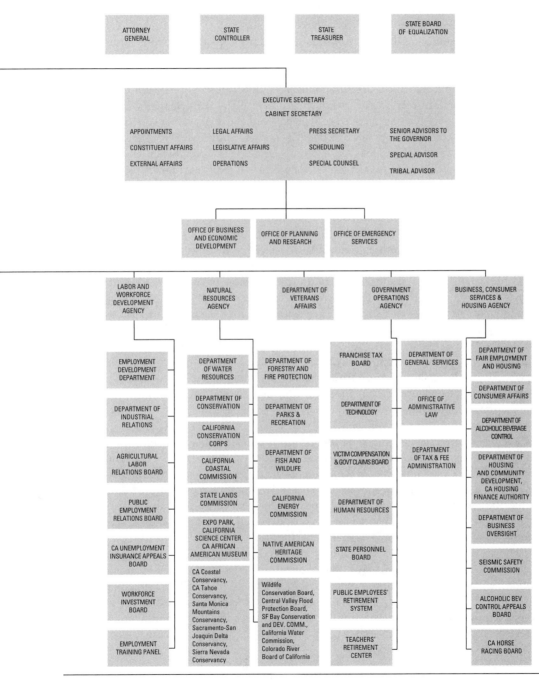

Source: Adapted from California Online Directory, "California State Government—the Executive Branch," http://www.cold.ca.gov/Ca_State_ Gov_ Orgchart.pdf. Updated July 1, 2017.

Administrators and Regulators

A great checkerboard of agencies, departments, administrative offices, and boards form the state's "bureaucracy," or bulk of the executive branch. Almost all are linked to the governor through secretaries whom he or she designates to head each agency or directors who run departments. Collectively the agency secretaries constitute the governor's cabinet, and in practice, they report to the *cabinet secretary*, a gubernatorial appointee who is considered one of the governor's most powerful staff members. Every organization within the executive branch is designed to help the governor execute state law faithfully, but bureaucratic reorganization is periodically needed to streamline operations and eliminate haphazard structures that have been added over the years. Citizens may not have noticed, but Governor Jerry Brown's overhaul of state government, approved by the legislature and implemented by 2013, reduced the size of government by consolidating several entities. Brown's plan aimed to make government "easier to manage, and more coordinated and efficient" so that it could provide "better and more cost-effective service"—the object of all reorganization plans, to be sure.[9]

The "**superagency**" scheme of Governor Pat Brown—the late father of Governor Jerry Brown— has stuck since the 1970s, with a few alterations. The superagencies act as umbrella organizations for the smaller departments, boards, and commissions nested within them. The seven superagencies are (1) Business, Consumer Services, and Housing; (2) Natural Resources; (3) Government Operations; (4) Transportation; (5) Health and Human Services; (6) Environmental Protection (EPA); and (7) Labor and Workforce Development. For example, the relatively new Transportation Agency houses six entities, including Caltrans, the Department of Motor Vehicles (DMV), and the state highway patrol. The state EPA oversees the State Water Resources Control Board, a headline-grabber during the drought; the Air Resources Board, tasked with implementing the state's carbon cap-and-trade program and other regulations related to AB 32; and four other major offices that regulate or assess pesticides, toxic substances, and other health hazards. Five "superdepartments" also house critical divisions and employ many specialists: Corrections and Rehabilitation (prisons); Government Operations (for tax collection and such); Finance (governor's budget); Food and Agriculture; and Veterans Affairs (see Figure 5.2). In all, about 208,700 full- and part-time public employees constitute the state administration or "state bureaucracy"—a 15 percent smaller workforce in 2017 than in 2009.[10]

About a dozen salaried state commissions and boards possess independent advisory, regulatory, or administrative authority and are led by gubernatorial appointees who must be confirmed by the Senate or are chosen by legislative leaders. Among these are the Public Utilities Commission, which regulates all private electric, gas, transit, water, and telecommunications companies operating in the state. About 300 boards, councils, and commissions also help run state programs, manage public works like the L.A. Coliseum, and handle professional licensing for dentists, nurses, accountants, and so forth. Most consist of four or five members, and some meet only twice a year. Full membership turnover of a board rarely occurs during a governor's term; thus, competing ideological viewpoints are often represented on boards depending on who appointed whom. In addition, many organizations operate autonomously, meaning that they don't need to consult the governor or other elected executives before acting on an issue, although state elected officials are ultimately responsible for actions taken. Together, these unelected authorities make rules affecting Californians in virtually every imaginable way, from making beaches accessible to determining where waste can be dumped.

Conclusion: Leading State Government

California's plural executive means that separately-elected individuals both share and compete for power. The division of labor among many offices provides checks against the concentration of authority, but, perversely, this arrangement also obscures accountability. Most Californians believe the governor is all-powerful and blame him or her when things go awry, even if he or she has no more authority to tell the controller what to do than the secretary of state can.

The governor sets the tone for state administration by using instruments of power such as the signing of legislation, vetoes, executive branch reorganization, appointments, and annual budgeting to coordinate "the big picture." Yet each constitutional officer brings a different kind of energy and focus to his or her specialized role in the executive branch. They may formulate their own initiatives and maximize their own budgets to reflect their priorities, and they use these to build their individual reputations, campaign skillsets, and policy knowledge in ways that enable them to pursue other offices—even each other's offices. Latent tensions tend to surface during crises and economic hard times, and occasionally their ambitions may put them at odds, but similar political views and shared partisanship certainly help them find mutual agreement on policy and campaigns. All in all, California's executive officers coexist in pursuit of the same basic goal: to allow the state to prosper.

California's quasi-national status also provides a stage for ambitious individuals and creates both national and international audiences for policy-oriented leaders with ambitious plans. Although the basic structure of the Golden State's executive branch resembles that of other states, the ways in which California's players maximize their roles—recently as chief antagonists to the Trump administration and as global economic and environmental policy drivers—help set California politics apart from the rest.

Key Terms

Department of Finance (DOF): organization in the governor's office that compiles information about state agency finances and population demographics and constructs the governor's version of the state's annual budget. (p. 69)

executive orders: a governor's written instructions to state employees about how to implement a state law or policy. (p. 68)

executive power: the power to carry out or implement laws and policies. (p. 73)

gubernatorial: of or relating to the governor. (p. 69)

line-item veto: a governor's ability to cross out or veto items within a spending bill, also known as "blue pencil authority." (p. 69)

superagency: large state agency that oversees smaller departments, boards, and commissions relating to a general area of state policy, headed by a secretary who is part of the governor's cabinet. (p. 76)

CHAPTER **6**

The Court System

our federal Immigration and Customs Enforcement (ICE) officials were hiding from their target in plain sight. As the Pasadena courtroom door opened, they alighted from the hallway bench and rushed the unsuspecting man. After asking for his name and announcing themselves, they informed him that they were taking him in.[1] Deportation was imminent.

Using state courts to nab undocumented immigrants has inflamed Chief Justice Tani Cantil-Sakauye, who promptly requested the U.S. Attorney General and Secretary of the Department of Homeland Security to refrain from making such arrests. In a letter to both officials, she called out ICE for violating the separation of powers principle and jeopardizing public trust in the court system. "Our courts are the main point of contact for millions of the most vulnerable Californians," she wrote. "Trial courts strive to mitigate fear. . . . Our work is critical for ensuring public safety and the efficient administration of justice."[2] Unmoved by arguments that courthouse arrests could scare off witnesses and prevent crimes from being reported, the federal officials promised more of the same, absent full cooperation from state and local law enforcement to promote deportations.[3]

California courts play a central role in preserving the rule of law, a function that is challenged not only by federal interventions such as these but also by chronic state underfunding. Economic recession prompted deep budget cuts that have not been fully redressed some ten years later, causing deficits that are still visible in a persistent shortage of judges, trial court delays and huge backlogs, insufficient numbers of court interpreters and court reporters, and archaic technological infrastructure, among other shortcomings. For millions of people who rely on the courts to deliver justice, it will be years before they find a system restored to full capacity.

Fundamentally, the state courts' place in a separated system of powers is to provide "fair and equal access to justice for all Californians." Judges also verify that the rules, laws, and policies that the executive and legislative branches produce and the initiatives that the voters approve are lawful. In one of the largest court systems in the world (and certainly the largest in the United States), over 2,000 judicial officers and 19,000 court employees handle about *7 million* cases annually.[4] Chances are good that every Californian at some point in his or her life will engage the justice system directly as a juror, to resolve family matters resulting from divorce or child custody disputes, or because of a traffic violation—the top reasons people connect to California's courts.

The Three-Tiered Court System

As in the federal judicial system, California courts are organized into three tiers, and the legislature controls the number of judgeships. At the lowest level are trial courts, which are also known as *superior courts*, located in each of California's fifty-eight counties. In a trial court, a judge or jury decides a case by applying the law to evidence and testimony presented. Working at this level are more than 1,725 judges and almost 300 subordinate judicial officers such as commissioners, and they deal with virtually all 7 million civil and criminal cases that begin here.

Most citizens who use the courts are involved in resolving minor **infractions** for which a fine rather than jail time is imposed, including traffic violations such as texting while driving. Infractions, which are heard by a judge only, make up about 65 percent of the superior courts' docket. A recent rule change allows traffic violators who challenge their tickets to avoid paying their fines until a trial is held. Strategies for moving all minor traffic violations out of criminal courts and into the civil courts are now being devised. The next-higher level is a category of crime called **misdemeanors**, for which the maximum punishment is a $1,000 fine and up to one year in a county jail. Examples include drunk driving, vandalism, and petty theft. Finally, an accused criminal may be charged with a **felony**, which is a serious and possibly violent offense, punishable by a state prison sentence or possibly death. Examples of felonies include murder, robbery, rape, and burglary of a residence. County district attorneys (DAs) bring cases against the accused, and anyone who cannot afford to pay for his or her own legal defense is entitled to help from a public defender. California's DAs have a conviction success rate of around 80 percent.[5] Sentencing outcomes depend on the severity of the crime, the offender's criminal history, and the court's discretion.

Civil suits, on the other hand, usually involve disputes between individuals or organizations seeking monetary compensation for damages, usually incurred through injuries, breaches of contract, or defective products. A *small claims* case is filed by a person seeking $10,000 or less, and attorneys are not allowed to be present at the court hearing. *Limited* civil cases involve damages valued at less than $25,000, and *unlimited* civil matters exceed that threshold. The huge number of civil lawsuits in the state, nearly 720,000 annually,[6] reflects a general acceptance of litigation as a "normal" way to resolve problems. The state attorney general can also bring civil cases against companies that break environmental, employment, or other types of state laws, or individuals who commit professional violations. Civil suits typically result in monetary judgments, not jail time, and the state does not supply legal representation for citizens who are involved in civil cases. The state does, however, support some legal defense assistance through services labeled "legal aid," a portion of which is dedicated to helping children and families navigate the citizenship process and avoid deportation.

Juvenile, family, and probate cases are specific types of civil cases that are also heard in superior court. Family matters typically involve divorces, marital separations, and child custody cases. Parties might also ask a judge to rule on a family member's mental competence, settle an inheritance dispute, or legally change a name. A single judge or a trial jury may decide a case at this level.

Building on the work of her predecessor, Chief Justice Cantil-Sakauye has focused on improving access to justice for vulnerable populations. To address fines and fees that disproportionately penalize low-income defendants, courts are testing an "ability to pay" calculator. Online "self-help" resources are available on the *http://www.courts.ca.gov* website to inform citizens about immigration rights, how to obtain legal aid in civil cases, prep for court appearances, or avoid going to court altogether. **Alternative dispute resolution** (ADR), also known as mediation or legally binding arbitration, offers a quicker way to decide cases and avoid the cost of hiring a private attorney. **Collaborative courts** have also become an important tool in dealing with repeat offenders. Known as "problem-solving courts" that operate through superior courts, they combine judicial case processing, drug and alcohol treatment services, and monitoring to help individuals rebuild their lives and avoid recidivism. Among the 415 collaborative courts in California are combat veterans' courts, mental health courts, homeless courts, drug courts, and domestic violence courts. When a veteran of the Iraq War pleads guilty to driving under the influence (DUI), for instance, in Veterans Court he may be placed on parole and ordered to enroll in a program to treat alcoholism or possibly be treated for posttraumatic stress disorder (PTSD) while being monitored closely, in lieu of paying a fine or serving jail time.

If the losing party in a case believes the law was not applied properly, he or she may ask the next-higher district *court of appeal* to hear the case. There are no trials in district appellate courts, although three-judge panels commonly hear lawyers argue cases. Spread across six different geographical areas in nine court locations are 105 appellate justices who review approximately 22,000 cases for errors, improprieties, or technicalities that could lead to reversals of the lower courts' judgments; they dispose of more than half these cases without issuing written opinions. On the whole, appellate court decisions clarify and actually establish government policy, as the state supreme court allows the great majority of these decisions to stand.

The highest judicial authority is vested in a seven-member *supreme court*, whose decisions are binding on all California courts. Headquartered in San Francisco, supreme court justices also hear oral arguments in Los Angeles and Sacramento for cases appealed from the intermediate-level district courts throughout the year, but they automatically review death row cases and exercise original jurisdiction over a few other types. Of roughly 7,870 cases appealed to it in 2015–16, the court issued a mere 76 written opinions, made available to the public on the court's website and through published official reports. The justices are not required to review every case and therefore have wide discretion over case selection, concentrating mostly on those that either address important questions of law or promote uniform judgments across the system. By law they must, however, analyze complex death penalty case records to generate internal memoranda and written opinions that often exceed one hundred pages apiece; the court acted on twenty-seven such cases in the 2015–16 term. It can take more than twenty years to exhaust the appeals process due to the immense legal resources that death penalty cases command. Voters approved a measure in 2016 designed to speed the processing of death penalty cases, and executions were set to resume after California's highest court ruled Prop 66 to be constitutional (subject to resolving a separate issue regarding the toxic formula used for lethal injections).[7] In Prop 66, voters directed the courts to resolve death penalty cases within five years, but based on the separation of powers principle, the court clarified that voters cannot place hard deadlines on courts.

Automatic appeals aside, justices spend considerable time choosing cases, and each justice employs support staff and permanent staff attorneys to assist him or her. Their interpretations of the law define the boundaries of acceptable behavior for businesses, government, and citizens. As the principal supervisor of the lower courts, the chief justice shoulders more responsibility than the other justices. As spokesperson for the judicial branch, Chief Justice Cantil-Sakauye delivers the "state of the judiciary" address annually to the legislature and has become the "chief lobbyist" for restoring state funding to the court system. The court's reputation at any given time reflects its collective policy decisions, both in the questions the justices choose to address or ignore and in their interpretation of the wording and intent of specific laws.

Controversy often stems from the supreme court's review of ballot initiatives, political measures that can only be ruled on *after* passage and are often overturned in whole or in part for violating the state constitution. Proposition 8, a constitutional amendment that eliminated same-sex marriage by defining marriage as between a man and a woman only, became a hot potato in 2009 for the justices, who were threatened with recall if they overturned it. (They didn't, although three supreme court justices in Iowa did legalize same-sex marriages and were ousted by that state's voters in 2010.)

Courtesy of the Supreme Court of California. Photo by Bob Knapik.

Consisting of six associate justices and one chief justice, California's Supreme Court is one of the most racially/ethnically diverse in the nation. The supreme court building is located in San Francisco. From left to right: Mariano-Florentino Cuéllar (confirmed 2015), Kathryn Werdegar (retired August 2017), Carol Corrigan, Chief Justice Tani Cantil-Sakauye, Goodwin Liu, Ming Chin, and Leondra Kruger (confirmed 2015).

On and Off the Court

An attorney who has practiced law in California for at least ten years may become a judge, but individuals usually enter the position through gubernatorial appointment rather than by first running for office. Those who are interested in becoming judges may apply through the governor's office. The combination of a recent state supreme court ruling and a new law known as AB 1024 now allows undocumented immigrants to gain admittance to the state bar and to practice law in California.

A governor has ample opportunity to shape the long-term ideological bent of the judiciary by selecting individuals whose partisanship and political principles are reflected in their judicial philosophies. When then-Attorney General George Deukmejian (1982–1991) was asked why he was running for governor, he replied, "Attorney generals don't appoint judges. Governors do."[8] Governor Arnold Schwarzenegger was perhaps the least partisan in his judicial appointments than any governor in recent times: about 40 percent of his appointees were Democrats, whereas Jerry Brown has appointed fewer than 10 percent Republicans.[9] Governors also directly affect the demographic composition of the bench, which today remains disproportionately male, middle-class, and White—in contrast to the state's heavily racial/ethnic prison population (see Table 6.1 and Box 6.1). However,

FIGURE 6.1 California Court System

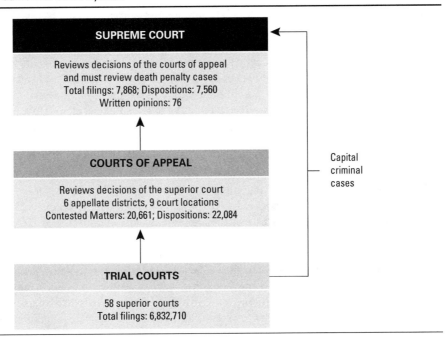

Sources: Judicial Council of California, *2016 Court Statistics Report: Statewide Caseload Trends, 2003–2004 through 2014–2015* (San Francisco: Judicial Council of California, 2016), http://www.courts.ca.gov/documents/2016-Court-Statistics-Report.pdf.

Note: Missing and/or incomplete data from eight courts affect these totals.

Brown has diversified the bench throughout his tenure, boosting gender equality with almost 40 percent female, 5 percent who identify as LGBT, and 40 percent ethnic and racial minority appointees, including 17 percent Latino, 11 percent Black, and almost 10 percent Asian persons.[10] Vacancies are unpredictable. Governor Schwarzenegger made 627 judicial appointments over seven years, and in the six years between January 2011 and March 2017, Governor Brown appointed 356.

Supreme court replacements seldom occur, but coincidentally, retirements enabled Schwarzenegger to appoint two of the seven supreme court justices, thereby fortifying the conservative court with his selections. Jerry Brown's four supreme court appointees are likely to tilt the court in the opposite ideological direction. Interestingly, none of Brown's first three appointees had prior judicial experience, although all three graduated from Yale law school, excelled as attorneys, worked in U.S. presidential administrations, and are prolific scholars. Goodwin Liu was born to Taiwanese immigrant parents; Mariano-Florentino Cuéllar is a naturalized citizen of Mexican parentage; and Leondra Kruger is a Black woman who was age 38 when selected in 2014. His fourth appointee (not announced at the time of this writing), fills the spot left by Justice Kathryn Werdegar, retiring after 23 years on the state's highest court.

Superior court judges serve for six years without term limitations, and if they were first appointed to office and not elected, they must become nonpartisan candidates for their offices when their terms expire. Longer terms are intended to increase the judiciary's independence and stability over time by reducing the frequency of distracting campaigns that can create potential conflicts of interest with campaign contributors. Contested elections are rare, and unopposed judges usually win.

Appointees to the six appellate courts and the supreme court also require the governor's nomination, but they must first be screened by the State Bar's Commission on Judicial Nominees, a state agency whose members represent the legal profession, and then be confirmed by the Commission on Judicial Appointments. Together they evaluate appointees' fitness for office. Confirmation allows a justice to fulfill the remainder of his or her predecessor's twelve-year term, but the judge must participate in a nonpartisan "retention election" at the next gubernatorial election, at which time voters are asked to vote yes or no on whether he or she should remain in office; no challengers are allowed. The judge may seek unlimited terms thereafter and must face the voters every twelve years.

Voters rarely reject judges. Defeat requires public outrage fueled by provocative, media-driven campaigns, as three supreme court justices discovered in 1986. Having earned reputations for being "soft on crime" at a time when rising crime rates were rattling the public, Chief Justice Rose Bird and two of her colleagues were targeted for their opposition to the death penalty. For the first time in California history, three justices lost their retention bids, and Governor George Deukmejian replaced them with conservative justices.

Although judges rarely lose elections, they are not immune to campaign or interest group pressures. Progressives realized this when they established nonpartisan judicial elections in 1911, but many judges must run retention campaigns in which outspoken donors or independent "super spenders" try to influence election outcomes. In their primary role as defenders of law and order, judges are expected to be independent arbiters of justice, but elections can jeopardize their impartiality. In the thirty-three states that directly elect judges, the price of judicial campaigns—even for retention elections—is rising, a trend that alarms court observers. Nationwide in 2013-14, special interest groups and political parties reportedly spent an unprecedented $34.5 million on state supreme court races, amounts that continue to swell.[11]

TABLE 6.1   Diversity of California's Justices and Judges (in percentages)

Court (persons reporting)	Female (N = 566)	Male (N = 1,118)	Black or African American (N = 116)	Hispanic or Latino (N = 169)	Asian (N = 110)/ Pacific Islander (N = 4)	White (N = 1,159)	Native American (N = 9)/ Other/ More than one (N = 75)	Information not provided (N = 42)
Supreme Court (7)	57.1%	42.9%	14.3%	14.3%	28.6%	28.6	14.3%	0%
Court of Appeals (93)	33.3	66.7	9.7	5.4	2.2	76.3	6.5	0
Trial Court (1,551)	33.5	66.5	6.7	10.3	7.0	68.6	4.9	2.7
Total	33.6	66.4	6.9	10.0	6.7	68.8	4.9	2.5

Source: California Courts, "Demographic Data Provided by Justices and Judges Relative to Gender, Race/Ethnicity, and Gender Identity/Sexual Orientation," December 31, 2016, http://www.courts.ca.gov/documents/2017-Demographic-Report.pdf?1511514088990.

Judges can also be dismissed for improper conduct or incompetence arising from a range of activities, among them bias, inappropriate humor, and substance abuse. Hundreds of complaints are filed each year with the Commission on Judicial Performance, the independent state agency that investigates allegations of judicial misconduct. The commission does not review a justice's record but focuses instead on personal behavior that may warrant a warning letter, formal censure, removal, or forced retirement. Only a tiny fraction of judges face disciplinary action; the great majority have internalized the norms of judicial propriety that are imparted through law school and the legal community.

Court Administration

Like the U.S. federal court system, the state judicial branch is headed by a chief justice. However, a formal voluntary organization, the *Judicial Council of California*, which the chief justice chairs, sets policy for the state's court system. The twenty-one voting members (plus nine advisors, bringing the total to thirty members) of this public agency are tasked with policymaking, establishing rules and procedures in accordance with ever-changing state law, making sure the court is accessible to citizens with diverse needs, and recommending improvements to the system. The council also controls the judiciary's annual budget and reports to the legislature and responds to its mandates. A subagency of the Judicial Council, the Administrative Office of the Court (AOC), is made up of staff members who actively implement the council's policy decisions. Administrative officers throughout the state manage the court system by supervising a supporting cast of thousands who help run the court system day to day. Among many other activities, they keep records, hire interpreters, schedule hearings, and create task forces to study and find ways to address issues that affect court caseloads and court operations, such as foster care or domestic violence.

Juries

Barring a traffic violation, jury duty tends to be the average citizen's most direct link to the court system, and roughly 9,450 juries will sit in judgment at trial every year.[12] Names of prospective jurors are randomly drawn from lists of registered voters and also provided by the Department of Motor Vehicles. Under the "one day or one trial" program, prospective jurors are excused from service at the end of a single day if they have not been assigned to a trial, and they only need to respond to a summons to serve once a year. If assigned to a trial, jurors consider questions of fact and weigh evidence to determine whether an accused person is guilty or not guilty. Convincing citizens to fulfill their duty to serve as jurors isn't easy, and juries tend to overrepresent those who have relatively more time on their hands, such as the elderly, the unemployed, and the wealthy. About 8 million people are summoned to serve on juries each year in California, although only about 3 million of them are eligible and able to sit on a trial; in all, about 150,000 people serve as jurors annually.[13] All jurors are compensated $15 per day starting with the second day of service plus thirty-four cents for mileage one way. There are no plans to raise this rate, although it is well below the national average of approximately $20 for the first day and $25 for the second day of service.[14]

Grand juries are impaneled every year in every county to investigate the conduct of city and county government and their agencies. Each contains nineteen members, except for Los Angeles's grand jury, which has twenty-three members due to the city's large population. During their one-year terms, grand jurors research claims of improper or wasteful political practices, issue reports, recommend improvements to local programs, and sometimes indict government officials for misconduct, meaning they uncover sufficient evidence to warrant a trial.

Criminal Justice and Its Costs

About 90 percent of cases never make it to trial. High costs and delays associated with discovery, investigations, filings, and courtroom defense encourage out-of-court settlements and mediation, and the chance to receive a lesser sentence for pleading guilty results in plea bargains that suppress prison crowding. Although California's crime rates have declined over the past two decades, the state's prisons have been bursting at the seams for years. Under federal court orders, the population has been forcibly reduced through a combination of measures, including the reclassification of crimes, resentencing under the new rules, and the transfer of prisoners to county jails and probation.

Mandatory and enhanced sentencing laws are largely to blame for the blistering growth of the prison population—a trend that finally has been reversed. In 1994, voters were horror-struck at the abduction and murder of twelve-year-old Polly Klaas, a crime perpetrated by a man with a long and violent record. Klaas's family and others lobbied vigorously for tougher sentencing of repeat offenders, and their efforts culminated in the "**three strikes and you're out**" (or "three strikes") law: anyone convicted of a third felony is sentenced to a mandatory prison term of twenty-five years to life without the possibility of parole, with enhanced penalties for second-strikers. Twenty years later, approximately 42,500 inmates were serving time for second and third strikes, most of which were nonviolent offenses.

Since then, at Governor Brown's urging, voters passed three initiatives that changed the rules to ease the phenomenon known as "mass incarceration." Prop 36 revised the three-strikes law to impose a life sentence only when a new third felony conviction is serious or violent, and it also authorized resentencing for current inmates if they were imprisoned for nonviolent offenses. Prop 47 reclassified some drug-related crimes as misdemeanors rather than felonies. Prop 57, passed in 2016, makes all nonviolent offenders eligible for parole consideration, and it awards sentencing credits for good behavior and rehabilitative or educational achievements.

Governor Brown and the legislature also crafted the "Public Safety Realignment" law in 2011 to meet a federal court mandate to reduce the prison population to 137.5 percent of capacity. **Realignment** policy has shifted the responsibility for locking up low-level nonserious, nonviolent, nonsex (so-called *triple-non*) offender adult felons to county governments, and thousands of state parolees have also been transferred to county probation departments.

These new laws continue to reduce the felony caseload and total incarceration rates, which dropped 31 percent between 2006 and 2016.[15] They will continue to draw down the state prison population while placing more pressure on counties that provide probation programs and house nonviolent offenders in county jails that are aging; in fact, half of all facilities were built before 1980.[16] County sheriffs are opting for alternative management systems such as electronic monitoring and community service, even as they seek ways to reduce recidivism rates, but varying economic environments, local policies, and politics across fifty-eight counties translate into differences in the ways that inmates are treated, raising questions about fairness and equality.[17] Another consequence of realignment is that state prisons are now packed with the most violent, most serious offenders, and relatively high recidivism rates do not appear to have changed much.[18] Importantly, two major studies have demonstrated that at least in the short term, prison downsizing has not affected overall violent or property crime rates in California, which remain at historic lows.[19]

Longer sentences bring about an aging prison population with expensive health care issues, and under the Eighth Amendment's prohibition against cruel and unusual punishment, inmates are the only population in the United States guaranteed the constitutional right to receive adequate health care—although the quality of that care is often in doubt. Prompted by a class-action lawsuit in 2001 alleging dire conditions and the state's slowness to reform, a federal court removed control of prison health care from the state and appointed a federal receiver to help raise standards to an acceptable level. Immediately, the receiver demanded that at least $8 billion more be invested in upgrades to compensate for historically insufficient funding.

Underfunding of the correctional system has been the default option for state lawmakers because prisoners are esteemed by no one: spending cuts to prisons represent a rare convergence point for those on the left, who would prefer more spending on rehabilitation and crime prevention programs, and those on the right, who tend to equate spending with unfair comforts for criminals who deserve to pay for their crimes. In fact, cuts to prisons and corrections are the only ones that a substantial majority of citizens consistently say they would make in order to balance the annual budget.[20] This attitude may also stem from a popular misconception that prisons and corrections are *the* top spending category in the state budget, but at 7.6 percent of general fund spending, this area is the fourth largest item in the state budget (well below health and human services, consuming 32.9 percent).[21] The receiver has remained in charge since 2005, and with lawmakers' authorization, major improvements to on-site medical facilities have been made, including a new inmate medical complex in Stockton, which absorbed over $1 billion in building and operational costs by the end of its first year.[22] Despite those investments, budget neglect over the years has led to deteriorating infrastructure, and the state has failed to build more penitentiaries; the result is a prison system that remains well over capacity.

Skyrocketing costs are also connected to overcrowding. In 1980, the total prison population was 22,500, and in 1985 it cost less than $100 million to run the entire correctional system. Today the system devours $13.869 billion (from all sources, 2017–18). Although its per prisoner costs are not the highest in the nation, at about $76,000 *per inmate,* California pays far more than other states where the average is closer to $30,000 per offender.[23] The comparatively higher costs are attributable mainly to expenses for security personnel and medical care. For each inmate, approximately $21,600 is spent on pharmaceuticals and medical, mental, and dental care; in 2017–18 the general fund costs for treating inmates with hepatitis-C alone were $76.2 million. About $34,000 per prisoner goes to staff salaries and benefits, and the remainder covers facilities, food, record keeping, rehabilitation, administration, and educational and drug treatment programs—associated costs that generally do not shrink as the prison population declines. It costs less to send California prisoners to out-of-state facilities in Arizona or Mississippi, where approximately 4,400 prisoners are incarcerated. In addition, felons who are not legal U.S. residents impose direct costs on the state of about $500 million per year because the federal government reimburses less than 10 percent of the costs associated with

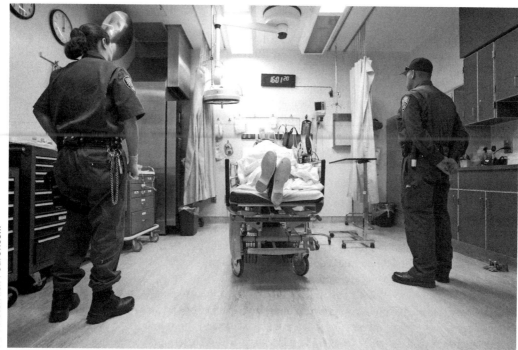

AP Photo/Rich Pedroncelli

An aging inmate population has made prison medical care a costly business; the average annual cost per person is $21,600, with much higher price tags for specialized care—for example, it costs close to $1 million a year to care for and guard a prisoner lying in a vegetative state not only because of necessary medical equipment and round-the-clock care but also because of the high-security environment.

BOX 6.1 **FAST FACTS on California's Criminal Justice System**

Enacted budget 2017–18:	$11.2 billion (general fund), $13.87 billion (total)*
Cost per inmate, 2016:	$76,000*
Staff, 2017–18:	56,600*
Average daily number of inmates (projected):	127,693*
Average daily parolee population:	47, 274*
Prisoners on death row:	748 (including 22 women)
Average daily parolee population:	47, 274*
Most common crime:	Property crime (86% of reported crimes)
Number of prisons:	34, minimum to maximum security, and including 1 medical prison, plus 42 adult firefighting camps, 1 community prisoner mother facility, and 1 female rehabilitative correctional center
Mean age:	39 (male), 38 (female)
Gender of inmates:	95.3% male, 4.7% female

Racial composition of inmate population:

Category	Inmate population
White, non-Hispanic	23.0%
Hispanic/Latino	41.3%
Black	29.4%
Other	6.3%

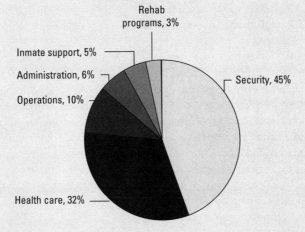

ESTIMATED ANNUAL PER INMATE COSTS, 2017–18 (%)

Rehab programs, 3%
Inmate support, 5%
Administration, 6%
Operations, 10%
Security, 45%
Health care, 32%

Sources: Larger figures have been rounded. California Department of Corrections and Rehabilitation, Offender Information Services Branch, Estimates and Statistical Analysis Section, Data Analysis Unit, "Weekly Report of Population as of July 19, 2017," http://www.cdcr.ca.gov/Reports_Research/Offender_Information_Services_Branch/Population_Reports.html.

*State of California, 2017–18 State Budget, enacted June 27, 2017, http://www.ebudget.ca.gov/, and LAO, July 2017.

their imprisonment.[24] Costs are also driven by housing and managing approximately 650 juveniles residing in three facilities and a conservation camp and supervising and treating about 47,000 adult parolees who need to be apprehended if they commit new offenses.[25]

Conclusion: Access to Justice

Can Californians count on gaining access to justice when needed? Chief Justice Cantil-Sakauye has stated that current underfunding of the judicial branch "unfairly affects members of the public seeking their day in court."[26] The cumulative impacts of budget cuts have been spread broadly, and they fall especially hard on Californians who live far from an operating courthouse, or don't own a car, or have little daytime to spare outside their jobs, or require interpreters, or don't have the money to hire lawyers to defend themselves in civil suits. Year after year, budget reductions have forced those who run the courts to make unsatisfactory decisions that inevitably cause certain subpopulations to suffer more than others. It will take years for the court system to dig out of the fiscal hole that the legislature has created for it and years to achieve the "fair and equal access to justice" guaranteed by the state constitution.

Unsustainable underfunding has also beleaguered the correctional department, which suffers from continuously deteriorating state prisons and county jails. The health care system is recuperating under the treatment of a federal receiver through higher injections of state cash, but an aging prison population with increasing medical needs and high personnel expenses including employee benefits has driven up costs that California taxpayers find difficult to stomach. Voters find it hard to justify spending more on prisons when the state spends an average of $13,812 (direct costs plus financial aid) to support students attending the University of California or California State University, yet it costs over $76,000 to house one inmate for a year.[27] Where the courts and prison populations are concerned, the lack of lobbying on behalf of inmates—the kind perfected by most special interest groups—and virtual absence of public sympathy are problematic in a political system that is responsive to such pressures.

Impartiality forms the judicial system's core, but the branch is political nevertheless—and it fights to suppress the forces that politicize it. Judicial branch politics and flaws in the correctional system also shed light on the complexity of governing. Prison overcrowding, an inmate population that is about three-quarters ethnic minority, and crowded court dockets are outcomes of other political and social issues that require legislators' attention, namely, poverty, lack of education, racism, unemployment, access to mental health care, and homelessness. Such social problems are manifest in all kinds of crimes and are inherent indicators of Californians' quality of life. California policymakers face criminal justice issues that exist in all states, but they have wrestled with them using the muscle of the ballot box and laws such as realignment. However, only a governing approach that comprehensively addresses the relationships among these issues can bring about fair, equitable, and accessible justice for all Californians—a daunting responsibility indeed.

Key Terms

alternative dispute resolution: an alternative to a court trial; mediation or legally binding arbitration to which two parties freely agree to submit, usually led by a retired judge or trained arbiter. (p. 81)

civil suits: lawsuits involving disputes between individuals or organizations that seek monetary compensation for damages, usually incurred through injuries, breaches of contract, or defective products. Types involve *small claims*, and *limited* and *unlimited* civil matters. (p. 80)

collaborative court: specialized "problem-solving courts" that operate through superior courts, combining judicial case processing, drug and alcohol treatment services, and monitoring to help individuals rebuild their lives and avoid recidivism. Examples include combat veterans' courts, mental health courts, homeless courts, drug courts, and domestic violence courts. (p. 81)

felony: a serious or violent offense, punishable by a state prison sentence or possibly death. Examples include murder, robbery, rape, and burglary of a residence. (p. 80)

infraction: a minor crime in which a fine rather than jail time is imposed, including traffic violations such as texting while driving. (p. 80)

misdemeanor: an intermediate level of crime, for which the maximum punishment is a $1,000 fine and up to one year in a county jail. (p. 80)

realignment: a California state policy established by legislation and ballot measures in which low-level offenders in state prison are transferred to county jails and probation departments. (p. 87)

Three strikes law, or "**three strikes and you're out**": Under laws passed as Proposition 36 and revised under Proposition 47, anyone convicted of a violent or serious third felony is sentenced to a mandatory prison term of twenty-five years to life without the possibility of parole, with enhanced penalties for second-strikers. (p. 86)

Other Governments

*T*housands of governments operate within California's borders. Unnoticed by most residents yet working in plain sight, counties, cities, special districts, and regional governments share responsibility for delivering essential services that both protect and enhance residents' quality of life—from maintaining police forces to making sure clean water flows beneath paved streets and from every tap. These multiple governing bodies stretch scarce taxpayer dollars across a huge range of services that residents mostly take for granted. Regular trash pickup, cemeteries, bus routes, sewage treatment, street lighting: these are the type of services either provided, managed, or contracted out to private companies by a patchwork of subgovernments in California. Their abundance reflects historically high demands for services, citizens' willingness to pay specific taxes but not higher general taxes, and strong desires to maintain control over local matters, or to exercise what's known as self-rule. Bottom-up solutions are thus joined to state and federal mandates in a functionally segmented system—one that works with surprising efficiency considering the enormous number and scope of issues encompassed and the limited budgets available to local governments today. As measured by number of entities, California places among the top five states—rivaled by Illinois, Texas, Pennsylvania, and Ohio[1]—but the complexity and depth of regulation arising from them in California is virtually unmatched.

County Government

Almost half of California's fifty-eight counties were created in the constitution of 1850, and, in 1907, a portion of San Diego County was cleaved off to form Imperial County, the last county added to the list. County boundaries have remained static for about a hundred years while their populations have changed dramatically. All carry out programs authorized by the

MAP 7.1 California, 2017 Population by County

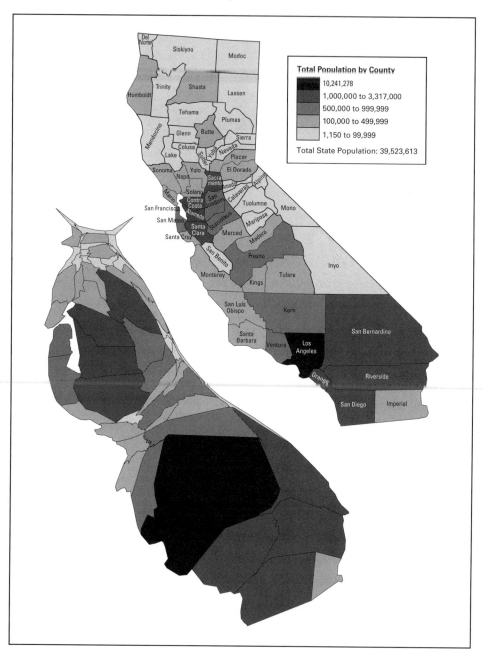

Total Population by County

- 10,241,278
- 1,000,000 to 3,317,000
- 500,000 to 999,999
- 100,000 to 499,999
- 1,150 to 99,999

Total State Population: 39,523,613

Source: State of California Department of Finance, "Demographics," http://www.dof.ca.gov/Forecasting/Demographics.

Notes: Geographic area and population are two variables used to measure the size of California's fifty-eight counties. Geographic boundaries are shown in the top map with shadings for population density, and the lower "cartogram" illustrates the relative distribution of population by county.

BOX 7.1   FAST FACTS on California's Other Governments

Number of counties:	58
Number of cities:	482
Number of federally recognized tribes:	110
Number of public school districts:	1,025, containing 10,453 schools
Number of special districts:	4,700; 2,800 county- and city-funded*
Five largest cities by population:	Los Angeles, 4,041,707
	San Diego, 1,406,318
	San Jose, 1,046,079
	San Francisco, 874,228
	Fresno, 525,832
Largest county by area:	San Bernardino, 20,052 square miles
Smallest county by area:	San Francisco, 47 square miles
	(10,000 people per square mile)
Largest county by population:	Los Angeles, 10,182,961
Smallest county by population:	Alpine, 1,160
Number of chartered cities:	121 (25%)
Number of general law cities:	361 (75%)
Number of cities with directly elected mayors:	149 (30%)

Sources: State of California, Department of Finance, "E-1 Population Estimates for Cities, Counties and the State with Annual Percent Change—January 1, 2016 and 2017." Sacramento, California (May 2017); California League of Cities, "Learn about Cities," https://www.cacities.org/Resources/Learn-About-Cities.

*Note: Numbers vary depending on what kinds of districts are counted. These actively report to the State Controller's Office yearly. More than 5,100 were listed in their online database as of September 2015, including an unknown number of inactive entities. The number in the table was reported in the State Controller's "Special Districts Annual Report, 2011-12," Appendix B, http://www.sco.ca.gov/ard_locarep_districts.html (the most current report available as of September 2017). The U.S. Census Bureau counted 2,864 based on their definition in their Census of Governments, 2012.

state government and provide critical services to Californians. The relationship between the state and counties is like that of a restaurant owner (the state) who creates a master menu, gives its fifty-eight "top chefs" (boards of county supervisors) a wad of cash, directs them to buy the right ingredients and to prepare the meals according to the plan, and then makes them serve the finished dishes to their customers (California residents).

Each county can be pictured as a partially finished jigsaw puzzle, with a defined outer frame and solid portions taking up most of the space inside, empty spaces interrupting the picture. The completed areas represent cities, and counties are filled with them: some almost completely, some only partially, and three without any (Alpine, Mariposa, and Trinity Counties do not contain cities). San Francisco is the only combination city/county, having consolidated the functions of both into one government. The blank spaces are considered **unincorporated** because they fall outside city boundaries, and all counties contain large swaths of unincorporated areas, where more than 20 percent of Californians live. County governments directly provide services and local political representation to those residents.

Original county lines bear no relation to population density or economic activity today, and all counties are expected to provide the same kinds of services to their constituents regardless of population size or geographic area. This means that the largest county by population, Los Angeles, with over 10 million people, maintains the same baseline agencies, elected officials, and responsibilities as tiny Alpine, population 1,160. The state legislature endows each county with the responsibility to provide for residents' safety, health, and welfare and can either delegate functions to the counties or revoke them.

The constitution permits general law and charter counties, with the main difference lying in how officers are selected and organized. Each county is governed by a five-member *board of supervisors* (San Francisco's board has eleven members and a mayor). Supervisors face nonpartisan elections every four years, and most are reelected overwhelmingly unless they cannot run due to term limits, and that depends on whether voters in a specific county have enacted such limits via local initiative. Many termed-out state lawmakers are prolonging their political careers as county supervisors, putting their knowledge and "institutional memory" about state issues and systems to good use by helping run the state's largest subgovernments. Forty-four counties are the *general law* variety, organized according to state statute. Each county must elect a sheriff, district attorney, and assessor and may appoint or elect a variety of other officers, such as a medical examiner and public defender. Fourteen counties are organized under *charters* that allow flexibility in governing structure: apart from elected supervisors and the above-named officials, they can determine the other types of offices, whether they will be combined (will they have an assessor/recorder/clerk or a recorder/clerk?), whether they will be appointed or elected, and whether they will be elected at-large or by district.

County officials such as the sheriff and assessor help the board of supervisors supply basic but vital social and political services in many areas:

- *Public safety:* courts, jails, probation, public defense, juvenile detention, sheriff, fire, emergency services, animal services
- *Public assistance:* housing, services for the homeless, food stamps, state welfare programs
- *Elections and voting:* voting processes, voter registration, signature verification
- *Tax collection:* county, city, special districts, school districts
- *Environment and recreation:* parks, sports, and entertainment facilities; open space; waste removal and recycling; air quality; land-use policy; water
- *Public health:* hospitals, mental health clinics, drug rehabilitation programs
- *Education:* libraries, schools
- *Social services:* adoptions, children's foster care
- *Transit:* airports, bus and rail systems, bridges, road maintenance
- *Vital records:* birth, death, marriage certificates

Counties finance these operations by levying sales taxes and user fees and through state government funding, property taxes, and federal grants. They spend the most on public safety and public assistance (see Figure 7.1). When state budget crises stem the flow of revenue, counties must lay off employees, cut services, and raise fees to make ends meet. Even when economies are in recovery mode, it takes years before the state restores funding to previous levels, and counties continually struggle to fulfill their state-mandated obligations—from preventing disease to ensuring foster children's safety—with relatively meager funding. Some of their financial woes today stem from their payment obligations to employees and future retirees for salaries and benefits, which are consuming larger chunks of their budgets over time.

Municipal Governments

Communities in unincorporated areas of a county may want more control over land use in their neighborhoods, better services, or a formal identity. They can petition their state-chartered local agency formation commission, or LAFCO, to incorporate as a city or municipality if the residents generate enough tax revenue to support a local government. The average population of a California city is 65,000, with a huge span between the smallest (Vernon, population 209) and the largest (Los Angeles, population 4 million).

Much like counties, cities provide essential public services in the areas of public safety and emergency services; sewage and sanitation; public health; public works, including street maintenance; parks and recreation; libraries and schools; and land-use planning. Sometimes these overlap or supplement county programs: for example, a city might maintain its own library and also contain two or three county library branches. If lacking their own facilities, cities can contract with counties for services, pool their resources in a joint-powers agreement, or contract with private firms. A prevalent trend among cities has been to cut personnel, benefits, and public works costs through outsourcing. One such "**contract city**" is the town of Half Moon Bay, which since 2011 has outsourced recreation services, engineering, legal services, code enforcement, and police protection, mostly to private contractors, the neighboring city of San Carlos, and San Mateo County. Similarly, as cities in Orange County (OC) have multiplied, the OC Fire Authority has continued to provide critical fire services to them under contract, and contracted county sheriffs patrol municipalities that cannot afford their own police forces.

More than 75 percent of California's 482 cities are incorporated under general law, meaning they follow state law in form and function. The remaining *charter cities* are creatures of local habits, formed through city constitutions that grant local government supreme authority over municipal affairs. This *home rule* principle permits municipal law to trump similar state laws. The city of Bell in the Los Angeles area serves as an uncomfortable reminder of this fact: using home rule to evade salary limitations that are set by state law, Bell's city leaders voted themselves exorbitant pay raises that technically were legal. When finally exposed, the city manager was raking in $1.5 million a year in total compensation—about nine times the governor's salary. In all, they stole more than $10 million from one of the state's poorest cities.[2]

Virtually every city is governed by a five-member *city council* that concentrates on passing and implementing local laws, called *ordinances*. Thus, unlike how state and federal governments separate powers among different branches to ensure checks and balances, city councils blend legislative, executive, and quasi-judicial functions (they hear certain appeals stemming from land use, for example), just as county boards of supervisors do. City councils rely heavily on small *boards* and *commissions* filled by local volunteers or appointees to help recommend and set policy relating to the special needs of citizens and businesses. For example, the city of Oakland has more than forty, including a Citizens' Police Review Board and a Youth Advisory Commission that is tasked with creating appealing community programs for kids and youth. To facilitate public participation in these public processes, all board members and commissioners must follow the *Bagley-Keene Open Meeting Act*, just as all city, county, and state governing institutions must abide by the *Ralph M. Brown Act*.

FIGURE 7.1   County Revenues and Expenses, 2014–15

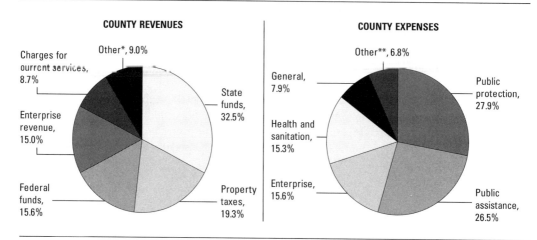

COUNTY REVENUES

Charges for current services, 8.7%

Other*, 9.0%

State funds, 32.5%

Enterprise revenue, 15.0%

Federal funds, 15.6%

Property taxes, 19.3%

COUNTY EXPENSES

Other**, 6.8%

General, 7.9%

Health and sanitation, 15.3%

Enterprise, 15.6%

Public protection, 27.9%

Public assistance, 26.5%

Source: California Budget Center, "Dollars and Democracy" (April, 2017), http://calbudgetcenter.org/wp-content/uploads/Dollars-and-Democracy_A-Guide-to-the-County-Budget-Process-4.2017.pdf.

*Reflects a range of smaller revenue sources, including other taxes, fines, licenses, and permits. Percentages do not sum to 100% due to rounding.

**Reflects spending for public facilities, debt service, recreation and cultural activities, and education.

These two laws mandate advance notice of all meetings, "open" meetings that do not take place in secret, and full public disclosure of the proceedings.

City council members are reelected every four years in nonpartisan elections, usually by the entire city's electorate in an *at-large election* rather than by voters separated into *districts* or *wards*. A wide range of local governments, including cities, are moving to district-based elections because plaintiffs in lawsuits have successfully shown that racial and ethnic minority candidates are disadvantaged by at-large elections. In addition, many city councils are now subject to local voter-imposed term limits, and the list of term-limited cities grows each year. If the *mayor* is not elected at-large (meaning that the whole city votes for mayor), council members designate one among them to act as a ceremonial mayor, typically on a rotating basis, for one or two years at a time. Each city makes its own rules regarding how long and how often city council members can act as mayor and whether the appointment will be automatic or by a vote. Automatic rotation creates opportunities for many young council members to assume the role of mayor. Ceremonial mayors lack veto power, and their vote on the council is equal to the votes of their colleagues. In place of an elected mayor, the council hires a manager to run city operations.

If the mayor proposes the city budget, has the power to veto city council actions, and can hire and fire high-profile appointees to help run city operations, then a *strong mayor* form of government is in place. Some 30 percent of California cities maintain this form of municipal government, partly because a sole individual can offer a clear agenda and be held accountable as the city's chief executive officer (CEO) for its success or failure. The far more popular *council-manager system* exists in nearly 70 percent of cities, an institutional legacy of Progressives who believed that efficient city management required technical expertise because "there is no partisan way to pave a street." In most cities, then, a council retains a ceremonial mayor but hires a professional **city manager** to budget for, manage, and oversee the day-to-day operations of a city. As a city's CEO, the city manager is authorized to make decisions independent of the council and thus wields great power behind the scenes. The office handles hiring and firing decisions and supervises all city departments. Most city managers possess a master's degree in public administration and have experience managing local government departments. Typically, the highest-paid city employee is the city manager, who earns more than $175,000 per year on average—although again the numbers vary widely, with some making little (less than $20,000) and others making a lot (more than $300,000). The average annual wage for all types of California city employees is $65,100, but the pay scales vary immensely and so do the numbers of city employees, resident-to-employee ratios, and the types of professionals in any given municipality.[3] Those earning over $300,000 a year tend to be police or fire chiefs or city attorneys working for large cities.

Cities depend heavily on taxes and fees to finance operations. Prior to Proposition 13, property taxes constituted 57 percent of combined city and county revenues annually; forty years later, property taxes represent roughly 10 percent of the average aggregate city budget. The bulk of funding now comes from service charges for public utilities and transit; sales taxes; property taxes; a variety of taxes and fees on hotels, developers, other businesses, and property use; and state and federal agencies. Bond money also enlarges budgets.

State representatives perform economic gymnastics to balance the state budget during hard times, and their routine includes yanking property taxes and other fees previously committed to cities to backfill the state's budget hole. In an effort to stop such state "raiding" of local funds, cities and counties sponsored a constitutional amendment (Proposition 1A in 2004) to prevent state legislators from transferring locally generated property taxes, vehicle license fees, and sales taxes into the state's general fund. The state, however, can override some of those restrictions during fiscal crises to take what they deem necessary.

Ever since Prop 13 eliminated the ability of local school boards to raise taxes at their discretion, local governments have hunted for revenues continually. It's common to charge developers heavy fees for new construction projects or saddle them with the costs of constructing new streets, schools, lighting, sewers, or any infrastructure improvements related to population growth. These fees are then imposed on homebuyers. **Mello-Roos fees** are assessed as a special lien against each property that will be in effect for twenty-five years on average, and the annual charges can vary dramatically from area to area and even house to house. In counties such as San Diego, the average homeowner in a Mello-Roos Community Facilities District pays an additional $1,826 per year on top of property taxes, with these fees totaling $195 million in San Diego County in 2012 alone.[4] Another strategy is to base land-use decisions on a project's net fiscal impact, a phenomenon known as the **fiscalization of land use.** In practical terms, this means that cities have incentives to entice and keep retail businesses that can generate substantial sales taxes, as local governments receive 1 percent of state sales taxes collected in their jurisdictions. Auto dealerships, shopping malls, and big-box retailers like Home Depot are therefore favored over low-income housing for people who will further stress city resources or service-based industries that will not generate tax revenue—in other words, decisions are made without regard to the intrinsic value of, or need for, a project. Research by the Legislative Analyst's Office (LAO) has shown that this phenomenon does not seem to have affected recent land-use patterns significantly, but cities use tax breaks, public financing, and low-priced land to entice business and spur the local economy.[5]

Borrowing large sums to build new stadiums or to rebuild schools, for example, has also become a favored tool for local governments of all types, especially school districts. Debt typically takes the form of voter-approved *bonds*, which can range into the hundreds of millions of dollars. Taxpayers

AP Photo/Dami an Dovarganes

City councils make local laws (their legislative function includes passing *ordinances*) and also execute laws by implementing city plans or programs. The San Bernardino city council meets twice weekly, compared to Los Angeles's city council, which meets three times a week, and the councils of smaller cities, which commonly meet twice a month. At a typical meeting, council members might listen to citizens' concerns, discuss pending regulations, decide land-use matters, pay tribute to community heroes, approve expenses and payments for city services, and/or vote on contracts for city services.

"issue" (sell) bonds to lenders and are obligated to repay them, with interest, usually after twenty or thirty years. Bond-related tax obligations appear as a line item on residents' property tax bills and are based on a property's value. The state treasurer estimates that California city and county bond debt exceeds $421 billion, and K-12 school and community college district debt hovers around $247 billion.[6] In addition, voter-approved *parcel taxes* can be used to pay for large local programs. Residents pay a flat fee, or the tax is based on a property's square footage or other characteristic. These taxes are also attached to a property tax bill.

Debt can also take shape in long-term commitments to pay for hefty projects that may or may not generate income, such as a water treatment plant that local citizens pay for through higher sewage bills. So-called **unfunded liabilities** probably constitute the most hazardous type of debt; this catchphrase refers to whatever a city or county legally owes in future payments but does not yet have the financial reserves to cover. Historically, California's cities and counties have negotiated retirement and health care benefits in contracts with public employees, such as firefighters and police, but some of those obligations have drained—and continue to threaten—public treasuries. Generous

100   *Chapter 7   Other Governments*

FIGURE 7.2 City Revenues and Expenses, 2015

CITY EXPENSES

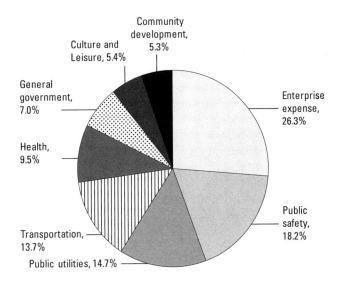

Community development, 5.3%

Culture and Leisure, 5.4%

General government, 7.0%

Health, 9.5%

Transportation, 13.7%

Public utilities, 14.7%

Enterprise expense, 26.3%

Public safety, 18.2%

CITY REVENUES

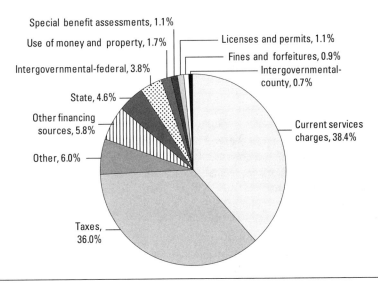

Special benefit assessments, 1.1%

Use of money and property, 1.7%

Intergovernmental-federal, 3.8%

State, 4.6%

Other financing sources, 5.8%

Other, 6.0%

Taxes, 36.0%

Licenses and permits, 1.1%

Fines and forfeitures, 0.9%

Intergovernmental-county, 0.7%

Current services charges, 38.4%

Source: California State Controller's Office, https://bythenumbers.sco.ca.gov/City-Expenditures/2015-City-Expenditures-by-Function/yc8x-v6ch.

Notes: Includes the city/county of San Francisco. Figures may not add to 100 percent due to rounding. In 2015, total city revenues were $68.64 billion, and expenses totaled $67.81 billion.

employee labor contracts have been based on optimistic projections of tax receipts and returns on investments, but those investments temporarily tanked along with the economy. Even with higher rates of return, municipalities and counties owe billions of dollars in pension payments—*plus* health care benefits (which are likely to *triple* those outlays). How will local governments fulfill their colossal pension obligations without going broke? Residents in some cities, as in San Diego, have passed local initiatives eliminating pensions and switching to 401(k) plans for new city employees. Other cities simply can't avoid running out of money. Following Vallejo's lead, the cities of San Bernardino, Mammoth Lakes, and Stockton filed for Chapter 9 bankruptcy protection in 2012 in hopes of erasing soaring debt that had been pushed into the stratosphere by employee compensation and pensions, bond repayments for ill-advised infrastructure projects, and general financial mismanagement by city officials. To recover, a bankrupt local government must raise taxes to pay its bills and curtail virtually every service it provides to citizens even as it charges higher fees. Crime rises as the police force dwindles, the city's ability to borrow vanishes along with its good credit ratings, the roads become gutted with potholes, and tourism evaporates. Creditors are repaid pennies on the dollar, and the city's long-term debt is reduced through the renegotiation of current labor contracts—yet huge pension obligations remain.

California state employees' earned retirement benefits have been shielded by court decisions that amount to a "California Rule": promised pensions must be honored as ironclad throughout an employee's career and cannot be reduced without equal compensation. Public workers in twelve other states are now similarly guarded. However, two recent California court rulings (one of which is being visited by the state supreme court at this writing[7]) weaken the "rule" by allowing certain benefit enhancements to be repealed or eliminated. If pension contracts could be broken entirely, then cities would have an incentive to declare bankruptcy in order to avoid their payment obligations, and retirees would see drastic changes in their long-anticipated retirement incomes. Municipalities considered financially vulnerable by big credit-rating agencies, including Los Angeles and San Jose, which spend tens of millions of dollars (roughly 20 percent of their annual budgets) on these expenses, might find this option irresistible. For municipalities and counties, big questions about their long-term pension obligations remain.

Special Districts

A *special district* is a geographic area governed by an autonomous board for a single purpose, such as running an airport or providing a community with street lighting or a cemetery. Abundant but virtually invisible to the average citizen, special districts proliferate because they are created to meet critical needs that cities and counties lack the will or capacity to address. Like regular governments, they can sue and be sued, charge users for their services, and exercise the right to *eminent domain* (the taking of property for public use). Unlike most governments, however, they may cover only a portion of a city or stretch across several cities or counties.

Close to 4,700 special districts operate in the state, about two-thirds independently with their own boards of governors chosen by voters in low-profile elections; the remainder are controlled by counties or cities through appointments. About 2,800 special districts independently generate their own revenue as fee-based enterprises or by charging their customers, while the remainder are funded by counties and cities. The majority of special district services are paid for through parcel taxes or service charges that initially require a two-thirds majority vote. Hospital, rat and mosquito control, trash disposal, fire protection, irrigation and water delivery, bus and rail transit, and utility districts are a few types. The Southern California Metropolitan Water District (MWD) epitomizes this type of fee-based service organization: created by the legislature in 1928, its mission is to provide adequate, reliable supplies of high-quality water to current and future residents in Southern California. A water wholesaler, it owns and operates major infrastructure, including the Colorado River aqueduct, hydroelectric plants, pipes, and water treatment facilities; it is also backing the Sacramento-San Joaquin Delta "twin tunnels" project. Twenty-six cities and water districts buy more than 1.5 billion gallons of drinking water from MWD every day, supplying 19 million people in six counties. In addition to paying their local water district for the water they use, Southern California residents see charges listed on their annual property tax bills for MWD operations.

School Districts

School districts constitute a separate but most familiar category of special district: more than a thousand provide K–12 education for about 6.2 million students attending over ten thousand different schools; an additional 72 districts encompass 114 community colleges.[8] Created by state law, nonpartisan five-member boards of education (Los Angeles's board has seven) govern their school districts by following the detailed operating instructions of the state's education code and heeding the State Board of Education's mandates. A superintendent manages the local system, which may be responsible for more than 640,000 students—as is the case in the gargantuan Los Angeles Unified School District—or fewer than twenty students. School boards handle issues relating to nearly every aspect of student life, from regulating students' cell phone use to defining nutritional standards to designing appropriate curricula, and they must weigh the concerns of vocal parents and special interests trying to influence their decisions along with the concerns of those who do not speak up so forcefully.

State-funded, K–12 public *charter schools* operate outside the jurisdiction of the local school board; 1,248 of them are organized by parents, teachers, and/or community groups to provide specialized education programs that may have a particular emphasis in the performing arts, sciences, languages, or college preparation, for example.[9] The school's mission is spelled out in its charter, or contract. The 1992 state law that permitted charter schools to form dictates that charter schools must be free and open to all students, and if a school receives more requests to attend than it has spots available, it must hold a blind lottery to determine which students can attend.

Proposition 98 dedicates approximately 40 percent of the state's general fund budget to K–12 and community college education, yet elementary and secondary schools rely on multiple source of funding. Using the 2017–18 fiscal year as a point of reference, just over 70 percent of K–12 public school money is sourced through Prop 98 with state general funds and local property tax revenue. The rest comes from a variety of sources: approximately 8.3 percent from the federal government, and about 20 percent from miscellaneous sources, including bond payments, the state lottery (a mere 1.3 percent), special local parcel taxes, and donations funneled through private foundations that have been formed to supplement operations by buying equipment or hiring specialized teachers (such as music or arts instructors) that districts cannot afford otherwise.

Public water agencies are tasked with providing clean, reliable water to the cities, farms, and businesses within the special districts they govern. The San Diego County Water Authority diversified its supplies with a $1 billion desalination plant in Carlsbad that filters nearly 50 million gallons of sea water daily for 400,000 San Diegans. Other desalination projects include Huntington Beach (2019), Santa Barbara (reactivated 2017), and Monterey (under development). The large plants occupy prime real estate, and high-pressure pumps needed for reverse osmosis consume tremendous energy, a costly process.

Regional Governments

Unlike governments that make and enforce binding laws, **regional governments** provide permanent forums in which local elected officials can exchange ideas and information, plan, and coordinate their policies across county and city boundaries, usually for land-use and development-related activities arising from population growth and change. State law allows for the creation of a variety of regional governments with **joint powers authority** (JPA), and these *councils of government* (COGs) plan for future populations by addressing common issues that encompass a wide spectrum of infrastructure-related needs, including housing and transportation, water and food availability, toxic waste disposal, and environmental quality. COGs in California, therefore, are a collection of local officials and agencies that voluntarily agree to share responsibility for solving collective problems. At least forty-six major COGs operate in California and have formed joint-powers agreements, plus there are many localized JPAs.[10]

COGs coordinate rather than dictate because they cannot force decisions on local governments. Their governing boards are composed of mayors, city council members, and county supervisors, making them *intergovernmental* entities. In these collaborative forums to promote regional planning, they receive input from research specialists and advisers from federal departments, special districts, state agencies, and even sovereign nations such as California Native American tribes and Mexico. Their planning activities include reviewing federal grants-in-aid and proposing legislation. They do not deliver public services.

COGs can take the form of *transportation planning agencies* or *commissions,* such as the Contra Costa County Transportation Authority, which coordinates freeway expansions and improvements, maintains emergency roadside call boxes, helps fund bus transit, oversees bicycle paths, and encourages ridesharing. Eighteen COGs are also federally designated *metropolitan planning organizations* (MPOs), legally responsible for researching, designing, and finding funding for regional transportation plans for areas with more than fifty thousand people. MPOs include associations like the San Joaquin COG (SJCOG) and the Merced County Association of Governments (MCAG). Other COGs are *planning councils* with wider scope, like the Tahoe Regional Planning Agency, through which elected officials from surrounding areas create overarching plans that have vital impacts on construction, recreation, water quality, and the environment around Lake Tahoe. Their boundaries can be extensive: for example, the Association of Bay Area Governments (ABAG) unites local elected officials from nine counties and 101 cities to deal with housing, open space, employment, waste, transportation, recreation, and equity challenges posed by a population that is seven million and growing.

Regional government may also take the form of regulatory entities that set rules for environmentally sensitive activities. These bodies are authorized by state law to set rules and enforce them. For instance, California's thirty-five "air districts" are dedicated to controlling pollution from stationary sources (Air Pollution Control Districts, or APCDs) and promoting air quality (Air Quality Management Districts, or AQMDs) through comprehensive planning programs that include the setting of compulsory rules for residents and the enforcement of those rules, air quality monitoring, research, public education, and the issuing of special business permits.

Federalism

To what extent is California at liberty to act without the federal government's permission? Whereas the state authorizes county governments, local jurisdictions, and special districts to perform necessary functions, the U.S. Constitution guarantees that states *share* governing power with the national government, and they possess primary authority over certain policy areas such as education and elections, although their authority has diminished as both the federal purse and federal capacities have grown. The U.S. Congress discovered long ago that *funding* is a convenient instrument for enticing states to adopt federal goals by granting or withholding moneys in exchange for their compliance. In this way, federal highway funds have been exchanged for lower speed limits and a minimum drinking age of 21—issues that only the states can legislate.

As several California cities and the state (such as San Francisco, and the state through SB 54) have provided sanctuary for undocumented immigrants that Immigration and Customs Enforcement (ICE) officials have targeted for deportation, federal officials have threatened to "cut off federal money" that flows to California, although in the first court case to test this principle, a federal judge has ruled that the executive branch cannot do so unilaterally or arbitrarily. In 2017–18, a whopping $107.5 billion in direct payments to the state covered housing subsidies, medical care, school lunch, the cost of educating low-income students and those with disabilities, transportation projects, and much more. Local governments also reap direct funding in the range of $8.2 billion a year, mostly in the form of grants.

Finally, individuals receive payments in the form of student financial aid, income support (tax credits, housing and food assistance, Medicare, Social Security benefits), civilian and military wages and salaries, and universities benefit from research contracts and grants. All told, annual federal expenditures in California exceed an estimated *$376 billion*.[11] Congress can pass laws financially penalizing cities or states for failing to cooperate with federal agents,[12] and federal courts will ultimately determine whether existing national laws can be weaponized to bring states into compliance.

California is also subject to **unfunded mandates**. These are federal laws that require the states to provide services, but no funds are supplied to implement them. Such mandates amount to hundreds of millions of dollars in state costs for social services, transportation, education, health care, and environmental cleanup. For example, the cost of holding about 11,400 undocumented immigrant inmates with active federal ICE holds in state correctional facilities is equal to operating an extra prison and absorbs nearly a half billion dollars per year (roughly $430 million, according to the LAO), but in 2016, the federal government's State Criminal Alien Assistance Program (SCAAP) provided counties only $50 million to cover related correctional officer costs.[13] Federal funding was awarded in 2017 with a public notice for all jurisdictions to comply with federal law and a warning that if sanctuary policies (i.e., those preventing the release of information or prisoners to Homeland Security agents) were found to violate federal law, then criminal and civil penalties would apply, and repayment would be extracted.

Demands like these are consistent with President Trump's 2017 executive order to strip federal funds from states and localities that his administration designates as "sanctuary jurisdictions." The executive order raises questions about states' legal obligations to the federal government in immigration matters. Attorney General Xavier Becerra has maintained that "the Trump Administration does not have the right to coerce states, counties or municipalities to do the federal government's job," stressing instead local law enforcement's mission to ensure public safety, not deportation.[14] Before SB 54 rendered California a sanctuary state, he wrote a friend-of-the-court (*amicus curiae*) brief in support of California sanctuary cities and was joined by attorneys general for nine other states, New York and Oregon among them. Federal courts had accepted this interpretation at the end of 2017.

Mandates also can take the form of *preemptive legislation*, which prohibit a state from passing certain laws; the federal government has used legislation of this kind to "regulate commerce" to prevent some of California's progressive environmental rules and legislation from taking effect, such as a proposed ban on ride-on lawn mowers—a move that could negatively affect workers and businesses in states where the mowers are manufactured.

California remains dependent on the federal government to balance its ledgers, and unanticipated changes to major programs such as health coverage severely impact its ability to deliver promised services. In fiscal year 2017–18, federal dollars ($107.5 billion) represented 37 percent of total state spending, which topped a staggering $290.7 billion. Given California's bursting population, position as a military gateway to the Pacific, and importance to the nation as an agricultural hub and economic powerhouse, federal funds will continue to backfill permanent and growing needs, despite potential cutbacks.

Tribal Governments

An often-overlooked class of government functions alongside state and local entities and also under the thumb of the federal government: that of sovereign tribal nations. Tribal governments operated in relative obscurity until recently. Isolated on 100,000 acres of mostly remote and frequently inhospitable reservations throughout California, the state's 110 federally recognized tribes had minimal

BOX 7.2 **California's Landmark Climate Change Law: AB 32**

California set itself apart yet again when the state's majority-Democratic legislature joined Republican Governor Arnold Schwarzenegger in crafting the Global Warming Solutions Act of 2006, otherwise known as Assembly Bill 32 (AB 32), the world's first law establishing a program of regulatory and market mechanisms to curb emissions of greenhouse gases. Voters beat back an initiative to rescind it in 2010 (Proposition 23), but businesses and anti-regulatory interests continue to oppose the law strongly, anticipating higher costs. AB 32 aims to promote a low-carbon, sustainable economy by encouraging jobs that promote more efficient, renewable energy sources that improve air quality, and it authorizes the state's Air Resources Board (ARB) to set new fuel efficiency standards for new vehicles sold in California, establish a statewide plan to reach an emissions cap in 2020 based on 1990 emissions levels, require mandatory reporting of greenhouse gas outputs, create advisory boards, and collect fees from significant sources of greenhouse gases.

Most notably, ARB has enacted the nation's first cap-and-trade program for greenhouse gas (GHG) emissions. Modeled on other successful market-based pollution reduction programs, California's version is designed to reduce the overall amount of GHGs by setting an upper limit, or cap, on the aggregate amount of statewide emissions from 85 percent of GHG sources. About 360 "polluters" (businesses creating carbon and other gases linked to climate change, representing six hundred facilities) were initially given trading credits, or allowances, for the normal amount of GHGs they produce. Chevron's Richmond refinery is the biggest source, producing 4.5 million metric tons of an overall estimated 447 million metric tons in the state yearly; the University of California is another large emitter. Every year the total cap on statewide emissions will decline by 2 to 3 percent (the total number of allowances will decline), providing incentives for polluters to invest in more efficient technologies or fuels that will reduce their own emissions, thereby creating for them a surplus of carbon trading credits that they can sell at a quarterly online auction, which commenced November 2012. Companies in capped industries must register and report their emissions annually (also subject to independent verification), and ARB has designed the process to protect against collusion, cheating, and price manipulation. Advocates of the cap-and-trade approach extol the facts that no new taxes are directly assessed, businesses have flexibility to alter their practices to be compliant, and revenues support "green" initiatives. Opponents bemoan the new layer of regulations and paperwork and costs of compliance and equate new costs with indirect taxes, dubbing them "carbon taxes" that they promise to pass along to consumers. California and Quebec, Canada linked their cap-and-trade auctions on January 1, 2014.

2015 EMISSIONS BY SECTOR

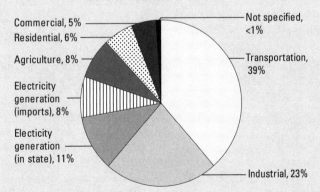

Commercial, 5%
Residential, 6%
Agriculture, 8%
Electricity generation (imports), 8%
Electicity generation (in state), 11%
Not speciial, <1%
Transportation, 39%
Industrial, 23%

Source: California Environmental Protection Agency, Air Resources Board, "California Greenhouse Gas Emission Inventory," last reviewed on June 6, 2017, https://www.arb.ca.gov/cc/inventory/data/data.htm.

Note: Total California emissions for 2015: 440.4 million metric tons of carbon dioxide equivalent.

(Continued)

BOX 7.2 (Continued)

Initially the act was fiercely opposed by a tight coalition of automobile, shipping, manufacturing, and energy industries, which challenged the new law as going "too far" by setting stricter standards than the federal government—despite the fact that the federal Environmental Protection Agency (FPA) had never set a greenhouse gas emissions standard. Ruling that AB 32 superseded federal authority to maintain clean air standards, the EPA under the George W. Bush administration denied California a waiver from adhering to lower clean air standards than set in the Federal Clean Air Act. On June 30, 2009, the EPA under the Barack Obama administration reversed the ruling, giving California and thirteen other states the green light to proceed with implementation and enforcement of laws like AB 32. Governor Schwarzenegger crowed: "After being asleep at the wheel for over two decades, the federal government has finally stepped up and granted California its nation-leading tailpipe emissions waiver. . . . A greener, cleaner future has finally arrived."* Assuming the public is willing to pay the costs associated with stricter standards (as reflected in higher gas prices, for example, but the overall costs are uncertain), California's ability to lower GHGs through innovative policies hinges on the Trump Administration's EPA. If they decide to rescind the clean air waiver, the program's core—including the state's harsher standards for auto emissions—will crumble. Meanwhile, led by Governor Brown, state legislators have continued their crusade against climate change. In 2016, they upped the ante by setting ambitious new carbon emissions standards under the new SB 32, which aims to lower them to 40 percent of 1990s levels by 2030. In 2017, a few Republicans joined majority Democratic legislators in rejecting the "command and control" approach to managing GHG emissions and extended the cap-and-trade program through 2030. Some lawmakers would also like to reach a "zero carbon" threshold by 2045, whereby 100 percent of California power would come from renewables; the current standard is 50 percent by 2030.

Source: California Environmental Protection Agency, Air Resources Board, "Assembly Bill 32 Overview," last reviewed August 5, 2014., https://www.arb.ca.gov/cc/ab32/ab32.htm.

*California Governor's Office, "Governor Applauds EPA Decision Granting California Authority to Reduce Greenhouse Gas Emissions," Press Release, June 30, 2009.

---

impact on neighboring cities or state government. Native groups were defined politically by their interaction with the U.S. Congress and federal agencies such as the Bureau of Indian Affairs, as well as by prior case law that treated them as wards of the federal government rather than as fully sovereign nations. In the main, California governments could ignore them.

Gaming changed all that. As bingo halls flourished in the 1970s and blossomed into full-scale gambling enterprises by the late 1980s, states began looking for ways to limit, eliminate, tax, influence, or otherwise control this new growth industry, one whose environmental and social effects on surrounding communities were proving significant.

After the U.S. Supreme Court ruled in 1987 that tribes do indeed have the right to run gambling enterprises on their lands, Congress exercised its supreme lawmaking authority (to which tribes are subject) and wrote the *Indian Gaming Regulatory Act (IGRA)*, a law that restricts the scope of gaming and defers regulatory authority to the states. The IGRA also stipulates that tribes within a state and the state itself must enter into compacts to permit certain forms of gaming irrespective of tribal sovereignty. In California, casinos with 350 or more slot machines are considered Class III gaming operations and are subject to compacts. Class II gaming includes card rooms and bingo played for monetary prizes.

FIGURE 7.4 Tribes Are Recognized Sovereigns

The U.S. Constitution explicitly recognizes four sovereigns:

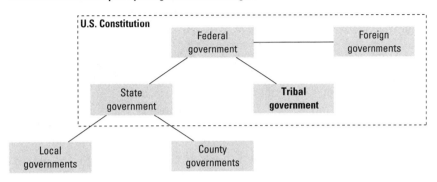

Source: K. A. Spilde, J. B. Taylor, and K. W. Grant, II, *Social and Economic Analysis of Tribal Government Gaming in Oklahoma* (Cambridge, MA: Harvard Project on American Indian Economic Development, 2002). Reprinted with permission of the authors.

No state can tax a tribal nation, a law that California Governor Gray Davis kept in mind during contract negotiations with sixty-one tribes in the late 1990s. The final compact specified that in exchange for permitting Las Vegas–style gambling, tribes would participate in revenue sharing with nongaming tribes and also contribute to a fund for reimbursing casino-related costs to cities and counties, such as those stemming from traffic congestion, public safety concerns, and gambling addiction. California voters overwhelmingly approved this first compact as Proposition 5, which was superseded two years later by constitutional amendment Proposition 1A in 2000. Gaming compacts that are renegotiated must be ratified by the legislature and may be challenged through referenda, subject to the voters' will. This occurred when several Southern California tribes arranged a deal to add thousands of slot machines in exchange for millions more paid annually into the state's general fund (contributions that can no longer be enforced). Native American groups then spent a combined $108 million to convince voters to approve four referenda on their amended gaming compacts in 2008 (Propositions 94 through 97), and each passed by at least 55.5 percent.[15] Today, the state's casino industry is exceeded in size only by that of Nevada, and more than half of the state's slot machines are located in three Southern California counties: San Diego, Riverside, and San Bernardino.

Sensing opportunity, a few smaller, more remotely located tribes have recently angled into the gaming business. As of 2017, California had ratified gaming compacts with seventy-five tribes; sixty-two casinos were operated by sixty of those tribes, plus card rooms and a smattering of satellite slot arcades that do not require compacts. The fact that casinos must be located on existing tribal lands limits their proliferation, but a few tribes have successfully taken additional land into trust with the consent of the federal government, enabling them to erect casinos in higher trafficked areas. Other tribes are actively scouting properties that can be redesignated as trust lands that would be open for casino development. Voters rejected a proposed compact in 2014 that would have allowed the North Fork Rancheria of Mono Indians and Wiyot Tribe to build a casino on new land they acquired for that purpose in Madera County some thirty-eight miles from the North Fork reservation. Recent rule changes implemented by the federal government's Bureau of Indian Affairs make it more likely that casinos will crop up in urban centers as additional tribes petition for federal recognition, a number of which plan to build casinos in places like San Francisco, Orange County, and Kern County, should they acquire the land. Seventy-two tribes without casino operations receive an annual payout from the Indian Gaming Revenue Sharing Trust Fund (to which large gaming tribes contribute) amounting to $1.1 million per tribe annually.

Clearly, "tribal sovereignty" has limits with regard to both federal and state law. Tribes retain control over political activities within their reservations' borders, and their governments usually take the form of all-powerful tribal councils vested with executive, legislative, and judicial powers. Councils have full control over tribal membership, which numbers more than fifty thousand registered individuals in California alone, and they implement federal assistance and grants covering health care, education, and other social needs. Gaming operations have laid the foundation for socioeconomic and political development in and around tribal territories. Relative prosperity has transformed tribal governments into fully staffed operations that have increasing institutional capacity to provide services that the state can't or won't provide; however, local governments are obligated to provide services such as law enforcement, road access and repairs, and emergency services. Tribes are now important participants in regional planning, and cities, counties, and local

Morongo Band of Mission Indians

The Morongo Casino Resort and Spa rises above the desert floor near the San Jacinto Mountains. The Morongo Band of Mission Indians in Cabazon, California, operates one of sixty-two Class III tribal gaming enterprises in the state; California has ratified compacts with seventy-five tribes, some of which were renegotiated recently.

communities benefit from their charitable donations as well as from the jobs and tax revenues the casinos generate. Additionally, the state benefits from the tribes' ability to obtain federal dollars for improvement projects such as widening roads and building bridges, especially when such upgrades are otherwise unaffordable. State and local governments will also continue to negotiate with California tribes over mitigating the local impacts of casinos, although the tribes must agree to the terms. Fourteen tribes have been making annual payments to the state's general fund (approximately $225 million out of a total estimated $8 billion in casino revenues in fiscal year 2015–16), but that number will drop as the state finishes renegotiating existing compacts in light of a federal court ruling that states cannot force tribes to share their revenues; moneys may be spent only on items that benefit tribes or directly offset local and state costs, such as promoting antigambling programs.[16]

Gaming enterprises have transformed tribal governments into major players at both the state and national levels, enabling them to lobby for or against policies of interest to them and to donate heavily to political campaigns. Tribes nationwide contributed approximately $18.3 million to federal candidates, parties, and outside groups in the 2015–16 election cycle and since 2014 have been spending over $25 million on lobbying activities annually.[17] California tribes constituted four of the top ten donors at the national level, and among them were Southern California's San Manuel, Pechanga, and Morongo bands. The Table Mountain Tribe alone spent over $12 million in support of the tribal gaming compact referendum discussed above (Prop 48, which failed), helping to bring the political expenditures of the top ten heaviest spending tribes to $20 million in the 2014 off-year election cycle.[18] Like many other special interests, Native American tribes have "found a voice" in the political system through the power of money.

Conclusion: The State's Interlocking Systems

California's state government is much more than a mega-institution with a few major components. Thousands of local and regional entities are responsible for countless directives that have immediate impacts on everyday life—laws and rules that are crafted by thousands of people working in elected and unelected capacities across county, city, special district, and regional governments, as well as in tribal nations. Operating mostly out of sight, their day-to-day work attracts little attention from either the public or the media, but in ways both small and large, their decisions directly condition the health and livelihoods of communities throughout the state. These entities safely dispose of millions of cubic feet of trash daily, kill mosquitoes that spread disease, employ nearly 300,000 teachers across the state, and assume responsibility for solving these and other significant collective action problems that transcend boundaries but require local input and cooperation to solve. When they're doing their jobs right, virtually no one hears about them.

The state's government should therefore be viewed as a complex organism, with approximately six thousand identifiable working parts that have specialized and localized functions. Each part contributes to the welfare of the whole, either singly or in conjunction with others, but never in total isolation. When dissected, the system appears as a bewildering mess of overlapping boundary lines, yet with remarkable success, these interlocking systems provide essential services that citizens need and will continue to demand.

As the federal government pressures California to fall into line on immigration, environmental, and other major policies, the state's Democratic political leaders seem ever-more committed to "going it alone," and largely they have the support of the state's residents—most Republicans excepted. However, the deep-rooted need for federal dollars constrains California's ability to be independent. The same can be said for the cities and counties in California: state government funding for basic services is a critical lifeline. *Interdependence* is a hallmark of the modern state.

Key Terms

city manager: a professional public administrator who oversees the day-to-day operations of a city, usually in charge of supervising all city departments and budget implementation. (p. 98)

contract city: a municipality that outsources (or contracts with) one or more neighboring local governments to provide city services. (p. 97)

fiscalization of land use: a city practice whereby land-use decisions are driven by the need to collect sales tax revenues, which leads to favoring large retailers and decision making without regard to the intrinsic value of, or need for, a project. (p. 99)

joint powers authority (JPA): a regional governing entity formed by two or more governments that enacts a binding agreement to provide services (also known as a joint-powers agreement). (p. 104)

Mello-Roos fees: fees on new construction to support infrastructure development, usually paid monthly by homeowners for a period of time (such as 25 or 40 years). (p. 99)

regional governments: planning organizations that bring together local elected officials to facilitate the exchange of ideas and information, enabling them to plan and coordinate their policies across county and city boundaries. Councils of government (COGs) are a type of regional government. (p. 104)

unfunded liabilities: financial obligations to make payouts in the future but insufficient funds have been set aside to cover them. (p. 100)

unfunded mandates: laws that require a lower-level government or agency to provide services, but no funds are supplied by the higher-level government to implement them. (p. 106)

unincorporated areas: geographic areas of a county that lie outside city boundaries; governed by a county board of supervisors. (p. 95)

CHAPTER

8

The California Budget Process

*The best evidence of the fairness of any settlement is the fact
that it fully satisfies neither party.*

—Winston Churchill, 1926

Annual budgeting at the state level is a grueling process of translating social and political values into dollars, a set of interrelated decisions that creates winners and losers. A budget is a statement of priorities, the result of intense bargaining, and the product of a sophisticated guessing game about future income and economic trends that provides risk-averse politicians with incentives to respond to the most vocal and powerful interests participating in the political system. All the while, larger economic conditions provide a context for decision making that can set the stage for massive heart attacks (from ballooning deficits that require terrifying cuts, for instance) or just mild heartburn (from conflicts over how best to spend unexpected revenues). National politics, such as partisan changeover in the U.S. presidential administration, can also leave marks on the state budget.

California's annual spending plan, $183 billion in 2017–18, represents a temporary answer to the state residents' infinite needs and wants and, despite its enormous scale, still makes many Californians wonder, "Why do we pay so much in taxes, but the state never has enough?" This chapter examines the budgeting process and explores the reasons for California's budgetary dilemmas that, more often than not, force representatives to make painful choices among alternatives.

California Budgeting 101

California's fiscal year (FY) begins July 1 and ends June 30. By law, a new budget must be passed by June 15 or lawmakers are supposed to forfeit their pay. The governor must then sign the budget by July 1, or the state cannot write checks for services or goods in the new cycle. In past years, the budget was routinely completed late, triggering more uncertainty and panic for Californians dependent on state services, but the on-time budget seven years in a row (2011–17) attests to the power of unified government (that is, when one party dominates both the legislative and executive branches), as well as rules (the budget now passes with a simple majority—rather than a two-thirds—vote).

Advance work begins in the governor's *Department of Finance (DOF),* an office staffed by hundreds of professional analysts who continuously collect data about state operations. Each branch of government and executive department itemizes its own programmatic budget needs, from personnel to project costs, including items such as habitat restoration (Department of Fish and Game), in-home care for people with disabilities (Department of Health and Human Services), and trial court funding (judicial branch)—merely a sampling from among thousands of state government activities. The DOF's projections about how much money will be available through taxes and fees provide baselines for estimating how much *must* be spent on major existing programs and how much *can* be spent on new desired programs or services. *Mandatory spending* already committed through existing laws, such as Medi-Cal and debt payments, absorbs most of the approximately $180 billion annual budget, leaving limited room for legislators to duke it out for the *discretionary funds* used to cover all other state services, from monitoring the safety of amusement park rides to sheltering victims of domestic violence.

Guided by the governor's initiatives, political values, and stated objectives, the DOF prepares a budget by assigning dollar amounts to state programs and services. The governor submits his or her budget to the legislature by January 10 in the form of a **budget bill,** whereupon it is routed to the legislature's own Legislative Analyst's Office (LAO) for scrutiny. Heeding recommendations from policy specialists in the LAO and anticipating the governor's updated version that accounts for actual tax receipts (the **May Revision** *or "May Revise"*), throughout the spring, Assembly and Senate budget committees and subcommittees develop their own version of the budget. State analysts testify before the committees, as do officials, lobbyists, and citizens representing every sector of society and local government as they seek protection for existing benefits or beg for more.

Once the budget committees finalize their work and the two houses resolve their differences (usually through the help of a conference committee made up of three members from each house), legislative leaders and their staff members negotiate with the governor and his or her staff to reach compromises over the final numbers in the comprehensive budget bill. Will tuition at state universities and colleges remain flat, be lowered, or increase? If lowered, will it be paid for through cuts to mental health programs or after-school care? Will reentry programs for former prison inmates be enhanced? Hundreds of decisions like these play into negotiations both at the committee level and in high-level negotiations that routinely include the party leaders from both houses. When the same party controls the governorship and both legislative chambers, minority-party leaders will ultimately be excluded from the top-level negotiations if their votes are not ultimately necessary for passing the budget. Thus, the **Big Three,** or the governor, the speaker, and the Senate president pro tem (all Democrats), have been the key negotiators since 2011.

Budget committees in both the Assembly and Senate chisel the governor's budget into shape throughout the months of spring, in advance of a June 15 deadline. Democrat Shirley Weber chaired the Assembly Budget Committee in 2015; here she is trailed by fellow Assembly members as they leave the Assembly floor after a vote on the $117.5 billion budget plan for 2015. The budget bill must also go through the Senate Budget Committee, be approved by the Senate, and signed by the governor to become enacted.

Final agreements also hinge on the governor's *line-item veto power* (see Chapter 5). The governor excised only $1.3 million from the 2015–16 budget with this authority and $0 from the following two budgets. Eventually, often after considerable debate and struggle, the budget bill is passed and signed into law, as are "*trailer bills*"—a package of omnibus or large bills that make the necessary policy changes to the state laws and codes outlined in the budget plan.

Mechanics of Budgeting: Revenue

A budget reflects the governor's and legislature's educated guesses about how much money the state will collect in taxes, fees, and federal grants during the coming year, as well as the state's commitments to spending or saving what it collects. All budgets are built on economic data, assumptions, and formulas designed to produce accurate forecasts about dollar amounts and the numbers of people who will demand the services and products these dollar amounts cover. Relatively small numerical shifts in these formulas can equal hundreds of millions of dollars over time. The state controller reported that receipts from all sources in June 2017 had fallen short of projections revised just a month earlier by just 0.2 percent, equating to *$295.7 million*.[1] Discrepancies like these simply cannot be estimated precisely in advance. Nevertheless, sophisticated assumptions about how much will be coming into the state's coffers serve as a foundation for balancing the budget—or at least making it temporarily *appear* balanced.

Revenue is another word for income. The largest revenue streams are provided by *taxes* and *fees* for services, and in FY 2017–18 these helped raise the state's general fund revenues to an estimated $127.7 billion.[2] Taxes are deposited into the state's main account, the **general fund**, or redistributed to county and local governments; special fees and taxes go into separate funds, such as gas taxes that are funneled into the transportation fund. It should be noted that property taxes are raised at the local level and mainly used to fund schools; they do not augment the general fund.

A separate stream of revenue, *federal grant money*, is funneled through the federal fund, representing billions of dollars from the U.S. government that go to state and local governments to subsidize specific programs, such as job retraining, or to local entities for a variety of items, such as low-income housing or special districts. The Department of Finance anticipated federal transfers of $107.5 billion for FY 2017–18. When these federal dollars are combined with all sources, the entire state budget in FY 2017–18 is actually *$290,754,400,000.*

The state relies on three major categories of taxes, all of which are highly sensitive to larger economic trends. In other words, taxes rise and fall with the economy, creating unpredictable swings in tax collection. The "big three" are personal income taxes, also known as the *PIT*; sales taxes; and the corporate tax. Considering all taxes (including those earmarked as special funds), the state expected to bring in over $178.4 billion in in FY 2017–18.

Personal income taxes represent the greatest portion of state revenues in California (as they do for most all states), totaling $90.7 billion in FY 2017–18, or 51 percent). California's personal income taxes are *progressive*, meaning that tax rates increase along with income so that people at the higher end of the income scale are charged a greater percentage in taxes than those at the lower end. On top of base taxes, marginal tax rates (as of 2017) for single or married individuals range from 1 percent to 12.3 percent, reflecting an increase of 1 to 3 percent for those making $250,000 or more, temporary tax hikes that were approved by voters in 2012 (Prop 30) and extended to 2030 with Prop 55. Tax rates are also indexed to inflation.[3] To illustrate how this works, excluding credits and exemptions, a single person making $15,051 would pay a base tax of $80.15, plus a 2 percent "marginal rate" on the amount over $8,015. A person in the next bracket would pay a 4 percent marginal rate, up to the highest bracket of 12.3 percent for those making over $250,000. Millionaires also pay 1 percent extra to help fund mental health services. This policy of "soaking the rich" means that California relies disproportionately on higher-income taxpayers to fill its coffers, although taxpayers can receive various exemptions and credits to offset the total they owe. In fact, in 2015, some 2,457 Californian taxpayers with incomes of over $200,000 paid no state income tax because of the deductions, credits, or tax breaks they were allowed to take.[4] Even so, the top 1 percent of personal income tax filers pay almost *half* of all income taxes in California.

Retail sales and use taxes are the second-largest source of California's income, accounting for 19.8 percent of the state's total revenues. Consumer spending on everything from cars to clothing directly affects how much money is available to cover state expenses. Sales taxes on goods and special taxes on fuel and other activities were anticipated to bring in $35.3 billion in FY 2017–18, an amount based on the base state sales tax rate of 7.25 percent. Of the taxes on every dollar spent, 6 cents go to the state (some of which fund local activities), and 1.25 cents are reallocated to local governments (and additional sales taxes can be imposed in counties and cities). Special taxes and fees can add more to a bill, such as an extra $1.75 for a new tire.

FIGURE 8.1 State Revenue, Fiscal Year 2017–18

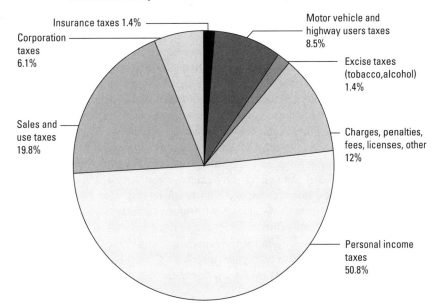

General Fund and Special Fund Revenues 2017–18 = $178.4 billion

- Insurance taxes 1.4%
- Corporation taxes 6.1%
- Sales and use taxes 19.8%
- Motor vehicle and highway users taxes 8.5%
- Excise taxes (tobacco, alcohol) 1.4%
- Charges, penalties, fees, licenses, other 12%
- Personal income taxes 50.8%

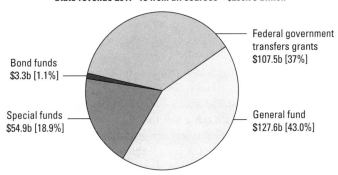

State revenue 2017–18 from all sources = $290.75 billion

- Bond funds $3.3b [1.1%]
- Special funds $54.9b [18.9%]
- Federal government transfers grants $107.5b [37%]
- General fund $127.6b [43.0%]

Sources: California Department of Finance, "California Budget, 2017–18," http://www.ebudget.ca.gov; California Department of Finance, "Chart B Historical Data," http://www.dof.ca.gov/budget/summary_schedules_charts/documents/CHART-B.pdf

Note: Percentages in the top chart are based on general fund and special funds of $178.4 billion (bond funds excluded). Figures may not add to 100 percent due to rounding.

Corporation taxes have declined over time and represent a much narrower piece of the budget pie (estimated to be $10.89 billion in FY 2017–18, or 6.1 percent of the total budget). A smattering of other sources include motor vehicle fees (4.6 percent), fuel taxes (3.8 percent), insurance taxes (1.4 percent), and taxes on tobacco and alcohol (1.4 percent). Marijuana sales will probably add only $1 billion to the total—about .0005 percent of total revenues. The remainder comes from fees and fines imposed on a wide range of activities (parking at state parks, traffic tickets, professional licensing, and so forth), rental income on state property, and surcharges on energy and other commerce; these total approximately 12 percent. Apart from taxation, **bond** funds are borrowed funds that supplement the budget and are designated for specific purposes. In 2017–18 bonds contributed $3.3 billion to the total state budget.

Borrowing to finance megaprojects has become so commonplace that the average bond measure is in the $5 billion range, and the state now carries more than $84 billion in bonded debt principal, plus $58.4 billion in interest, for a total of $142.4 billion in **general obligation bond** commitments alone.[5] Most of the debt comes from voter-approved general obligation bonds dedicated to school construction and remodeling, public transportation projects (including a record-setting $19.9 billion omnibus transportation bill approved in 2006), and environmental and natural resource projects such as beach restoration or above-ground water storage. These measures veer sharply from the "pay-as-you-go" schemes typically used to finance large infrastructure projects in the past. Unfortunately, bonds will cost about twice their "face value" in the long run because of compounded interest, though the total cost is lower if inflation is taken into account and if lower interest rates can be obtained (about $1.40 paid for every $1 borrowed). The state's credit ratings (assigned by the nation's independent credit-rating agencies) dictate the interest rates: dismal credit ratings force the state to borrow at higher interest rates, adding billions more to the state's bond repayment obligations; higher credit ratings translate into lower rates. During his first two years in office, Treasurer John Chiang banked on improved credit ratings to renegotiate and restructure bond debt, saving taxpayers $5 billion over the life of those bonds.[6]

Mechanics of Budgeting: Expenditures, Deficits, and Debt

The state commits to a spending plan before it knows how much will actually arrive in its coffers. Legislative and Department of Finance analysts do their best to predict how much unemployment compensation, welfare, housing assistance, health coverage, and a host of other services and benefits will be needed, but the costs of these services depend on how the economic winds blow. A struggling economy typically means that more residents lose jobs and pay less income taxes; financially distressed consumers also spend less, so the state's sales tax collections falter. Meanwhile, the state has already committed to a spending plan, but government expenses in the form of unemployment checks, health coverage, and other social services spike during economic hard times, and these imbalances translate into billions of dollars that policymakers cannot quickly replace. Actual revenues in FY 2014–15 surpassed original budget projections by $6.8 billion, a windfall; the state underestimated revenues two years later and ended FY 2016–17 with $2.68 billion less than anticipated.[7]

When expenses exceed revenues, *deficits* result. Legislators and the governor must return to the negotiating table to "close the budget gap," which they can accomplish through reducing benefit checks, cutting state workers' salaries and/or benefits, eliminating or reducing services, changing tax policies, borrowing, deferring payments to schools or other government agencies, or a combination

TABLE 8.1 California in Debt (as of end of FY 2016–17)

California state government carries several types of debt. **General obligation bonds** and **lease-revenue bonds** generally cover investments in infrastructure that shape the quality of life and commerce, such as better roads and water supplies. When times got tough in the late 2000s, to cover general fund expenses the state "raided" special accounts and also deferred payments that had been guaranteed to schools with promises to repay what it borrowed. That kind of **budgetary borrowing** amounted to a $35 billion "wall of debt" in 2011, which has almost been paid off. Then there are **unfunded liabilities**: pension and health care promises made to state employees in labor contracts; they are hardest to tame. The overall debt load looms large.

Category	Description	Main types	Amounts owed
Bond debt	Long-term loans to cover infrastructure that shapes quality of life and commerce, authorized by voters or the legislature. Must be repaid in time (often 5, 20, or 30 years) with interest (included here).	• General obligation bonds (GO) • Lease-revenue bonds (LR)* • Other; self-liquidating special funds (SF)	GO: $127.20 billion LR: $14.10 billion SF: $1.02 billion ***Approximate total bonded debt: $142.4 billion***
Budgetary borrowing	Long-term loans or payments deferred to cover shortfalls in the annual budget (most were incurred in late 2000s)	• Bonds ("economic recovery") *paid off, 2016* • Internal loans • Unpaid costs to local governments and schools • Underfunding of mandated programs • Deferred costs and payments • Borrowing from special funds • Unemployment Insurance Fund loans (to U.S. government)	Internal loans, borrowing from special funds: $1.763 billion Unpaid costs to schools: $1.026 billion $308.2 million ***Approximate amount owed from budgetary borrowing: $3.1 billion***
Unfunded liabilities**	Promised benefits for current and future state retirees, negotiated and set in labor contracts but underfunded based on obligations. Note that costs are subject to change over time.	• Underfunded (future) pension payouts for state employees (CalPERS, CalSTRS, UC, Judges) • Future health care	Pension liabilities: $82.6 billion Health care liabilities: $95.2 billion ***Estimated total unfunded liabilities: $177.8 billion***
TOTAL	Total for all categories		$323.3 billion

Sources: California State Treasurer's Office, "Bond Debt Summary as of July 1, 2017," http://treasurer.ca.gov/bonds/debt/07/summary.pdf; Department of Finance, "Complete Debts and Liabilities," January 31, 2017, http://www.dof.ca.gov/Reports/Budget/documents/Complete_Debts_and_Liabilities_2017-18_GB.pdf.

*"Lease-revenue" refers to debt incurred for facilities construction that will be repaid through revenue generated by the activities or projects being financed.

**Unfunded liabilities are difficult to estimate because fund levels depend on fluctuating rates of return over time, human longevity, and unknown future costs. CalPERS is the California Public Employees' Retirement System; CalSTRS is the California State Teachers' Retirement System, partially funded by the state. Health care costs will be affected by changes to the Affordable Care Act.

of these. Elected officials have relied on all available options, including borrowing billions to cover portions of the deficit during the 2000s, deferrals, and "borrowing" from the state's other accounts, such as those dedicated to schools—about $35 billion, part of the state's "wall of debt" that has been repaid (see Table 8.1). State officials have also sliced state programs by billions of dollars (more than $14 billion in cuts negotiated in spring 2011 alone) and resorted to "gimmicks" such as unrealistically assuming a much higher employment rate. Governor Brown rejected some of these tactics in June 2011 by vetoing the budget for the first time in state history, calling it "unbalanced" and citing "legally questionable maneuvers, costly borrowing and unrealistic savings."[8] The state hit a milestone in 2013 when Brown erased a long-term structural deficit, which refers to a built-in imbalance between the amounts the state spends and collects.

What does the state pay for? *Education* dominates the budget, and funding levels for this area are typically locked in through initiatives and statutes. For example, except in times of fiscal emergency, Proposition 98 mandates a minimum spending threshold that usually results in 40 percent of the budget being dedicated to K–12 schools and community colleges, systems that include 6.2 million schoolchildren and 2.1 million full- and part-time community college students. In FY 2017–18, general fund expenditures of $53.5 million on K–12 equaled 42.7 percent of revenues. Historically low per-pupil spending has been bumped up to $11,067 for each student, up from $8,757 four years ago.[9] These increases have boosted California's ranking on the U.S. Census Bureau's per-pupil spending list to thirty-first, still below the national average. Spending would need to double to launch it into the top ten.[10] Funding for the two major public university systems, California State University and the University of California, is not included in Prop 98. After tuition was hiked to help balance the budgets 2011–2012, resident tuition was frozen or increased incrementally through 2018. California dedicated $69 billion from the general fund for all education in FY 2017–18; it spends about $135 billion on education annually from *all* sources. This amount could increase by at least $31 million if lawmakers agree to waive per-credit fees for all full-time, first-year community college students as a 2017 state law allows.

Health and human services eat up the second largest slice of the budget pie and are the most difficult to project, and uncertainty surrounding national health care mandates adds to budget-makers' worries. These services represented almost 33 percent of the general fund in 2017–18 and typically exceed $60 billion in expenditures. This category encompasses a range of essential services such as Medi-Cal, food assistance, residential care for the elderly, health care for children, and benefits for the disabled. Health care spending dominates. To help meet the state's needs, the federal government transfers billions of dollars in welfare and other payments, which are both coordinated and redistributed through state agencies such as the Department of Health and Human Services. To implement the Affordable Care Act, total Medi-Cal coverage (the state's version of Medicaid) has been expanded to include 13.5 million people, including adults near the federal poverty level, disabled Californians, and low-income children regardless of immigration status. Medi-Cal covers roughly one-third of the state's population and depends heavily on federal funding, which Congressional Republicans have proposed to slash. Covered California, the state's own insurance exchange that was set up in 2014 as part of the national health care law, is now self-sustaining and has cut the state's uninsured rate in half. Ninety percent of the 2.5 million now covered under the state exchanges also depend on federal health subsidies to pay their premiums, which remain imperiled.[11] The state has recently expanded coverage for dental, vision, and mental health services, including behavioral treatment for individuals with autism, up to age 21. In FY 2017–18, $60.3 billion from the general fund was dedicated to health and human services, plus $100 billion from other sources.

FIGURE 8.2 State Expenses, Fiscal Year 2017–18

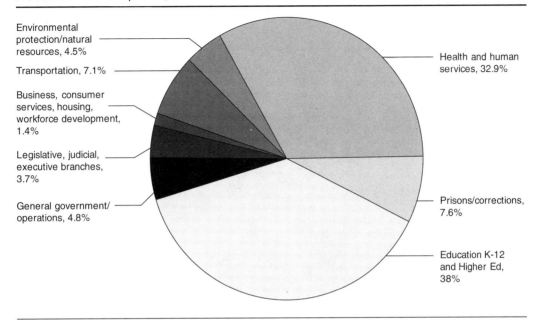

Environmental protection/natural resources, 4.5%

Transportation, 7.1%

Business, consumer services, housing, workforce development, 1.4%

Legislative, judicial, executive branches, 3.7%

General government/operations, 4.8%

Health and human services, 32.9%

Prisons/corrections, 7.6%

Education K-12 and Higher Ed, 38%

Source: California Department of Finance, "California Budget," http://www.ebudget.ca.gov/2017-18/pdf/Enacted/BudgetSummary/Summary Charts.pdf.

Note: Percentages are based on combined general, special, and bond fund expenditures of $167.6 billion. Total state revenues were projected to be $267 billion, including $162.2 billion in general and special funds (an additional $1.9 billion was diverted to a "rainy day" fund), $6.5 billion in bond funds, and $100 billion in federal transfers and grants. Figures may not add to 100 percent due to rounding.

The reorganized Transportation Agency manages $13 billion for the state's *transportation* infrastructure, which encompasses Caltrans, the California Highway Patrol, and the Department of Motor Vehicles. Much of the agency's budget is derived from bonds and special funds in the form of fuel taxes, which cover the construction of state highways, mass transit projects including high-speed rail, and maintenance of fifty thousand miles of road and highway lane miles, all overseen by Caltrans. As hybrid, electric, and alternative fuel vehicles have swarmed the roads, less and less money has been generated by gas taxes to address the deteriorating condition of the state's roadways (a common situation across the U.S.). In 2017, California lawmakers raised fuel excise taxes; one of at least seven states to do so in 2017 and one of 26 states to have raised fuel taxes since 2013. California's rate hikes are higher than others at 12 cents per gallon of regular fuel, and 20 cents for a gallon of diesel. Also new is a $100 annual fee for hybrid and electric vehicles. These could generate over $5 billion a year to address basic road repairs that will require nearly $60 billion to fix over the next ten years.[12] A Republican-backed referendum on the tax will likely be on the 2018 ballot.

State government also incurs *general operational* costs: about $7.9 billion is spent to run the major branches, including the state administration, which runs all government programs, from elections to veterans' services to state hospitals. This category also includes the courts and lawmaking operations.

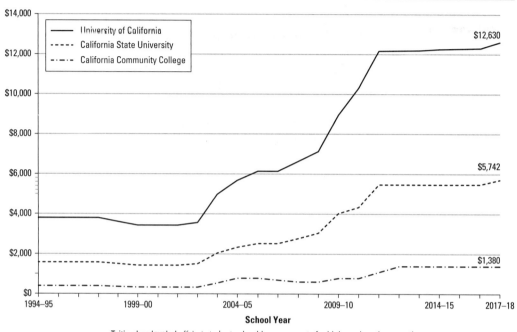

FIGURE 8.3 Full-Time Undergraduate Tuition for California Residents Attending Public Universities and Colleges, 1994–2017

Tuition has leveled off, but students shoulder more costs for higher education over time.

Source: California Legislative Analyst's Office.

Other government operations entail managing the state's employee retirement systems (CalPERS, and CalSTRS for teachers) and providing tax relief to local governments ($7.9 billion total).

At least another $15 billion goes to the *prison system*. Corrections covers inmate medical care and rehabilitation programs, as well as prison guard salaries and operating costs. Almost $14 billion of this comes from the general fund. As discussed in Chapter 6, on average it costs California over $76,000 annually per adult inmate, a price tag that reflects the high costs of medical care and correctional officer compensation. Prison spending is at its highest in state history.

It should also be noted that about 4.5 percent of the general fund budget is dedicated to paying interest on both general obligation or **lease-revenue bonds**, which represent the state's investments in infrastructure. This figure varies with market conditions, such as the rates at which different bonds were (and are) sold.

Finally, voters and their representatives agree that the state should set aside funds for unanticipated economic situations or emergency spending. Mandatory annual deposits into a "rainy day fund" have increased it to over $8.5 billion in reserves. Governor Brown supports such "fiscally prudent" steps to "counter the potential fiscal impact of federal policy changes on California" and the potential end of an economic expansion.[13]

Political Constraints on Budgeting

The budgeting process is far more than a series of steps. By nature it is political, involving many factors that condition and constrain policymakers' ability to make decisions collectively. These factors help explain how budgets can be late and out of balance by billions of dollars within weeks of their passage, and why millions of Californians are skeptical of elected officials' ability to solve problems and remain dissatisfied with the budget in any form.

Above all, the budget reflects the *larger economic climate*. State governments suffer the same economic miseries when the U.S. economy falters, and rise with the tide when the economy recovers. As unemployment climbs, recessions decimate revenue sources such as the PIT and sales taxes, which happen to be the state's top two largest sources of revenue—quite volatile, unpredictable sources on which state government stakes its fortunes. Moreover, the state's tax policies have recently shifted some of the tax burden away from corporations onto high-income individuals who largely rely on earnings from capital gains and business activity. The top 2.8 percent of taxpayers (those making more than $300,000 per year) paid 60 percent of all personal income taxes in the 2014 tax year. The 185,930 people making $500,000 or more, *the top 1.2 percent of taxpayers, paid 49.8 percent of the state's income taxes*. Thus, the entire state budget critically depends on the financial fortunes of this small group.[14]

The *political climate* also influences what kinds of programs receive funding and how much. Public opinion shifts cause some issues to gain political traction; sometimes this happens in response to sudden events, the major election outcomes, or changes in environmental conditions. Crime led the political agenda in the 1990s; the drought dominated for several years until a wet winter drowned it out in 2017. Today, a housing crunch and income inequality command attention, along with immigration and climate change. Furthermore, lawmakers know who their loyal supporters are, and they privilege some special issues and interests over others. Citizens who don't share the values of those in charge will view these choices as wasteful, offensive, or just plain ridiculous.

Anyone who has observed lawmaking will know that *special interests* and their *lobbyists* also unduly prevail throughout the process. Not only do they actively educate legislators about the effects of proposed budget changes, but they also threaten to use the initiative process to achieve what legislators may not deliver. Because they are usually at the table when the language of laws is being spelled out, their concerns are heard and can be accommodated. Business and union lobbyists vigorously promote their own companies, workers, industries, and causes, but among the most active advocates in California are those who work for local governments of the type described in Chapter 7, *stakeholders* that include schools, counties, cities, and special districts. All send swarms of policy experts and lobbyists to press their cases to state lawmakers and legislative staff, who help determine how much money they will receive and how it must be spent. Well-organized special interest groups are also behind some of the initiatives deliberately designed to limit legislators' budgeting flexibility. For example, a coalition of educators successfully endorsed Proposition 98, which guaranteed minimum funding levels for public education.

Term limits have also contributed to the tangle by continually stocking and restocking the legislature with many novice lawmakers who lack big-picture understanding of how systems in the state interrelate and how cuts in one area will affect others. It takes more than one budget cycle for a legislator to gain a working understanding of how the process itself unfolds; it takes much longer to grasp how different constituencies are affected by changes. Legislators who stay twelve years will hone their perspectives over time, but every election will renew the freshman class.

Use of the ballot box, or *ballot-box budgeting,* has fundamentally reshaped budgeting practices throughout the state as well. *Proposition 13* is a case in point. Prior to 1978, cities, counties, and schools relied on property taxes to finance their budgets. When Prop 13 capped property taxes at 1 percent of a home's or commercial building's purchase price and limited property assessment increases to no more than 2 percent per year, local governments were forced to look for other ways to pay for services (now mainly sales taxes and fees), and state government assumed responsibility for refilling local government accounts and funding schools. However, when times got tough, as they did in the early 1990s, the state substantially changed the way it allocated education funds, resulting in the redirection of yet more revenues away from local governments. Since then, state lawmakers have adopted the practice of occasionally "borrowing" property taxes from local jurisdictions to pay for schools or simply to plug large holes in the state budget. Thus, the burden of low property taxes has been shared by local governments, which have struggled to find alternative sources of revenue, and the state government, which must borrow to meet its obligations to local governments and schools when the general fund is empty. Other ballot measures, such as mandatory minimum sentences for repeat or drug offenders (three strikes and automatic sentencing enhancements), unintentionally impose costly obligations on the state that drive up prison budgets.

In all of this, *rules matter.* Today the *two-thirds supermajority vote requirement to raise any tax or fee* hamstrings the majority Democrats, who—unless they hold supermajority status in both houses—must secure a few votes from the minority Republicans, who consider raising taxes a nonstarter. Unless 54 Assembly members and 27 Senators are willing to hike sales taxes or vehicle license fees, the majority party needs several minority-party members' votes to implement such increases.[15] California is only one of seven states to impose this stringent threshold. Ironically, however, it takes only 50 percent plus one to *reduce* taxes and fees. Until 2010, one rule mattered most above all others: the two-thirds vote requirement for passing the budget. Because of their power to control the budget vote, minority-party members regarded the budget as their only opportunity to meaningfully influence public policy and force the majority to meet their demands. Overdue budgets became routine. In 2010, Californians lowered the threshold for passing the budget to a simple majority, meaning 50 percent plus one (41 Assembly members and 21 Senators), thus shifting the burden of constructing a balanced budget entirely to the Democratic majority. Budgets have been on time ever since.

Generally speaking, representatives would rather give their constituents what they want than risk losing the next election because they voted for a law that caused their constituents to lose an important state service such as in-home elderly care for an aging mother; they don't want to be blamed for a lower unemployment check or loss of health care coverage. Thus, *risk-averse politicians* who may want to promote the general welfare but shy away from making painful cuts help drive up deficits. This calculation underlies the phenomenon of structural budget deficits. In other words, when times are good, lawmakers are happy to commit more dollars to new programs or neglected needs, but they find it agonizingly hard to reduce spending levels when revenue sources dry up. Imbalances carry over to the following year, further deepening the hole and underscoring the fact that every budget builds on the prior one. A structural deficit that existed from 2000 was finally plugged with state

FIGURE 8.4 The Annual Budget Process

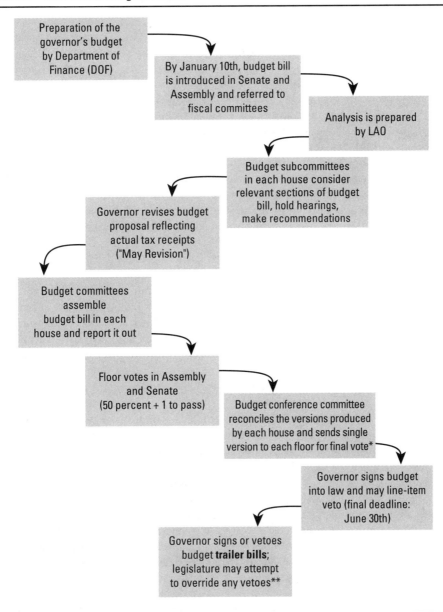

Preparation of the governor's budget by Department of Finance (DOF)

By January 10th, budget bill is introduced in Senate and Assembly and referred to fiscal committees

Analysis is prepared by LAO

Budget subcommittees in each house consider relevant sections of budget bill, hold hearings, make recommendations

Governor revises budget proposal reflecting actual tax receipts ("May Revision")

Budget committees assemble budget bill in each house and report it out

Floor votes in Assembly and Senate (50 percent + 1 to pass)

Budget conference committee reconciles the versions produced by each house and sends single version to each floor for final vote*

Governor signs budget into law and may line-item veto (final deadline: June 30th)

Governor signs or vetoes budget **trailer bills**; legislature may attempt to override any vetoes**

*More typically, the Senate and Assembly **leaders debate and negotiate with the governor** over final figures, with their staff members working overtime. If a conference committee meets, usually three people from each house participate. From this point, permutations of the process occur with regularity.

**Leaders in each house help members construct many separate, omnibus "*budget trailer bills*" that contain new policies or formalize legal changes reflected in the final budget figures. Trailer bills are processed through the houses, and the governor signs (or vetoes) each one. The legislature may attempt to override the governor's vetoes, but achieving the required two-thirds threshold is rare.

program reductions, higher revenues from an improving economy, and a temporary sales tax hike (Prop 30), all of which has finally brought state spending in line with income.

Tax Burden: Highest in the Nation?

It is a common complaint among Californians that they pay more in taxes than the average person in other U.S. states. California's ranking in terms of overall state and local debt burden tends to justify that view: according to the state's nonpartisan Legislative Analyst's Office (LAO), the state placed tenth among the fifty states in 2010. However, if state and local revenues are considered as a share of economic wealth or income, the state's ranking is considerably lower.[16] The LAO has called the overall burden "somewhat above average" based on its 2010 calculation of state and local taxes: $11.30 per $100 of personal income, just above the national U.S. average of $10.59.[17] California's taxes are generally among the highest across many major categories, but the bottom line is that whether one feels overburdened tends to be a function of one's place in the economy.

The statewide base sales and use tax rate of 7.25 percent places California among the highest in the nation (the national median is 6 percent), and because localities can charge extra sales taxes, California ranks tenth for combined state and local tax rates, which are 8.5 percent on average across the state.[18] California doesn't tax food or services, and what's taxed or not varies greatly among states. New regulations related to greenhouse gas reduction programs and an increase in November 2017 helped boost California's gas taxes to the number two spot among the states, second only to Pennsylvania.[19] Corporate taxes are relatively high on paper, but because of tax credits and changes to corporate tax law in recent decades, corporate taxes as a percent of profits have sharply declined, so many firms pay a fraction of the 8.84 percent main rate. Personal income taxes are also deceiving: the top rate is among the highest in the nation, but as of 2017, single Californians whose taxable income is less than $30,769 pay a base tax ($0, $82, or $308 depending on the income category), plus 1, 2, or 4 percent (marginal rates before exemptions), formulas that include roughly 40 percent of all Californians and are about average for all states. Individuals making between $53,980 and $275,738 a year pay bumped up rates ($2,377 base tax plus a 9.3 percent marginal rate, the highest among all states) and the base tax jumps to $23,000 plus a 10.3 percent marginal rate for those in the next income bracket. Marginal rates are highest (12.3 percent) for those earning $551,473 or more (they pay $53,606 base taxes)—but again, deductions and tax credits often reduce their tax burden significantly. On the other hand, thanks to Proposition 13, Californians pay among the lowest property taxes in the nation (a significant category) but can get stuck paying Mello-Roos fees or other local parcel taxes. "Sin" taxes on alcohol and tobacco are also comparatively low.[20] For example, as of 2017, California ranked twenty-eighth in beer taxes ($0.20 per gallon), and only Louisiana had lower taxes on table wine ($0.11 versus $0.20 per gallon in California; by comparison, both Florida and Alaska tax wine more than $2.00 per gallon). It should be noted that this category represents less than 1 percent of the state's revenues.

These figures show that the amount of taxes paid varies greatly from individual to individual and among socioeconomic classes. It is crucial to note that on an individual basis, whether a Californian pays more or less than taxpayers in other states depends greatly on how much the person earns, homeowner status, regional location, and what goods and services that person consumes. These factors also influence individuals' perceptions of being overtaxed at least as much as their attitudes about public spending and the proper role of government do.

Yet, when it comes to budgeting, not enough revenue has been collected to cover all that Californians appear to collectively want. Solid majorities oppose spending cuts to education and health and human services, but less than half support higher sales taxes, and the only category most citizens would slash is prisons and corrections—which federal courts have determined to be *under*funded in recent years.[21] Majorities of Californians say that spending more money on roads, bridges, and infrastructure is very important for California's vitality and future, but they balk at raising the gas tax or vehicle license fees (60 percent opposed those options in May 2016; 54 percent opposed in January 2017).[22] However, it is worth noting that while Californians seem to have a penchant for keeping taxes low, time and again, it has been shown that while they oppose general tax increases, they are much more willing to support specific taxes if they are assured the funds are designated for popular, specific purposes—as they did in 2012 when they approved temporary tax hikes to pay for education.

TABLE 8.2   State and Local Governments Rely on a Variety of Taxes

Type of tax	Current basic tax rate
Personal income	Marginal rates of 1 percent to 12.3 percent*; additional 1 percent surcharge for taxable income over $1 million
Sales and use	7.25 percent, but an average rate of 8.5 percent,* varies by locality
Property	1 percent of assessed value, plus rate needed to pay voter-approved debt (Assessed value typically grows by up to 2 percent per year.)
Corporation	8.84 percent of net income apportioned to California (10.84 percent for certain bank and financial companies)
Insurance	2.35 percent of insurers' gross premiums
Vehicle license	0.65 percent of depreciated vehicle value; +$100 for alternative fuel vehicles**
Cigarettes	$2.87 per pack
Alcoholic beverage	Varies by beverage, from 20¢ per gallon of wine or beer to $6.60 per gallon of spirits (over 100 proof)
Vehicle fuel	41.7¢ per gallon (plus 2.25% state sales tax, plus local sales tax, plus 2¢ per gallon UST fee)**
Diesel fuel	36¢ per gallon (plus 13.00% state sales tax, plus local sales tax, plus 2¢ per gallon UST fee)**

Sources: Mac Taylor, *Cal Facts* (Sacramento, CA: Legislative Analyst's Office, December 2016), http://www.lao.ca.gov/Publications/Report3511.

*Includes temporary tax increases imposed by Proposition 30 (2012) and extended by Prop 55 (2016).

**These figures reflect additional vehicle license fees and fuel taxes effective November 2017 including $100 annual registration surcharge for alternative fuel vehicles and increases in the gas tax of 12¢/gallon and 20¢/gallon of diesel. Also, federal taxes of 18.4¢ per gallon are added to vehicle fuel, and 24.4¢ per gallon are added to diesel fuel. "UST" refers to underground storage tank fees.

Conclusion: Budgeting Under Variable Conditions

As a U.S. state, California faces most of the same basic challenges as the other forty-nine, but as one of the world's largest "countries," its economy is intimately tied to global fortunes, and its fiscal dilemmas are comparable in scope and depth. Policymakers routinely deal with amounts in the billions, not just millions or thousands. The sheer volume of issues generated by nearly 40 million residents is staggering, and the majority of those issues are reflected, though not always resolved, in the state's annual budgets. Above all, annual budgets provide a blueprint for the state's priorities and the governor's perspective in particular. When one party controls both the legislature and the governor's office (2010–2018 is a case in point), the budget clearly reflects that party's outlook, and it becomes easier for voters to hold that party to account for policy decisions and consequences.

Budgeting by nature is a rough-and-tumble business. Financial analysts in the executive (DOF) and legislative (committee consultants and LAO) branches must perform the wizardry of forecasting without a magic crystal ball, relying on feedback, data, experience, statistical indicators, history, and tested formulas to predict the economic conditions for the coming year. Political representatives must then square their ideals with economic realities and reevaluate their preferences in the context of what is politically possible. Choices must be made, bargains must be struck, and solutions must be fashioned through compromise. Legislators' behavior is guided by rules, such as supermajority votes, that occasion either hard bargains or the marginalization of a minority party if its votes aren't needed. Budget meltdowns, delays, and austere spending cuts during the late 2000s and early 2010s illustrated that effective governing requires rules that will facilitate rather than obstruct compromise.

After negotiations have ended, the legislature has passed the budget bill, and the governor has signed it into law, the $180 billion (or so) annual budget is then assaulted by forces largely beyond the government's control. National and international crises may trigger severe and unanticipated drop-offs in tax revenues, leaving the state in the lurch. In times like those, representatives have almost no fiscally sensible ways to deal with such short-term crises because they cannot legally cut services immediately without undermining the state's contractual commitments to people and companies. On the other hand, unanticipated surpluses allow state officials opportunities to fulfill more promises. Although the budget is assembled for the coming year only, its very design conditions future choices: commit to new programs with ongoing obligations or one-time items only? Pay down old debts or stash away cash for emergencies? Invest in infrastructure or ignore long-term needs? California's brand of politics is clearly reflected in the choices and compromises that emerge from the annual budgeting process; quasi-national in scope and dwarfing those of every other state, the budget unveils the complexities of the modern state.

Key Terms

Big Three: the governor, the Assembly speaker, and the senate president pro tem. (p. 114)

bond: a debt instrument enabling a state or local government to raise capital, usually for large projects, by borrowing large sums of money and committing to repay the principal and the interest by a specified future date (usually 20 or 30 years). A bond can be a piece of a large loan that is usually financed by multiple sources. (p. 118)

budget bill: the proposed annual spending plan for the state's next fiscal year, formulated as a massive bill that must be passed by the legislature and signed into law by the governor. (p. 114)

general fund: the state's main "bank" account, into which tax revenues are deposited. (p. 116)

general obligation bonds: a type of bond that is backed by the full faith and credit of a state or local government and will be repaid by taxpayers (see "bond"). Usually covers investments in infrastructure such as library or road construction, school upgrades, or water projects. (p. 118)

lease-revenue bonds: debt incurred for facilities construction that will be repaid through revenue generated by the projects being financed. (p. 122)

May Revision (also known informally as the "May Revise"): an updated version of the proposed annual budget that accounts for actual tax receipts; the governor's Department of Finance prepares and submits new estimates to the legislature by May 14. (p. 114)

revenue: another word for (state) income. (p. 116)

trailer bills: omnibus or large bills that make the necessary policy changes to the state laws and codes outlined in the budget plan; these are passed after the budget bill is signed. (p. 115)

CHAPTER

9

Political Parties, Elections, and Campaigns

Would you join a political party if it was a good reflection of your political views or do you prefer to be unaffiliated with any specific party? Political scientist E. E. Schattschneider wrote in 1942 that "modern democracies are unthinkable save in terms of political parties,"[1] and the same can be said of elections. Without parties, the scale and scope of conflict produced by countless unorganized groups would be unmanageable. Without elections, citizens would lack the means to hold their representatives accountable. Through both parties and elections, diverse interests are voiced, aggregated, and translated into policy.

Many Californians remain unconvinced. In response to the question above, 55 percent of survey respondents said they would prefer to remain unaffiliated (down from 69 percent in 2014),[2] a group that is saturated with college-educated and younger people (ages 18 to 34), and the "no party preference" or independent voter category is the only one to have climbed steadily upward since 1980, skirting the 25 percent mark in 2017. A solid majority of Californians think they make better public policy decisions than elected officials do, placing their faith in an initiative process that allows them to bypass state government—although less than half trust their fellow voters to make good public policy decisions through the ballot box.[3]

Political communities define themselves by how they use parties and elections, and in California, these institutions tend to reflect an antigovernment political culture and a strong independent streak. Furthermore, an ideological **east-west divide** has formed along liberal-conservative lines, whereby the more urbanized and suburbanized coastal regions are heavily liberal to moderate and trend Democratic, and rural, inland counties are much more conservative and strongly Republican. This active fault has displaced the old north-south divide that is still visible in policy disputes over water distribution (and maybe sports rivalries) but little else. Urban Californians share more with other urbanites today, and rural residents have more in common with each other than urban dwellers; their politics

MAP 9.1 California's East-West Partisan Divide

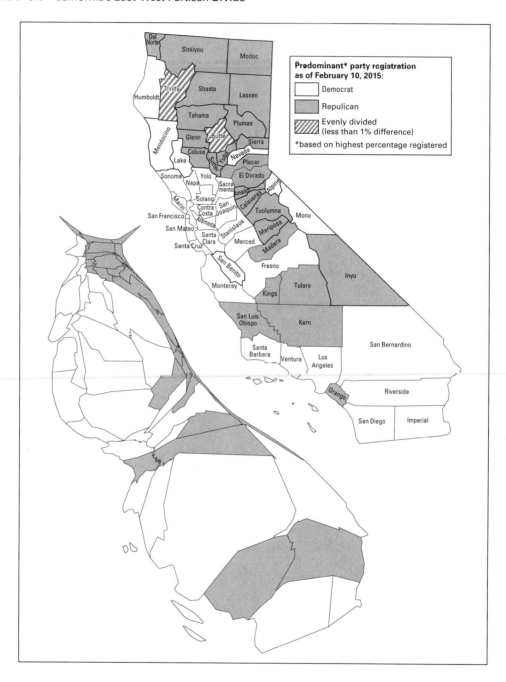

Predominant* party registration
as of February 10, 2015:

☐ Democrat

▨ Repulican

▨ Evenly divided
(less than 1% difference)

*based on highest percentage registered

FIGURE 9.1   Party Registration in Presidential Election Years, 1924–2016

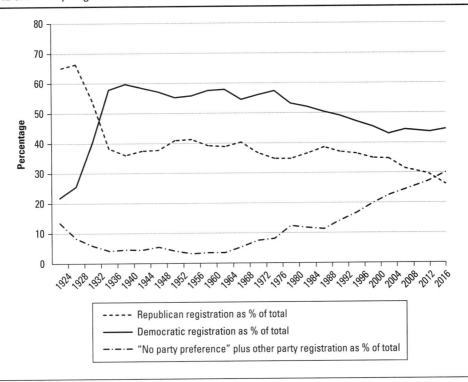

Source: California Secretary of State, "Report of Registration," November 2016.

Notes: Percentages are based on numbers from the closing date for registration in the general election. In previous years, "No party preference" voters registered as "Decline to State."

are reinforced by their sociopolitical environments (see Chapter 10) and the ground rules they have laid for political parties, candidates, incumbents, special interests, and each other.

Democratic Stronghold, but Weakly Partisan

Historically speaking, political parties in California have struggled for survival, not prospered. Much of their troubles date to Progressive reforms in the early twentieth century deliberately designed to strip them of their power. Idealizing politics without partisanship, Progressives overhauled election law by establishing new mechanisms for voters to sidestep parties altogether—the initiative, referendum, and recall being foremost among these. Other innovations included nonpartisan elections for local officials and judges and cross-filing at the state level for statewide elected officials (discussed in Chapter 2). Through secret ballots, direct primaries, nonpartisan local elections, and a ban on parties' preprimary endorsement of candidates, party members were able to choose their nominees without the blessings of party bosses.

A good deal of the Progressives' antiparty program flourishes today. Cross-filing was eliminated long ago,[4] but the long-term consequences of the Progressives' attack on parties are still visible: there is no absolute majority political party in California, state party organizations remain relatively weak, special interests in place of parties can affect some campaigns decisively through independent spending, and candidates tend to self-select and draw on their own resources rather than those of their parties. Almost one in four California voters (24.5 percent) lands in the "**no party preference**" category, having chosen to register to vote without a political party affiliation, and a version of cross-filing has been revived with the Top-Two primary.

Parties are far from ineffective in the state, however, and they thrive within government. The divergent goals, values, and agendas of the two major parties spur policy decisions. Democrats dominate state elected offices as well as the Congressional delegation (only 14 of 53 were Republican after the 2016 election). Yet, on balance, the evidence supports the judgment that California is not a strong party state, despite the left-leaning tendencies of the populace. This can also be seen through a more systematic examination of three interconnected parts of the party system: party *in the electorate* (PIE), party *in government* (PIG), and party *as an organization* (PO).

Party in the California Electorate

In one respect, a political party is made up of members who share similar beliefs about the role that government should play in their lives, but "party in the electorate" also refers to the generalized sentiment a party's members share about what it means to be a Republican, Democrat, or member of any other party. It is this sentiment that leads them to vote for certain officials and reinforces their attachment to the party's "brand name."

Seventy percent of registered California voters belong to one of the two major parties, Republican and Democratic, but that number is somewhat deceiving. According to a 2016 statewide survey, a majority of Californians think the state needs a third political party.[5] Because neither party has absolute majority status, independent, "no party preference" voters provide the swing votes necessary to win in general elections, and generally speaking they side with Democratic candidates. While California is commonly labeled a "blue state" based on registration statistics and statewide elections that have overwhelmingly favored Democrats, the reluctance of more people to join a party and the defection of many from the major parties have turned the state's political complexion slightly purple.

In terms of party registration, California was an absolute majority-Democratic state between 1934 and 1989; since then, Democrats have made up the state's plurality party, topping Republicans by almost 19 percent in February 2017. Democrats today are first in registration at 44.8 percent, Republicans take second at 25.9 percent, and other parties collectively hold third place with a combined membership of 4.9 percent. Individuals who affiliate with no party constitute 24.5 percent of the state's electorate.[6] A minority of "no party preference" voters actually consider themselves politically independent (27 percent), with most of them leaning toward the Democrats (41 percent) rather than toward Republicans (32 percent), even as they profess to dislike the parties: 55 percent of independents rate the Democratic Party unfavorably, but they rate the Republican Party even more unfavorably at 69 percent.[7] Historically they have cast more votes for Democrats than for Republicans in California elections. Exit polls showed that 50 percent of independents voted for Hillary Clinton versus 37 percent for Donald Trump; 57 percent of them voted for Democrat Jerry Brown two years earlier, evidence that corroborates political scientists' findings that self-identified independent "leaners" usually vote for the parties they say they tend to prefer.[8] Slightly more men have registered independent; independents also tend to be young and college educated (46 percent college grads) and are a fairly diverse group (43 percent "non-White").[9] San Francisco has the highest percentage of no party preference registrants in the state, nearing a third of all voters (31 percent in that city/county).

Current members of the Democratic Party in California tend to be ethnically diverse, in the low-to-middle income bracket, and younger than in the past. About one out of two Democrats is Latino, African American, or Asian, and 50 percent are White.[10] About a third of likely Democratic voters have household incomes of $40,000 or less per year, and a quarter of them are renters rather than homeowners. A disproportionate number of women are Democrats (60 percent).

Republicans, meanwhile, tend to be White and middle- to upper-class, and they count more evangelical Christians among their ranks. In contrast to Democrats, 77 percent of likely Republican voters are White.[11] More than half (55 percent) are over the age of 55. About the same number of people in both major parties are college graduates (about 40 percent), but almost half of Republican likely voters make $80,000 or more annually (50 percent), compared to 38 percent of Democrats.[12] Overall, these trends mirror those across the states.

About three out of four California Republicans describe themselves as **conservative**: they generally want strictly limited government, oppose taxes, respond more favorably to business than to labor, favor strong laws restricting illegal immigration, and believe that "individual destiny should be in the individual's hands." Considered to be on the right-hand side of the ideological spectrum, about 82 percent of Republicans want lower taxes and fewer government services.[13] Those who are strongly conservative oppose school districts designating themselves as sanctuary "safe zones" to indicate they will protect undocumented immigrants from federal enforcement efforts (71 percent oppose)[14] and believe the government goes too far in restricting gun rights. About half of them are against the legalization of marijuana, have a generally unfavorable view of the 2010 health care reform (Affordable Care Act), and favor restrictions on the right to an abortion.[15] California Democrats, on the other hand, tend to hold **liberal** views: 67 percent of them would pay higher taxes in exchange for more government services; they want the government to promote equal opportunity in education and the workplace, they want wider access to health care and favor a single-payer system, they favor prochoice laws, and they are more responsive to labor than to business. They feel government doesn't regulate or control guns enough (72 percent).[16] Regarded as being on the left-hand side of the ideological spectrum, slightly over half of Democrats say they are liberal, and about a third consider themselves moderates. In contrast, independents are distributed widely across the ideological spectrum: about a third of likely independent voters describe themselves as moderate or *middle-of-the-road*, and equal proportions (one-thirds) consider themselves liberal or conservative. They are about evenly split on raising taxes for more services or lowering them for fewer services (48 percent would pay more).[17] On climate change, a scientific issue that has become politicized, 76 percent of Independents agree that "global warming is a serious or somewhat serious threat to the economy and quality of life for Californians," compared to Democrats who almost universally agree with this statement (93 percent) and only 50 percent of Republicans who hold that view.[18]

Party in Government

Those most responsible for advancing a party's brand name through policymaking are current elected officials: the party in government. Approximately 20,000 officials in California hold elective office; of them, 132 hold statewide office and 55 represent Californians in the U.S. Congress. Governors,

BOX 9.1 How to Party in California

To qualify as a new political party in California, a group must first hold a caucus or convention at which officers are elected, and a name is chosen. After filing a notice with the Secretary of State, qualification may then proceed either by petition or by registration. Petitioners need to gather 751,308 signatures,* a number equal to 10 percent of the total number of people who cast votes in the most recent gubernatorial (governor's) election, and they must file those petitions in several counties at least 135 days before the next election. The more complicated registration option requires that 0.33 percent of registered voters complete an affidavit of registration at least 154 days prior to the next election (or 123 days prior to a presidential election) where they indicate their preference for the new party, affidavits that must be verified by county elections officials. The latter process is difficult to coordinate statewide, but a new party cleared those hurdles prior to the 2012 California primary election: Americans Elect, which qualified for the June 2012 primary election, was disbanded in May that year because the party was unsuccessful in nominating a candidate through its online voting process.

Registered Parties in California as of June 2017

- American Independent: http://www.aipca.org
- Democratic: http://www.cadem.org
- Green: http://www.cagreens.org
- Libertarian: http://www.ca.lp.org
- Peace and Freedom: http://www.peaceandfreedom.org
- Republican: http://www.cagop.org

Parties That Have Failed to Qualify

- California Pirate Party
- California Moderate
- God, Truth, and Love
- Open Party
- Pot
- California National Party
- Reform Party
- Superhappy Party
- United Conscious Builders of the Dream

Source: California Secretary of State, "Qualified Political Parties for the June 5, 2018 Primary Election," accessed July 25, 2017, http://elections.cdn .sos.ca.gov/ror/ror-pages/ror-odd-year-2017/qual-pol-parties.pdf.

*This number will change after the 2018 elections.

Assembly members, senators, federal representatives, and others pursue agenda items that become associated with a party's name through fulfilling their chief purpose: *to organize government in order to achieve their policy aims.* Through their messages and decisions and also by what they choose not to do, those in positions of power communicate what it means to be a member of a particular party.

Democrats have held the title of majority party for more than forty years in both legislative houses. The Assembly and Senate have been majority Democratic almost continuously since 1971, interrupted only once by Republican rule in the Assembly in 1995–96. A high degree of ideological polarization pervades the capitol, especially with regard to taxation and spending: Democrats are more willing to raise certain taxes (gas taxes or income taxes paid by millionaires, for example), and Republicans are unwilling to raise them, period, instead insisting on shrinking government through cutting services.

Although neither Democratic legislators nor Republican legislators are all exactly alike, they have expressed strong party solidarity and ideological rigidity over the years, which voters hoped to alleviate through redistricting and the Top-Two primary. In the past, district lines were engineered to guarantee the election of Democrats or Republicans, which led to the election of the most ideologically extreme candidates. The "real" competition took place during primary elections, as candidates of the same party vied for the votes of strong partisans in those low-turnout elections. Despite voters' intentions, however, the nonpartisan, citizen-led redistricting process created by Prop 14 did not eliminate the tendency for districts to favor one party or the other (more often the Democrats). Likewise, preliminary research shows that the Top-Two primary has fallen short of expectations that it would bring about the election of more moderates, but it has not been an utter failure. There is some evidence that, in certain districts, the relative moderate has been chosen over the more ideologically extreme opponent, even if the legislature has not noticeably moderated overall. Also, more elected Democrats have supported business-friendly agenda items such as by blocking fee and tax increases, but it is not clear whether that tendency can be attributed to the Top-Two system.[19] Underwhelming outcomes may be attributed to the difficulty average voters have in discerning candidates' positions, and voters usually resist crossing over to support opposing party candidates.

Democrats now dominate state government, having captured every executive office up for grabs in 2014 but one (on the Board of Equalization, joining one other Republican) and a supermajority in the legislature for much of the 2012–13 and the 2016–17 term. What accounts for their domination? Higher Democratic Party registration among voters, mainly. Historically, however, some success has come from Democrats' influence in the redistricting process. Competitive districts have not consistently materialized because of *natural sorting* and attempts at **gerrymandering**. Gerrymandering refers to the act of manipulating district boundaries to include or exclude certain groups in order to benefit a party or an incumbent. Until 2010, state lawmakers—in actuality, the majority Democrats *plus* the governor *and* ultimately the courts—were in charge of redistricting and tended to draw maps that guaranteed a Democratic majority and few competitive seats. "Bipartisan gerrymanders" were created when both sides agreed to maintain the status quo.

In 2010, Californians joined a category of twelve states that entrust redistricting authority to citizen-controlled independent commissions. Under Prop 11, party leaders and legislators are barred from playing an active role in forming their own districts, although they are allowed to plead their cases to fourteen citizen mapmakers on the **Citizens Redistricting Commission**—along with every other Californian. Factors other than gerrymandering help determine the level of competitiveness in districts: higher statewide Democratic registration, the Republican Party's relative unpopularity in the state, and natural *sorting*—that is, like-minded people with similar values tend to live near each other. These settlement patterns have produced a densely populated coastline that is more "blue" (Democratic) and an inland that is more "red" (Republican). Competitive districts are difficult to construct because the mapmakers must draw districts containing numerically equal populations that are as compact as possible, respect city and county lines, and keep communities of interest intact. These conditions pit practicality against ideals, and, in the end, interparty electoral competition seldom materializes. Regardless, citizens have been swayed by the argument that lawmakers in principle should not be in charge of drawing their own districts, whether or not more competitive districts are created.

FIGURE 9.2 Registration by Political Party in California, 2017

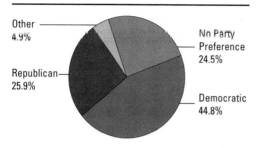

Other 4.9%

No Party Preference 24.5%

Republican 25.9%

Democratic 44.8%

Source: California Secretary of State, "Odd-Numbered Year Report of Registration, February 10, 2017," http://elections.cdn.sos.ca.gov/ror/ror-pages/ror-odd-year-2017/hist-reg-stats.pdf.

The governor's office remains one place where Democrats' hold has been historically weak. Republicans occupied the seat for almost fifty of seventy years after World War II. They have also managed to secure other statewide executive offices over the decades, preventing Democrats from monopolizing state administrative power. As noted, two of four elected Board of Equalization members were Republican as of 2017.

Party Organizations

The concept of party also encompasses formal organizational bodies and their rules. It should be noted that when citizens register to vote they actually become members of their *state* parties, organized according to election codes in the fifty different states and the District of Columbia. This is why voter registration forms are addressed to a country registrar of voters rather than a national party association, and voters are given the option to register when they visit the Department of Motor Vehicles, a *state* agency. The national organizations known as the Democratic National Committee and Republican National Committee have little to no control over the state parties.

Party organizations are well suited to fulfill another key party role: that of *nominating candidates for election and getting them elected*. At the top is the party *state central committee*, responsible for coordinating the local bodies that exist below it, for strategizing to win seats, and for assisting candidates with funding and other resources. These committees run their respective state conventions every year.

A state party chair acts as CEO of the party, and members of the state central committees include current statewide elected officials, nominees for statewide office, county-level party officials, and appointed and elected members from across the state. Democratic members of their state central committee number about 3,000, evenly divided between men and women and roughly balanced among age groups and races/ethnicities. The Republican state central committee has approximately 1,650 members, and there are no gender, age, or race/ethnicity quotas. Beneath the major state party organs are fifty-eight *county central committees* for each party, also organized by the state election codes. Further down are local and regional clubs that are home to dedicated party volunteers. The Democratic Party organizes these clubs by Assembly district, and in 2017, Bernie Sanders supporters who strongly support universal health care and reject "politics as usual" quietly concentrated on assuming these positions, devoting themselves to displacing establishment leaders by becoming delegates to the annual state party convention. They had almost enough votes to install their preferred state party chairperson, and should they continue to saturate local clubs throughout the state, they could succeed in 2018.

In California as elsewhere, *informal networks* formed by interest groups, media outlets, campaign donors, and other elites such as former officeholders also influence how the organization behaves and how it is perceived.[20] Working through ideologically based networks and groups, powerbrokers guide agenda priorities, help choose who is recruited or endorsed for elective office, pressure competitors to drop out of a race to clear the field for a preferred front runner, or donate money to the party and candidates. Increasingly, these activists are influencing elections behind the scenes by independently spending huge amounts of money for candidates they endorse and to defeat candidates they oppose.

Elections: Continuity and Change

Like political parties, elections are a keystone of democracy, and voters continue to find ways to improve them, usually in order to address what they perceive as unfair advantages held by groups or individuals. Elected officials also occasionally initiate electoral changes, which might take the form of readjusted rules targeting the conduct of parties or candidates. Sometimes those reforms perform as intended, but often there are unanticipated or unintended consequences.

Propositions 11 and 14, already discussed elsewhere in this text, illustrate such outcomes. For example, newly redistricted maps in 2012 forced many incumbents into the same districts, which caused an unprecedented number to decline to run for reelection (six Democrats, nine Republicans, one independent). New challengers entered the fray, and in the end, thirty-nine first-time legislators were elected, two seats switched parties, and only two Assembly incumbents were defeated (compared to *zero* incumbent defeats in 2010).

Proposition 14, the "**Top-Two primary**," triggered a different set of outcomes. For years, reformers tried to unlock primary elections so that a larger electorate (independents) could participate. Through a normal **partisan primary election** for various offices, party members nominate candidates who will later compete head to head with the other party's nominees in the general election. For instance, six Republicans may jump into an Assembly primary race, but only one will receive enough votes to become the Republican nominee for that seat (an incumbent invariably receives his or her party's renomination). That person will face the Democratic nominee in the **general election**, usually held in November.

Until 1996, the state had a *closed primary* system, meaning that only voters who declared their party affiliation prior to the election could participate in their own party's elections. At the voting station, a person would receive a Republican or a Democratic ballot listing party candidates for each office. Independent voters could not vote for partisan nominees, although they could vote on statewide initiatives, local measures, and nonpartisan offices. Proposition 198 (1996) changed the rules but only temporarily. Californians approved the *blanket primary*, a type of open primary, in which all registered voters could vote for any candidate. In 1998, primary election voters were given a single ballot listing each office and every possible candidate for it, just as in a general election. Two years later, the U.S. Supreme Court ruled the scheme an unconstitutional violation of political parties' First Amendment right to free association. A *modified closed primary* took its place, and independents' votes counted if a party allowed it.

In June 2010, California voters decided again to switch to a system that resembles an *open primary,* similar to the one Washington state adopted in 2004. In exchange for his vote to pass the budget in 2009, Republican senator Abel Maldonado demanded the legislature place a constitutional amendment on the ballot creating a nonpartisan "**Top-Two**" candidates primary, also known as a *voter preference election*, in which any registered voter may select a top choice from among all candidates for office. The system is not a traditional political party primary, because even if one candidate receives a majority of all votes cast for that office, the top two vote-getters advance to the general election for a runoff, be they two Republicans, two Democrats, one from each party, or otherwise. Reformers hoped to disrupt the status quo by encouraging the election of centrist candidates who would need to appeal to a wider electorate and discouraging the election of ideologically polarizing lawmakers; they also sought to allow greater ballot access. One consequence has been longer ballots, because all candidates for an office are listed, and wilder outcomes that have earned it the name "jungle primary." As noted above, preliminary analyses of the first two elections have obtained mixed results about its moderating influences; in some Democratic match-ups the dynamic favors the more moderate candidate, but this does not appear to be a factor in Republican vs. Republican races, for example.[21] Overall, there is little evidence that the legislature has become more centrist, but this is partly explained by the fact that party leaders work hard to keep their members in line on important votes and discourage behavior that undermines party unity.[22] Moreover, third party candidates have virtually no chance of winning seats, although a few of them have made it into general elections where one of the major party candidates is otherwise unopposed (by a major-party candidate).

Another extremely significant reform has been *term limits* for elected state officials, which have generated a slew of electoral consequences since their adoption in 1990. For one, the game of political office musical chairs now extends to all levels of government: competition for down-ticket elections, such as seats on county boards of supervisors and big-city mayoralties, has increased, and pitched contests over congressional seats have also multiplied as the pool of experienced candidates looking for jobs continues to swell. About two-thirds of all statewide officials attempt to run for another office within two years of being termed out. In the crusade to stay in office, it is also fairly common now for incumbents to be challenged by members of their own party—rivalries that used to be adroitly managed by party leaders or preempted by the advantages of incumbency that scared off good challengers (those with experience and money). Ironically, term limits have not affected incumbents' chances for reelection, however; officeholders continue to be reelected at near-perfect rates. Modifications to term limits affecting officeholders elected after 2010 will likely suppress the rate of turnover (they can now stay up to twelve years total in one or either house), although the goal of staying in public office will continue to motivate individuals to run when new opportunities arise.

Special elections to fill vacant seats are commonplace due to term limits, as politicians leave one office for another that opens up. A "domino effect" occurs when a state senator runs for an open U.S. Congress seat and a member of the Assembly then runs for the subsequently vacated state Senate seat; this then creates a third election needed to fill the empty Assembly position, and so on down the line. Between January 2011 and October 2017, thirty stand-alone special primary and runoff elections were held to fill congressional or state legislative seats, most of which were vacated by ambitious elected officials. Candidates who win a special election with over 50 percent of the vote are considered elected, and no runoff election will be held. Unfortunately for cash-strapped counties, the average price tag for special elections can approach $1 million, and voter turnout for these elections is usually dismally low, averaging *below 15 percent* turnout from 2013 to 2017. Turnout rates for special statewide elections called by the governor are usually only slightly higher and cost upward of $100 million. Costs should drop as vote-by-mail elections become standard in the state.

Recent noteworthy reforms continue to reshape California elections, partly to administer elections more efficiently, partly to save money, and partly to encourage higher voter registration (and ultimately, voter turnout). First, the failings of punch-card systems laid bare by the 2000 presidential election between U.S. Vice President Al Gore and Texas Governor George W. Bush prompted the U.S. Congress to pass the Help America Vote Act of 2002. Every state received millions of dollars to replace old voting equipment with more accurate touch-screen and optical-scan machines. California's secretary of state monitors the new equipment for software glitches and intentional mischief. All counties are now outfitted with advanced voting technology—the need for which is increasingly offset by the numbers of registered California voters who **vote by mail** or are *permanent absentee* voters, meaning they receive their official ballot through the mail and either return it by mail or drop it off at a polling place. They are at the forefront of a new system coming into vogue in California: all *vote-by-mail elections and regional voting centers*. Certain counties now have the option of abandoning traditional, neighborhood polling booths for this new system, in which voters will be mailed a ballot that can be dropped off at any regional polling center, open at least 30 days prior to election day. The law already authorizes cities and special districts with populations under 100,000 to conduct all-mailed ballot special elections.

One of the biggest technological developments affecting elections is VoteCal, a statewide database connecting all 58 county elections officials. Because voter information is now linked statewide, beginning in 2018, voters will be able to register to vote on the day that they cast a ballot—also known as *same-day registration*—without running afoul of laws designed to prevent voter fraud. This system also allows *16- and 17-year-olds to preregister* to vote. In addition, an existing **motor voter** law reduces barriers to vote even further: effective January 1, 2016, Californians are *automatically registered to vote* when they renew their driver licenses or register their cars with the Department of Motor Vehicles (DMV) unless they opt out. As of 2012, Californians can register to vote via the Internet; *online voter registration* is a service offered in thirty-four other states and DC. To register in California, applicants can go to *http://registertovote.ca.gov*. If an individual does not have a signature that can be accessed from his or her California driver's license record, then a hard copy of the form that the applicant fills out online will be mailed for a signature. It is too early to discern whether voter registration rates have increased because registration can be done online, but it appears that young voters prefer this method of registering over mail-in forms, so this change has the potential to improve this voting group's historically dismal registration rates. Eliminating barriers to vote is a priority in California, and voters are NOT required to show a form of identification at the polls. Election-day fraud, such as impersonating someone else, is a felony in California.

Other important changes affect the 2020 presidential election. First, California is poised to make a bigger impact in the selection process by holding its primary election in March instead of June. Second, California could allocate its Electoral College votes for U.S. president under a new scheme to which it has already committed. It works like this: under the U.S. Constitution, each state determines how it will cast its electoral votes. In order to avoid the dilemma that arises when a candidate receives the U.S. popular vote but loses the election, as was the case with Al Gore in 2000 and Hillary Clinton in 2016, California will direct its electors to cast their votes for the presidential candidate who wins the most popular votes in the United States. This proposed change will take effect only when enough states enact this *"national popular vote" law* (collectively they must possess 270 Electoral College votes, a simple majority, to activate the law). California was the ninth state to commit to implementing this plan.

FIGURE 9.3   Vote-by-Mail Statistics, 1976–2016

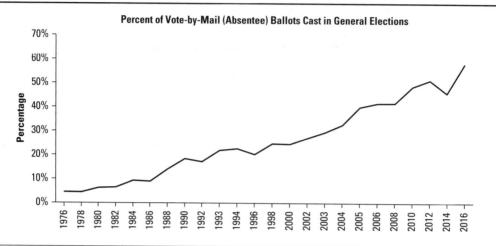

Percent of Vote-by-Mail (Absentee) Ballots Cast in General Elections

Source: California Secretary of State, "Historical Vote-By-Mail (Absentee) Ballot Use in California," http://www.sos.ca.gov/elections/historical-absentee. Data for 1993, 2003, and 2005 are for statewide special elections.

California Campaigns

Given parties' relatively weak hold over Californians, the frequency of elections, a mobile population, and the immense size and density of districts, campaigns serve the important role of connecting citizens with candidates and incumbents. Across the state, virtually all campaigners face the same basic challenges: raising huge sums of cash to buy access to potential voters and convincing enough of those voters to reject their opponents.

Former Assembly Speaker Jesse Unruh once proclaimed, "Money is the mother's milk of politics."[23] Indeed, incumbents cannot afford to stop raising money, waging what is known as the nonstop "permanent campaign." On average, a successful Assembly campaign costs about $837,000, and a Senate campaign $1.1 million—which means that Assembly and Senate candidates need to raise $1,000 and $1,500, respectively, *every single day of the year* to be viable.[24] Actual costs depend critically on how strong the competition is: incumbents running in a general election usually face "sacrificial lambs" who spend almost nothing in their own defense, and some incumbents *without* serious challengers still spend in excess of $2.5 million "defending" their seats (leaders can't afford to lose, so they might spend *thirty-five times* as much as their competitors, as Senate Pro Tem Kevin DeLeón and Speaker Toni Atkins did in 2014). These sums do not include multimillions more that outside groups expend independently to influence electoral races. The secretary of state recorded over $51 million in independent expenditures across 80 Assembly races, $37 million of which was spent in support of candidates; the amount was $28 million for twenty Senate races (again, most was spent in support).

Open-seat elections, created regularly now by term limits, require far higher sums. Candidates for open Assembly seats spend over $1 million on average; the most exorbitant races can cost each candidate more than $3 million. Costs are also higher when there is a good possibility that the seat could flip to the other party or be the race that denies the Democrats a supermajority, which can occur through special or regular elections. Democrat Josh Newman had already collected more than $1.2 million just a few months into the signature-gathering phase of a recall campaign against him; in the most expensive race of 2014, Republican Andy Vidak and his opponent spent $6 million. In both, the supermajority status of Senate Democrats hung in the balance. Candidates must raise funds from individuals who are limited to donating up to $4,400 per candidate, small contributor committees that can donate up to $8,800 per candidate, and political parties, which may give unlimited amounts.[25]

Among the most generous contributors to campaigns (by industry) are trade and public employee unions, banking and securities/investment, energy or oil and gas companies, general business (manufacturing, chemicals, food and beverage, tobacco), law, the two major state political parties, agriculture, real estate, health, and ideological or single-issue groups. Tribal governments tend to spend huge sums when gaming-related initiatives are on the ballot. It is important to note that *there are no limits on how much can be donated to ballot campaigns*. In addition, candidates enjoy the constitutional right to spend as much as they want of their own money in pursuit of a political office, but all other donors are subject to strict limits on how much money they may give directly to candidates, with one exception: recall elections are exempt from contribution limits. Out-of-state contributors are allowed to participate in campaign financing, and they, along with everyone else, must report to

Brian van der Brug/The Los Angeles Times

Wendy Carillo, here a candidate for Assembly, won an October 2017 special election primary in a crowded field of candidates that included ten Democrats. She faced a fellow Democrat, Luis Lopez, in the run-off election in December 2017, which she won. The special election was part of a "domino effect" generated when Congressman Xavier Becerra was appointed to replace Attorney General Kamala Harris, who had been elected to the U.S. Senate; Assemblyman Jimmy Gomez was then elected to represent Becerra's former U.S. House district, opening the 51st Assembly District seat mid-election cycle.

the secretary of state how much they spend independently plus the source of their contributions, a point the Fair Political Practices Commission (FPPC) drove home in 2013 when they fined two out-of-state nonprofits $1 million for improperly disclosing their contributors' names.

To clarify these rules further, all campaign contributions and expenditures must be reported to the California secretary of state's office, which makes fund-raising activity publicly available pursuant to Proposition 9 (see http://cal-access.ss.ca.gov). The state's disclosure rules (dictating that information about donors must be made available to the public) survived a legal challenge after the U.S. Supreme Court ruling in *Citizens United v. Federal Election Commission* (2010) lifted a seventy-year-old ban on independent federal campaign expenditures by corporations and unions in the name of free speech. Large sums are now being spent in independently run *federal* (Congressional and presidential) campaigns without strict reporting and disclosure requirements, principally in the form of mass mailings and television and radio ads designed to defeat or endorse candidates. However, in California, large sums could already be spent independently on state elections, so these were minimally affected by *Citizens United*.

Why do candidates require colossal amounts of campaign cash? In California's populous districts, paid media are the only realistic way to reach large numbers of potential voters. Advertising is especially pricey in urban media markets already crowded with commercial ads. Most candidates in the state invest heavily in this type of **wholesale campaigning**, or indirectly contacting voters through the airwaves and direct mail.

This is not to say that knocking on doors, attending community events, and "pressing the flesh"—types of **retail campaigning** that require a comfortable pair of shoes rather than large amounts of campaign cash—are unimportant in modern campaigns. Personal, face-to-face contact is particularly beneficial in local contests in which friends and neighbors help turn out the vote.

Professional campaign managers and consultants help candidates build efficient money-raising machines by coordinating other critical aspects of successful campaigns: access to donors, polling data, media buys, social media, targeted messages, and volunteers. Still, money isn't everything, even in statewide elections: in her losing gubernatorial contest with Jerry Brown, Republican candidate Meg Whitman spent a total of $178.5 million, or $43.25 per vote, compared to Brown's $36.7 million, or $6.75 per vote. Whitman, former president and CEO of eBay, spent $144 million of her own fortune on the race.

Conclusion: A Complex Electorate

Parties, elections, and campaigns have been the instruments of change and the targets of reform. Historical disdain for parties lingers in California's state election codes and permeates the conduct of elections, surfacing in initiatives that seek to empower individuals over organizations, such as Proposition 14, the "Top-Two primary," which reformed primary elections by opening them to all voters, regardless of political party affiliation. It is also manifested in relatively weak formal party organizations, active informal party organizations, and ever-increasing numbers of independents.

Political parties are far from dormant, however, and the strident partisanship that is displayed at times by legislators accentuates their viability. They are relevant at every level of government, from running elections to organizing government, and they still provide the most important voting cues for the average citizen. The ideological divisions they represent are real, and the fact that Democrats

Born and raised in Bakersfield, California, Vince Fong ran on a conservative platform and was elected to the Assembly at age 37. Mailers that advertise a candidate's qualifications, positions, and messages are standard elements of a political campaign strategy to reach potential voters.

TABLE 9.1   Top Contributors to Campaigns For and Against Proposition 61 (2016)

A measure to regulate prescription drug prices, requiring the state to pay no more than the U.S. Department of Veterans Affairs pays.

Top Contributors SUPPORTING Prop 61	Industry	State of Origin	Total Contributions
AIDS Healthcare Foundation	Nonprofit	CA	$18,717068
California Nurses Association PAC	Medical	CA	$264,138
TOTAL, Top Supporters			**$18,981,206**

Top Contributors OPPOSING Prop 61		State of Origin	Total Contributions
Merck & Co., Inc.	Pharmaceutical	NJ	$9,420,395
Pfizer, Inc.	Pharmaceutical	NY	$9,420,395
Johnson & Johnson	Pharmaceutical	NJ	$9,301,646
Amgen Inc.	Pharmaceutical	CA	$7,670,768
Abbvie Inc.	Pharmaceutical	IL	$6,859,873
Sanofi-Aventis U.S.	Pharmaceutical	NJ	$6,720,945
AstraZeneca Pharmaceuticals	Pharmaceutical	DE	$6,080,535
Allergan USA, Inc.	Pharmaceutical	NJ	$5,079,332
Novartis Pharmaceuticals Corp.	Pharmaceutical	NY	$4,728,302
Glaxosmithkline	Pharmaceutical	NC	$4,528,527
TOTAL, Top Opponents			**$69,810,718**

Source: California Fair Political Practices Commission, "Top Contributors to Primarily Formed Committees: November 2016 Election," Accessed November 24, 2017, http://www.fppc.ca.gov/transparency/top-contributors/nov-16-gen/nov-16-gen-v2.html.

hold a distinct party registration advantage and swept statewide elections 2010 through 2016 signals their advantage over Republicans in the state, as well as Republicans' need to regroup in order to regain lost ground. Democratic consolidation of power in both legislative chambers and executive offices enables greater accountability, in that the voters can blame or reward one entity, one party, for the governance provided. However, many voters aren't paying close attention to politics, and there's considerable bias among those who participate (topics of the next chapter), and Democrats' consistent electoral successes tend to mask citizens' growing detachment from parties. Voter-related reforms now in the pipeline are unlikely to strengthen partisan connections, but they do intend to increase political participation, however incrementally.

Having followed in the footsteps of other states that forged innovative party and election reforms, California has engineered its own set of rules that is clearly unique, but not particularly exceptional. It remains to be seen whether same-day voter registration, expanded motor voter registration, or switching to permanent absentee voter elections results in campaigns, candidates, and winners that embody the spirit of moderation and citizenship that Californians—indeed, most Americans—yearn for, or whether these will bring about the effective governance that citizens so strongly desire. The abiding hope is that they will—or that the *next* reform will.

Key Terms

Citizens Redistricting Commission: a group of fourteen mapmakers, chosen through a rigorous process stipulated in Proposition 11 (the Voters First Act), who redraw the district boundaries that determine representation for the state Assembly, Senate, Board of Equalization, and U.S. House of Representatives. Chosen once every ten years, following the decennial census. (p. 137)

conservative: an ideological disposition to strictly limit government, taxes, and illegal immigration; general favoring of business interests over those of labor; and a belief that the individual—not government—should be financially responsible for his or her own well-being and destiny. (p. 135)

east-west divide: a political division manifest in geography (where people live), whereby the more urbanized and suburbanized coastal regions are heavily liberal to moderate and trend Democratic, and rural, inland counties are much more conservative and strongly Republican. (p. 131)

general election: a regular election, usually held in November; a major (run-off) election that features two candidates who have been chosen through a primary election, and after which the winner takes office. (p. 139)

gerrymandering: the act of manipulating district boundaries to include or exclude certain groups in order to benefit a party or an incumbent. (p. 137)

liberal: an ideological disposition to more government services in exchange for higher taxes, including wider access to health care; favoring government action to promote equal opportunity in education and the workplace; general favoring of labor interests over those of business. (p. 135)

no party preference: a term designating that a citizen has chosen to register to vote without a political party affiliation. (p. 134)

motor voter law: citizens are automatically registered to vote when they renew their driver licenses or register their car with the Department of Motor Vehicles, unless they opt out. (p. 141)

partisan primary election: a preliminary election in which candidates vie to become their party's nominee for elective office, and; the winners later compete head to head with the other party's nominees in the general election. (p. 139)

retail campaigning: campaign activity involving direct, face-to-face contact with voters. (p. 144)

Top-Two primary: California's "open" voter preference election, in which any registered voter may select a top choice from among all candidates for office, and the top two vote-getters advance to the general election for a runoff, regardless of party affiliation. (p. 139)

vote by mail: a system of voting wherein voters receive their official ballots through the mail, and completed ballots may be dropped off at a voter's polling place or voting center. (p. 141)

wholesale campaigning: campaign activity involving indirect contact with voters through the airwaves and direct mail. (p. 144)

CHAPTER 10

Political Engagement

Citizens and Politics

The Greek words *demos* and *kratos,* or *democracy*, translate literally as "the people rule." Democracy is therefore rightly associated with voting, but self-governance requires more than filling in bubbles on a ballot. Being informed, discussing public affairs, and contacting elected officials are essential elements of self-governance that allow a citizenry's will, demands, and needs to be expressed and are a mere sample of the ways a person might engage politically. Subgroups of citizens with similar interests try to influence the political system through political parties (the subject of Chapter 9), the media, or organized interest groups, of which there are thousands in the state of California alone. Mass media in turn play a critical role in connecting Californians to their government by distributing and framing information that influences public opinion and political behavior. Political participation is strongly linked with certain demographic characteristics that are unevenly distributed across the population, as discussed in the next section.

Predictors of Political Participation and Disengagement

Despite the proliferation of social networking and forms of instant communication, like other Americans, most Californians do not follow state politics closely. Many across the state scorn politics altogether, an orientation that seems natural to them, whereas the impulse to participate politically comes almost automatically to others. What factors influence these tendencies?

Feeling that one can personally make a difference by participating in public affairs, or one's sense of *political efficacy*, provides a crucial stepping stone to active participation in civic or political settings.[2] Those who feel as if they will never be taken seriously or that their efforts will be wasted don't usually take the time to vote or contact their representatives to voice their concerns. On the other hand, those who perceive the impact of policies, recognize the immediate relevance of laws, and feel as if they can make a difference tend to become involved in politics. *Interest in politics* also makes a measurable difference in helping people connect to the political system; interest levels are generally higher among likely voters across all racial/ethnic groups.[3] Certain groups of Californians have "only a little" interest in politics, which is associated with lower levels of participation. For example, *60 percent* of Latinos have only a little interest or "none" at all, compared to 23 percent of non-Hispanic Whites—a 37-point gap.[4] Overall however, political interest has climbed since Donald Trump was elected to the U.S. presidency.

Socioeconomic variables are strong predictors of political activity. *Age, education*, and *income* levels are positively related to participation, meaning that the older, more educated, and wealthier one is, the more likely one will pay attention to government affairs and try to affect political outcomes. *Home ownership* and *length of residence* are positively associated with civic behavior and activism; retirees and older residents who have lived in their own homes for more than two decades are among the most reliable political participants.

Race/ethnicity and *nativity* (whether one was born in the U.S.) are the strongest predictors of political disengagement and help explain why participation rates in California generally lag behind the rest of the nation. California contains disproportionately large Latino and Asian populations with high percentages born elsewhere, and they are less inclined to discuss politics, to register to vote, or to cast a ballot than are others.[5] Having friends and family who talk about politics and who value voting—aspects of *living in a "pro-voting" culture*—matters greatly for political activity; for example, Spanish speakers who hardly ever talk about politics with their friends are far less likely than other groups either to register to vote or actually vote.[6]

While disengaging from politics can certainly be a conscious choice, *not participating* is associated with many factors that are often beyond an individual's control. Political science research shows that poverty and lack of education limit an individual's skill set, leading to language and knowledge deficits, fewer chances to be contacted or mobilized, and often a lower sense of confidence or lower political efficacy. Less disposable time to participate in activities is another limitation associated with lower socioeconomic status, and continued disengagement leads to even higher levels of frustration and political apathy.

These variables matter greatly because certain kinds of people are overrepresented in California politics. White, well-educated, older homeowners are most likely to get involved in local and state affairs, and therefore, that is the group that political representatives are most likely to hear from and respond to, creating imbalances in public policy.[7] As one set of researchers put it, "California's democracy is neither adequately participatory nor representative."[8]

The Five Californias

The characteristics mentioned above help predict who is most or least politically active in a community—but it should be kept in mind that these are general tendencies and do not necessarily explain any one individual's behavior. The same can be said of the "Five Californias," or five different

MAP 10.1 The Five Californias

	One-Percent California	Elite Enclave California	Main Street California	Struggling California	Disenfranchised California
Life expectancy at birth	86.2	84.3	82.0	79.7	77.6
At least a B.A. degree	71.4%	56.4%	34.5%	17.6%	8.3%
Median personal earnings (2012 dollars)	$69,552	$48,878	$33,975	$23,816	$17,204
Percentage living below poverty level in past year	6.1%	8.8%	12.6%	22.3%	36.3%
Married-couple family (% of households with children)	87.5%	79.4%	71.7%	62.9%	52.3%

GEOGRAPHIC BREAKDOWN

One-Percent California	Elite Enclave California	Main Street California	Struggling California	Disenfranchised California
2 Neighborhood Clusters 344,372 people	42 Neighborhood Clusters 5,733,945 people	102 Neighborhood Clusters 14,658,157 people	110 Neighborhood Clusters 16,109,333 people	9 Neighborhood Clusters 1,195,623 people

POPULATION BREAKDOWN (% OF ALL CALIFORNIANS)

1%	15%	39%	42%	3%

Source: Kristin Lewis and Sarah Burd-Sharps, "A Portrait of California, 2014-2015," California Human Development Report, Measure of America (2014).

groupings of Californians separated by relative levels of well-being and their access to opportunity. After measuring the overall health, income, and education levels of the state's residents, researchers sorted them into five major groups and placed them on a human development scale to indicate their relative differences—disparities that are reflected not only in the everyday challenges and problems that people face, but also in the demands they place on the political system.[9]

One Percent

Topping the charts with the highest human development scores are "one-percenters" (344,000 people) who both drive and benefit from innovation such as information technology and whose standard of living affords privileges unknown to the rest of society. With access to great healthcare and stable jobs and relationships (almost 88 percent are married), *One-Percent* Californians are extremely well-educated (almost 40 percent hold a graduate or professional degree), and can expect to live long lives. Over half of them are White, 34.5 percent are Asian American, 9.5 percent are Latino, and 1 percent are Black; over a third of them are foreign-born. Most have well-paying careers in management, business, science, and the arts, with annual median household incomes over $114,000. Nearly 75 percent of their children go to preschool, and they can afford expensive private schools. One-Percent Californians cluster in Santa Clara County towns where the median price of a home is over $2.1 million.

Elite Enclave

Elite Enclave Californians (15 percent of the population; 5,734,000 people) are also well-educated, affluent "knowledge workers" who reside in neighborhoods rich with amenities. Holding careers in business, the arts, and sciences but earning considerably less than One-Percenters (median $89,000 per household a year), they are mostly White (55.3 percent) and Asian American (22.4 percent); only 15.5 percent are Latino and 3.3 percent are Black. Almost all have graduated high school and over half have a college degree (56 percent); 23 percent have an advanced degree. Although housing consumes about a third of their income, they can pay their bills every month, including age-appropriate childcare, and experience low levels of crime. Located in pockets of Los Angeles, San Francisco, Sacramento, San Jose, and San Diego, most are married (79 percent), and about a quarter are foreign-born. Parents in this group are highly focused on getting their kids into college, and their kids bypass the hardships of poverty.

Main Street

Main Street Californians (39 percent of residents; 14,658,000 people) resemble what many think of as "middle class" America: largely they work in offices and service sectors, and while about 60 percent own their homes, their grip on financial security is weakening as secure retirement and better lives for their children remain just out of reach for many. Majority-minority, it includes 45.5 percent Whites, 30.2 percent Latinos, 15.7 percent Asian Americans, and 4.4 percent Blacks, and three out of four are foreign-born. Almost all have graduated high school (87 percent), whereas 34.5 percent have a Bachelor's degree, and only 12 percent hold a graduate or professional degree. Only half (53 percent) of children attend preschool, and their parents are able to provide afterschool enrichment activities as kids age; much of their income—the median hovers around $66,000 annually—goes to cover housing and health care. One in five children grows up in a single-mother household; 72 percent are in married-couple families. Good childcare is harder to find, and more of these youth aged

16 to 24 are unable to find work. Main Street communities cluster in large cities as well as inland counties of Fresno, Riverside, and San Bernardino.

Struggling

The largest number of people (16,109,000; 42 percent) in California struggle to hold it together. Living in suburbs and rural neighborhoods located mostly in disadvantaged, segregated sections of Northern and Central California and in the Inland Empire, *Struggling* Californians are majority Latino (52 percent), White (29 percent), 8 percent Asian American, and almost 8 percent Black; 28 percent are foreign-born. Mainly high-effort/low-reward jobs in sales, office, and service enable them to earn a median household income of $45,000 a year, not enough to keep many kids out of poverty (32 percent). One out of three households is headed by a single parent, and nearly one of five youth is neither in school nor working. Insecure jobs without benefits, more exposure to crime, little if any access to affordable childcare or extracurricular activities, and caring for a disabled family member take tremendous tolls on health; they live seven years less than the One Percent, on average.

Disenfranchised

Three percent of Californians (1,196,000 people), the *Disenfranchised*, experience "marginalization, segregation, and social exclusion" along with material scarcity and lack the skills, networks, and services that enable access to the "normal activities available to the majority."[10] Isolated from jobs and reliable health care and often living outside the formal economy with a median household income of $31,000, about half have at least a high school diploma and most work in production, transportation and moving, service, sales, and under-the-table jobs that are unreliable. Daily they experience the stress of living in survival mode, which often leads to riskier health behaviors. This heavily racial/ethnic minority group is 71 percent Latino, 13.5 percent White, 8.6 percent Black, and 5 percent Asian American, and they mostly live in parts of Los Angeles and the San Joaquin Valley in conditions rivaling the worst-performing states of Mississippi and West Virginia. About a third are foreign-born. About half of these children live below the poverty line, and many don't attend school; 22 percent of youth are not in school or working. These impoverished communities spend one-third less on public education than One Percent California. Roughly half of all children in California are either Struggling or Disenfranchised.

Although these categories do not map perfectly onto known patterns of political participation, this human development distribution allows us to better understand the capacity of certain groups to advocate for themselves. Enormous variation in educational background, basic needs, and stressors that Californians experience also creates different kinds of opportunity structures for political participation: whereas some people have plenty of time to read newspapers and donate to causes that concern them, others may not understand how politics works and feel intimidated by those who do, or only have time to focus on surviving.

News and Media Habits

Californians know extremely little about state politics unless a scandal breaks, a crisis develops, or an election occurs, and their attitudes, opinions, and beliefs about government are molded by the way public affairs are reported in the press, otherwise known as **framing effects**. For instance, a protest group might be portrayed as a motley collection of out-of-work complainers, or contrastingly, as honest patriots who are championing adversity. Different frames of reference that tap into viewers' emotional or psychological associations can strongly affect how fellow citizens, groups, and government are perceived.

Although most people consult a mix of sources for news, unsurprisingly, the Internet is quickly replacing newspapers as the "go-to" source for news.[11] About half of all adults and at least half of all young people (age 18–29) primarily access political news online,[12] although some formats such as Facebook and Twitter act like Petri dishes for manufactured or "fake" news, and lack of context also can promote confusion and misinformation.[13] Televised political reporting hasn't disappeared despite the rise of web-based news, but coverage of state politics tends to be scant and big-event-driven, appealing to voters over age 49.[14] Although almost no Californians aged 18 to 34 (*just 3 percent*) read a printed newspaper,[15] about forty percent of *voters* tend to rely on the in-depth, investigative coverage provided by newspapers[16] (*Los Angeles Times, Sacramento Bee, San Francisco Chronicle,* and several other major city papers are struggling to maintain readership). Independent sources continue to wither away through consolidation of operations and are owned by a few out-of-state corporations, a trend that translates into far less original local and state-level reporting of the kind that has been pivotal in uncovering wrongdoing or political corruption in the past. Nevertheless, viewers' ideological biases also drive news consumption, and Democrats (89 percent) and Independents (70 percent) today are more likely to value media's role as a watchdog over government, whereas nationally a majority of Republicans now view criticism of (Republican) political leaders coming from media as a hindrance that keeps leaders from doing their jobs.[17]

Types of Political Participation

How might a person get involved in politics? One entryway is through *working with neighbors* to solve a problem in the community, something about one out of three Californians say they have done.[18] It takes minimal effort to *like* a political item on Instagram or Facebook or *follow* a political candidate on Twitter. Individuals might also discuss politics with their friends and family, an important gateway to political activity, and three out of four Californians today report doing so weekly.[19] With some effort, they might post about politics online (about 29 percent of Californians do so[20]), plant a campaign *yard sign*, sport a campaign *sticker or T-shirt, encourage others to vote,* or *try to influence how others vote*. Higher up the scale, Californians *sign petitions* and may do so easily with electronic versions or e-petitions; still, digital access has not translated into higher rates of petition signing (36 percent of adults sign paper petitions, whereas 24 percent sign Internet petitions).[21]

It takes progressively larger investments to *contact elected officials* through a phone call, e-mail, or letter to complain about a problem or ask for help with an issue; about 17 percent of Californians have done so. One out of four Californians has *boycotted* a product or *changed their spending habits* for a political or social reason.[22] About 25 percent also *attend local public meetings, attend rallies* or *demonstrations, volunteer for campaigns,* or even *donate* to campaigns or incumbents (about one in five people).[23] A tiny fraction become *active party members* or *officers*.

Striking patterns emerge from recent surveys about Californians' political habits. Keeping in mind that Whites are now a minority racial group (39 percent), they dominate almost every category of activity except for attending public meetings and protesting. Among all adults, Latinos and Asian Americans generally do not contact their public officials, nor do they make political donations (totaling less than 25 percent of all those who did these things), in contrast to Whites (responsible for 70 percent of contacts and also donations). Whites are also more likely to change their purchasing habits for political reasons (63 percent of all consumer activists). Data also show that these same racial/ethnic patterns are being replicated among Millennials, but differences fade with protesting and signing e-petitions.[24]

Major Voting Trends

"California's turnout was even worse than you thought," taunted one headline following the November 2014 general "off-year" election, in which only *8.2 percent* of 18- to 24-year-olds voted, and only 42.2 percent of registered voters took part.[25] Widespread apathy and abstention contributed to record low voter participation in a regular election: the worst in California history. Of the 30.9 percent of eligible voters who bothered to cast a vote, grandparents crushed the other age groups: nearly 60 percent of voters fell into in the 65- to 74-year-old category. Two years later the numbers turned around. Registration and turnout rates picked up in 2016 as they generally do in presidential election years, with 33.4 percent of California youth voting in the June primaries, and total turnout rate for all registered adult voters reaching 75.3 percent in November.[26] Nationwide, Millennials (ages 18 to

Student protests have been provoked by Trump administration policy decisions that directly alter some students' legal status and disrupt their ability to travel. Protests have also erupted on campuses over speakers who position themselves as provocateurs or who align with hate groups; the concept of "free speech" is once again being questioned.

35 in 2016) combined with Generation Xers (ages 36 to 51) to cast a majority of all votes in the 2016 general election, outvoting those over age 51.[27]

In a representative democracy, the act of voting provides a critical check on officeholders, as it not only offers a means to reject undesirable representatives but also supplies cues about what policies a constituency prefers. In a direct democracy, the voters represent themselves and "check" each other by casting votes, but *the majority of whoever turns out to vote wins*. For these reasons, "who votes" in a hybrid democracy such as California's has profound implications for electoral outcomes, policymaking in the public interest, and, ultimately, the quality of representation and governance.

California's electorate is an exclusive, self-selected group, and their choices skew election outcomes. Stated differently, voters neither represent all Californians nor reflect the size, growth, or diversity of the state's population. Whites total just under 40 percent of California's resident population, but they constitute *sixty percent* of all voters, who also tend to be slightly older, U.S.-born, and more conservative than nonvoters. Latinos participate at lower rates than their population numbers would predict, and the same is true for Asian Americans, a trend that was less pronounced in the 2016 presidential election than it was in the midterm elections two years earlier. For instance, Latinos' votes were 19.7 percent of all those cast in California in 2012, but based on eligible voters it should have been closer to 26.3 percent that year.[28] Eligible African American voters tend to turn out at rates closer to their share of the population.

Excluded from the electorate are approximately 3.3 million legal permanent residents, another estimated 2.5 million undocumented immigrants who reside and work in the state, and approximately 182,800 in prison or on parole.[29] Additionally, almost one of four adults who are eligible to vote don't register; this equates to more than 5.5 million people who are not among what the Public Policy Institute of California calls the state's "exclusive electorate." Nonvoters differ from the pool of likely voters in several significant ways: more nonvoters are renters (66 percent of nonvoters), have only a high school diploma or less (only 17 percent graduated college), and are racial or ethnic minorities (77 percent).[30] They make less money overall than those who vote: 80 percent of nonvoting adults are in households earning $60,000 a year or less.[31] Not registering to vote largely accounts for the lower Latino and Asian American vote share in comparison to that of Whites.

Despite lower voter registration barriers in California, these groups have not registered relative to their share of the population as they have expanded, but rates have improved recently due to the state's efforts to expand into online registration, automatic "motor voter" registration, and all-mail ballot elections. Studies suggest that aggressive mobilization efforts could further accelerate registration rates.[32]

The fact that not all *eligible* voters vote in every election also skews election outcomes. Presidential elections combined with supercharged ballot issues such as the legalization of marijuana lure many more voters than off-year midterm elections, special elections, or primaries, which draw far fewer voters but more loyal partisans. Turnout over the past five presidential elections averaged 75 percent of all registered voters and a much lower percentage—56 percent—of all *eligible* voters (2000–2016). Turnout sinks in the off-year elections, averaging 52 percent of all registered voters (for the past four midterm elections, 2002 to 2014), or just *37.5 percent* of all those eligible to vote. Stand-alone municipal elections obtain gravely low turnout rates, usually ranging between 15 percent and 35 percent of registered voters. On the other hand, the revved-up presidential election of 2008 that resulted in the election of Barack Obama and the passage of Prop 8, the constitutional amendment defining marriage as between a man and a woman (invalidated in 2013), drew out 79.4 percent of registered voters (or 59.2 percent of those eligible to vote), one of the highest turnouts since the mid-1970s.

Among those who actually vote, different combinations of voters also produce different electoral outcomes. For instance, voters "grouped" into Assembly districts choose candidates who tend to reflect their characteristics and preferences, and, as a result, elected legislators resemble those localized voters. Initiative voters, on the other hand, hail from the entire state, and they reflect a wider set of characteristics and preferences. The same is true for governors and statewide executives, whose constituency is the entire state. Bias is also introduced through the phenomenon of "roll-off," which means that many voters cast their ballots only for the "big-ticket" offices such as president, the races that appear first, skipping lower offices and ballot measures located further down the ballot, often because they do not feel informed enough to vote on them or because they view "down-ticket" items or offices as unimportant. Fewer people actually choose the officials who are geographically closest to them, either because they don't reach the end of their ballots or because the many candidates for local offices are unrecognizable.

Finally, and importantly, it's important to note that the values and priorities of regular voters sometimes contrast strikingly with those of nonvoters. Those who cast ballots generally hold distinctly different views about the *proper role of government* than those who don't vote or don't register to vote—patterns that generally hold both at the state and national levels.[33] For instance, economic biases are reflected in voters' views about government: only 47 percent of California's registered voters would prefer to have a bigger government providing more services, compared to 70 percent of those who are not registered to vote would prefer a bigger government providing more services.[34] A whopping

FIGURE 10.1 Californians on the State's Role in Reducing Income Inequality

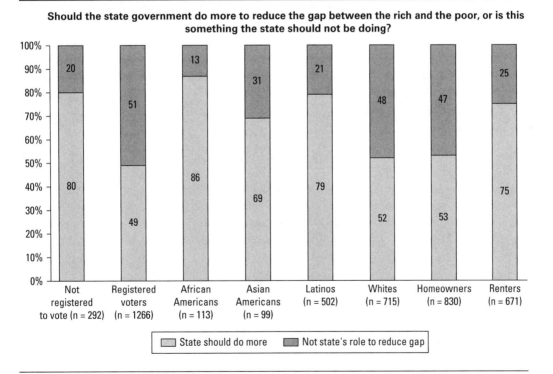

Should the state government do more to reduce the gap between the rich and the poor, or is this something the state should not be doing?

Source: PPIC Statewide Survey, "Californians and Their Government," May 12–22, 2017, sampling error +/–3.2% at 95% confidence level for unweighted sample of 1,707 adults. Numbers may not add to 100% due to rounding. "I don't know" answers excluded.

74 percent of Californians who aren't registered to vote think that the government should do more to reduce the gap between rich and poor in California, compared to 56 percent of registered voters.[35]

Gaps also surface in the policy preferences among groups. Only 42 percent of registered voters favor a pro-immigration sanctuary state law, compared to 60 percent of Californians who aren't registered. Where guns are concerned, a majority of registered voters (55 percent) think gun laws should be stricter, but 71 percent of unregistered adults feel that way. And legalizing marijuana? A majority of the unregistered want it to remain illegal (58 percent), compared to 64 percent of registered voters who favor legalization (and 57.1 who actually voted for it). It should also be noted that the results of low-turnout elections magnify the biases and policy choices of narrow electorates.

Special Interest Groups: Indirectly Connecting Citizens to Government

Interest groups representing practically every aspect of the human experience advocate for government policies that will advance or protect their causes, and the benefits or changes they seek often extend to anyone who shares a key characteristic—which could be a medical condition, a position on offshore oil drilling, or a business or professional affiliation. An organized group that makes its case to the government about its goal, or "**special interest**," is known as a **special interest group**. Such a group might therefore be an entity such as the Catholic Church, a progun rights organization, or a set of interrelated businesses such as the film industry. The term *special interest* can also be a vague reference to any group whose members share the same public policy concerns, such as beachfront property owners who want to protect their homes against erosion or noisy, nosy tourists. Virtually all politically active special interest groups want to protect their own interests by engaging government in pursuit of legal protections or material benefits.

Special interest groups are often regarded as self-interested, greedy political creatures because most are "not at all interested in the larger societal challenges—they never think about the 'big picture,'" as one state senator put it.[36] Most citizens are unaware that they are indirectly linked to government through the interests and goals they share with many of them. A typical California college student is "represented" in the public sphere by a multitude of interest groups and their lobbyists, among them the university or college itself; the city, county, and region in which the student resides; hobby-, sports-, or activity-related groups such as the National Collegiate Athletic Association (NCAA); groups based on demographic characteristics such as economic status, ethnicity, religion, and more; health-related groups focused on chronic conditions such as diabetes; values-based associations concerned with rights, the environment, moral issues; and too many more to name. That student might also be linked to politics through employment or a parent's affiliation with a trade association for professionals such as the 170,000-member California Association of Realtors, which facilitates state licensing requirements and advocates for laws and tax policies that will affect real estate agents or their clients, or a labor union, such as the mighty California Correctional Peace Officers Association (CCPOA), which represents more than 30,000 prison guards and parole officers. If that student comes from a family that owns a business, then the California Chamber of Commerce, which represents almost 13,000 California businesses both large and small (see Box 10.1), offers a symbiotic political connection.

Special interests are not equal, however, and some in California carry disproportionate political weight because of advantages stemming from their resources, size, and/or perceived importance. In other words, legislators pay more attention to some interests than others. Among the most prolific, active, and influential special interests in Sacramento are actually *local governments* and *public entities* and *agencies* that carry out state programs for thousands or millions of Californians: public officials and experts working for cities, counties, and special districts often are in the best positions to judge the impacts of programs or predict how proposals will affect the public. Collectively they shelled out $84 million in 2015–16 to press their case, or lobby, state government.[37] Other groups are valued for their important roles in communities, such as *large employers* that provide jobs and subsidize local governments through the taxes they collect from consumers and pay, and *labor groups* that defend workers' rights. Representatives have incentives to please politically active constituencies, so any group or business that has the *ability to mobilize voters* and *influence public opinion* possesses significant advantages. Lawmakers also pay attention to organizations that *share their issue positions or values*, and they respond to individuals and groups that provide *support for their campaigns* through volunteers, financial, or in-kind donations.

The political power of special interests, therefore, is largely derived from what they can provide to decision makers, principally in the form of *information, votes,* or *money.* In lawmaking environments, good information is always in demand, and legislators and their staff members crave answers

TABLE 10.1   Top Fifteen Spenders on Lobbying in California, 2015–2016

Name	Industry	Total amount spent
Western States Petroleum Assn	Oil and gas	$18,718,663
California Hospital Assn	Health services	$11,980,669
California State Council of Service Employees	Labor unions	$11,808,178
Chevron	Oil and gas	$7,179,341
California Chamber of Commerce	Business	$7,033,032
City of Los Angeles + County of Los Angeles	Government	$5,540,934
Kaiser Foundation Health Plan	Health services	$4,525,516
California Teachers Association	Public sector unions	$4,449,370
AT&T	Telecommunications	$4,307,774
CA School Boards Assn	Labor unions	$3,981,703
California Medical Association	Health services	$3,383,372
California School Employees Association	Labor unions	$3,456,039
California Manufacturers and Technology Association	Manufacturing	$3,430,589
PG&E	Electric Utilities	$3,337,245
Howard Jarvis Taxpayers Association	Taxpayer advocacy	$3,300,903

Source. California Secretary of State, http://cal-access.sos.ca.gov

to questions about the potential impacts of their bills. To provide persuasive information, groups hire *professional lobbyists* who can be "educators" about the negative or positive effects pending legislation may have—framing a case that is sympathetic to their own interests, of course. So powerful are special interest lobbyists in Sacramento that they are collectively known as the "**third house**," a reference to the fact that they are vital players in the lawmaking process. Lobbyists can make their clients' cases in face-to-face meetings with legislators or staff, but more often they do so by testifying in committee hearings where bills are vetted. They also perform research for bills and draft client-friendly legislation for lawmakers to sponsor.

Lobbyists also gain access to legislators by buying tickets to expensive fund-raising events (happening daily around Sacramento and elsewhere) and funneling campaign donations to state representatives, making sure that the interest groups they represent donate the maximum allowed. Although state law caps the amounts of direct donations that individuals, unions, and corporations can give to candidates, special interest groups may spend as much as they want independently to influence elections, and lobbyists help them decide how best to spread that money. There are more than fifteen paid lobbyists for every legislator, and they helped spend a record $623 million on lobbying activities during 2015 and 2016.[38] In state politics, organization, information, money, and status amplify voices and provide critical linkages to decision makers. The well-heeled few tip the playing field in their favor with the access their resources can buy. By extension, the unorganized and the disenfranchised are the biggest losers in politics.

BOX 10.1 **The Power of Organized Interests**

If education made the news this morning, chances are the powerful California Teachers Association (CTA) had something to do with it. As the state's largest professional employee organization representing more than 325,000 teachers, school counselors, and librarians, the CTA is a union that helps bargain for higher salaries and benefits in local districts and provides assistance in contract disputes. An advocacy group affiliated with the National Education Association (NEA), the CTA is committed to "enhance the quality of education" and "advance the cause of free, universal, and quality public education" by influencing state education policy.

Closely aligned with Democratic interests, the CTA participates at all stages of the bill-passage process by writing bills, testifying before committees, shaping legislation through suggesting amendments, donating to initiative campaigns, mobilizing citizens to support measures, and encouraging legislators either to support or to oppose bills. Most of this work is done through lobbyists, but members also are highly active, holding public demonstrations in local districts and loud rallies at the state capitol, organizing massive postcard campaigns, calling legislators, and contributing to both candidates' and initiative campaigns. When proposed ballot measures or laws appear to work for or against their interests, the CTA roars to life with ad campaigns and grassroots lobbying, asking teachers to flood legislators' inboxes with e-mails and phone calls. In 2017, when Pres. Trump chose charter school advocate, Betsy DeVos, to head the U.S. Department of Education, the CTA paired with the NEA to organize a national protest campaign. They also campaign in support of local and state school bonds and candidates by organizing volunteers and donating money, as they did for Prop 51, a $9 billion school bond, and Prop 58, a law regarding English proficiency. They spent over $29 million in the 2016 elections. The CTA also retained nine lobbyists and spent $4.5 million on lobbying activities in 2015–16.

Sources: California Teachers Association, http://www.cta.org; California Secretary of State, http://cal-access.sos.ca.gov.

Kevork Djansezian/Getty Images

When teachers speak, Democratic leaders listen. They influence education policy through strong lobbying and ballot initiatives. CTA was instrumental in mobilizing support for Props 51 and 55 in 2016 and Prop 30 in 2012 and helped reelect the superintendent of public instruction in 2014.

California Chamber of Commerce: Major Player in Business

Ever heard of a "job killer" bill? The California Chamber of Commerce (or CalChamber) has, and it aims to identify and destroy such bills before they impose new "expensive and unnecessary" regulations on California businesses. What is CalChamber, and why is it so powerful?

Unlike professional associations that represent individuals (such as the CTA), the Chamber's members are 13,000 California-based companies, from local shops to Microsoft, enterprises that employ a quarter of the state's private-sector workforce. The motto of the state's largest and arguably most important business organization is "Helping California business do business." Aided by eight in-house lobbyists, the Chamber tries to help shape laws or administrative rules by educating policymakers about how proposed laws will critically affect California companies. It also donates to sympathetic candidates and officeholders through its political action committees, supports and opposes ballot campaigns through independent expenditures and direct donations, and files friend-of-the-court briefs in court cases, among other activities. Member companies often team up to advocate for or against important bills. The Chamber reported lobbying expenditures during 2015–16 exceeding $7 million and campaign spending of about $2.25 million in 2016. These figures represent a fraction of what businesses generally spend to protect their interests in California. For example, the Walt Disney Company separately pays hundreds of thousands of dollars a year for ongoing lobbying activities, as do other California businesses.

Sources: California Chamber of Commerce, http://www.calchamber.com; California Secretary of State, http://cal-access.sos.ca.gov.

Dennis McCoy/Sacramento Business Journal

Calling attention to business-related issues is part of CalChamber's strategy to influence lawmaking and the regulatory environment. Chamber president and CEO Allan Zaremberg's days are filled with media appearances and interviews, meetings with policymakers, and more.

Conclusion: An Evolving Political Community

Patterns of political activity and the biases that arise from unequal participation among groups do not distinguish California sharply from the rest of the states, but if California's diverse population lived up to its extraordinary potential, local and state policies might reflect different priorities and choices. Regardless, most people scarcely pay any attention to state or local politics, even though their livelihoods are tied more closely to decisions at those levels than at the national level. By creating new challenges (such as longer bus routes, fewer state-run clinics), or breaking them down (such as in-state tuition for undocumented immigrants, tax breaks for housing developers), today's policy decisions shape realities and opportunities both for employers and for the Five Californias in ways that will help determine the state's collective future.

Social media, traditional mass media, and interest groups provide the means for citizens to connect to government affairs, officials, and each other. Being informed helps empower citizens to be politically active, and there is plenty of room for more citizen participation in all types and levels of governments and in politics generally, because even though political scientists disagree about the minimum levels of knowledge, trust, and engagement needed to sustain a governing system for the long term, they generally recognize that "inputs" from civically engaged citizens generally lead to more positive government "outputs." As it stands, better educated, affluent, and Whiter citizens, as well as big corporations, well-heeled unions, and resource-rich organizations are perpetual outsized contributors to California's political system and, consequently, benefit from their investments in politics. As the saying goes, the squeaky wheel gets the grease. And in California as elsewhere, the "haves" are far noisier than the "have-nots."

The most recognizable form of political participation—voting—carries intrinsic value as a democratic exercise and provides a vital link between citizens and their representatives, but so do other actions. Uneven levels of activity among various constituencies contribute to the governing dilemmas of policymakers as they weigh their responsibilities to serve the greater public interest but also respond to those who actually pay attention and care about the results. Until the electorate and the universe of campaign volunteers, e-mailers, public meeting attendees, callers, demonstrators, lobbyists, donors, and petitioners more accurately reflects the entirety of the state's population, elected officials' decisions will continue to reflect the political, cultural, geographic, and demographic biases of those who vote and those who donate, a dynamic that ultimately constrains how effective government can be. Government will also continue to be viewed as particularly ineffective by those who feel unable to influence it, regardless of its performance. In the search for greater governability, expanding the electorate and of the pool of regular political participants would be surefire ways to make California's government more accountable, representative, and positively exceptional.

Key Terms

framing effects: the way information is presented, usually by highlighting or ignoring certain elements, such that the viewer's attitudes, opinions, or beliefs are influenced. (p. 154)

political efficacy: a sense of confidence or feeling that one can personally influence government by participating in public affairs. (p. 150)

professional lobbyist: a person who is paid to try to persuade lawmakers and other government officials to create policies that benefit their special interest clients (also see Chapter 4). (p. 160)

special interest: any group that can be identified by a unique characteristic. (p. 159)

special interest group: an organized group that tries to influence the government to advance or protect its interests and goals. (p. 159)

third house: a term referring to lobbyists as a group and—as if they were on par with the other houses of the legislature—indicates their influence in the legislative process. (p. 160)

CHAPTER 11

Concluding Thoughts

Political Paradoxes, Policy, and Exceptionalism

"'Already a pandemonium' in 1848, and a pandemonium it remains," Carey McWilliams wrote nearly 70 years ago,[1] a description of California that continues to be cultivated by the headliner antics of its celebrities, voluminous natural resources and the natural disasters that endanger them, state leaders who perform on a world stage, and bold public policies that buck national trends. To an outsider, there's no need to question California's exceptional nature; the state is clearly an outlier.

Yes, California is different. As a potential nation, California stands apart for its hyperdiverse population that is spread across a giant landmass and generates a world-class economy that outpaces all but five or six countries. California has helped lead the United States out of recession, even as it repels federal policies generated by the Trump administration.[2]

"Going it alone" has entailed building a clean energy economy through a cap-and-trade market for carbon emissions, reducing greenhouse gases through promoting biofuels and zero-emissions vehicles, and incentivizing solar and wind energy investments. Setting its own course has meant shielding undocumented immigrants from deportation, including 216,000 children,[3] treating eligible college-age undocumented youth like citizens by giving them in-state tuition, covering 170,000 immigrant children's health care, and enabling the undocumented to obtain special divers licenses that bring them out of the shadow economy. Going against the grain has involved enhancing employment benefits: paid sick leave for part-time workers, minimum wage increases, and an expanded definition of disability that has warranted paid maternity leave. Trailblazing for equal rights has involved recognizing a third gender option ("X") on legal documents.

Other highly charged, attention-baiting policy experiments are also out of "left" field (figuratively *and* ideologically speaking). Guns can't fire more than ten rounds at a time; single public restrooms must be all-gender; patients may choose the right to die; only adults over age 21 can buy tobacco products. Universal health care coverage? Maybe, but the estimated *$400 billion* price tag—more than double the entire current state general fund budget—is a harsh reality check.

Reforms that make it easier to vote also distinguish California politics from those states that are tightening the voter rolls with strict voter identification laws and shorter early voting periods. California's Top-Two primary further cracks open the electoral system, enabling independents to have a say in primary elections, and the Citizens Redistricting Commission empowers citizens to control the redistricting process—innovations that are not California's alone, to be sure.

These reforms scratch the surface of California's deeply rooted problems, some of which stem from the design of its hybrid government. California's self-styled hybrid democracy splices the power of direct democracy with political representation, and the two coexist in a state of uneasy tension. Voters can change the rules of the game for each other and for representatives in any general election. This can be seen most clearly in voter-imposed budget mandates, such as in minimum funding guarantees for schools and practically unattainable two-thirds thresholds for raising taxes. Ballot-box reforms also promote "one-size-fits-all" policy solutions and hinder comprehensive approaches to problem solving. The initiative process itself is now an overworked policy machine, the gears of which are oiled by oversimplified messages and shifted into overdrive by massive amounts of campaign cash. Special interests parade as public interests, trying to drown out other voices in the political marketplace. Ironically, the initiative process itself is ripe for reform.

California politics is riddled with other ironies and paradoxes that go a long way toward explaining the current state of affairs. For example, even when things are going well, Californians are frustrated that they aren't better. They generally distrust politicians and disdain political conflict, so they continue to reach for ways to take politicians—and politics, for that matter—out of politics; they impose term limits that will automatically toss representatives from office at prescribed intervals, for example, and hope that citizen-driven redistricting will obtain more moderate legislators who are not beholden to political parties. Public grievance with politics continues, however, because political systems are by nature designed to expose conflicting interests in the struggle to reach consensus. The people not only need politicians to govern what is effectively one of the largest countries in the world, but they also need to organize in order to win, and political parties provide that reliable structure. Nevertheless, many Californians are unconvinced that parties matter, and increasingly they are registering as "no party preference" voters.

Californians also have a difficult time imagining how state government could need as much money as it rakes in, especially compared to other states, and over half of California adults believe that a lot of their tax money is wasted.[4] This partly explains the resentment people feel about higher fuel taxes, up 12 cents per gallon as of November 2017. Attitudes like these have led to a gross backlog of infrastructure projects (think roads, water storage, and so forth) and chronic underfunding of services such as education and transportation that local and state governments must provide for all Californians. The irony is that when infrastructure fails because governments have stretched scarce dollars too thinly (massive failure of the Oroville Dam spillway in winter 2017 comes to mind), citizens are quick to blame politicians for wasting or misspending funds and therefore are even less willing to help government do its work. However, voters do tend to make exceptions for new taxes that have concrete, dedicated purposes and when they believe that their money will be well spent, allowing most local governments to meet residents' immediate demands but often to the detriment of long-term critical needs.[5] These tendencies have resulted in a heavy reliance on upper income taxpayers to foot the state's bills, as well as a shift away from paying up-front costs and a pivot to long-term bond debt that costs about twice as much in the long run, generating interest payments that place stress on the state's general fund and local treasuries by siphoning off money that could be used for other necessary budget items.

Quite apart from the paradoxes of governing are socioeconomic issues that determine the political state of affairs—issues that involve 40 million people who live in distinctly different conditions and who place often incompatible and ever-changing demands on the state. Latinos constitute the largest ethnic group, and California is projected to be an absolute majority-Latino state around 2050, just as the population reaches 50 million.[6] The multiethnic mix of children today signals momentous change: 54 percent of all schoolchildren in 2016–17 were Latino/Hispanic; non-Hispanic Whites just 24 percent. How will decision makers nurture the educated workforce that will be needed to drive the state's service-based economy? Will voters be willing to extend helping hands to those at the bottom of the socioeconomic scale? Nearly a quarter (22.5 percent) of all Californians will be sixty-five years of age or older by that time: how will the state provide for a humongous elderly population that places immense demands on health and residential care systems?[7] Year after year, the equivalent of a Riverside or Anaheim (about 300,000 new people) are added to the state. To accommodate such growth, the state will need to invest more than $500 *billion* to upgrade, add, and expand crumbling transportation, school, water, and other systems in the next twenty years.[8] How will Californians be able to raise that kind of cash?

In many ways, political reforms brought California to this point, and political reforms will help transform its future. Yet institutional reforms can go only so far. Rules set boundaries for decision making but do not determine the choices people make, and choices must be based on realistic understanding about government's capabilities if the state's policies and laws are to work. For instance, many Californians presume that rooting out existing government waste would uncover enough revenues to pay for large government programs, as if saving millions of dollars could compensate for not raising billions through higher taxes. Would more meaningful involvement by a greater swath of the Five Californias in local problem solving reshape their expectations and make real change possible? Or is representative government still the best defense against mounting problems?

California's government faces many of the same challenges as the governments of other states. What helps make California politics exceptional are the scope and scale of the state's public policy issues, which pose enormous challenges as well as opportunities for state elected officials to exercise national and global leadership now and for the foreseeable future:

- *Education*: Only an educated workforce can sustain a sophisticated, diverse, service-oriented modern economy. California spends the most of all states on its K–12 students overall but ranked thirty-first in 2015 for per-pupil spending, despite hikes in funding. This equals inadequate instructional materials, lower pay for teachers, fewer days of instruction, and shortages of experienced faculty and reliable after-school care and programs that only certain communities can address with supplemental resources.[9] How will California schools bridge the gap to prepare future citizens to meet state, national, and global communities' changing needs? The fastest growing segment of the population is Latino, but as a group, these students trail behind in graduation rates and test scores. High school graduation rates have improved but remain

five percent below the national average. How will achievement gaps be closed and graduation rates be improved? State colleges and universities are still a bargain, but California's master plan for providing tuition-free higher education has been abandoned, forcing students to bear the escalating costs of tuition and fees. How will the state's education funding habits affect students' future job prospects and the higher education system's competitiveness nationally and globally? Education isn't just about earning more over a lifetime: research suggests that if every Californian could magically jump up to the next higher level of education, about one million fewer people would be in poverty, people would live over a year longer, 1,200 fewer Californians would be murdered every year, and 2.4 million more people would vote.[10]

- **Immigration:** California's immigrant population is the largest in the nation at about 10.6 million, equating to 27 percent of residents who were born outside the United States. Will voters be willing to extend to immigrants the same rights and public benefits that they have enjoyed? Should representatives push policies that advance assimilation or accommodation, especially for the 2.5 million undocumented immigrants who reside in the state, mostly in the shadows? Cities, and even the state, risk losing federal dollars to provide sanctuary to them. Still, 83 percent of Californians say that undocumented immigrants who are living in the United States should be allowed to stay; 63 percent believe they should also be offered the chance to become citizens.[11]

- **Environment:** Climate change threatens California's basic lifelines. Erratic weather patterns are difficult to plan for. Rising temperatures bring less rain and lighter snowpack, translating into limited water supplies for thirsty farms, manufacturing plants, and homes. Alternatively, unpredictable weather events such as El Niño can produce severe and costly flooding. Volatile weather patterns place stress on traditional recreation and tourism-related industries. Lower rainfall increases the risk of wildfires in bone-dry areas and increases airborne fine-particle pollution; wildlife unaccustomed to higher-than-average temperatures cannot quickly adjust, so biodiversity suffers. Rising sea levels threaten a densely populated coastline and imperil the Delta agricultural region (the source of drinking water for two-thirds of Californians and irrigation for 750,000 acres of croplands) with rising levels of salinity. California's AB 32, the nation's first greenhouse gas emissions law, promises to bring higher costs of implementing its requirements but lower greenhouse gas emissions. Can California continue to build a "green" economy without creating a more hostile business environment? Emergencies take huge tolls; the state Geological Survey estimates that a 7.8 earthquake on the San Andreas Fault would

168   *Chapter 11   Concluding Thoughts*

cause over $210 *billion* in damages in Los Angeles, and a 7.0 quake in San Francisco would cause even more losses.[12] Could local and state governments adequately respond if environmental crises like earthquakes, heat waves, extensive wildfires, extended droughts, and torrential rains and resulting mudslides hit in quick succession? Following in Schwarzenegger's footsteps, Governor Brown has exerted strong leadership on the issue of climate change by partnering with China to boost clean energy jobs, by hosting a global summit in California, by persuading the legislature to extend the state's carbon cap-and-trade market through 2030, and by signing new laws such as SB 32, which aims to take greenhouse gas (GHG) emissions to 40 percent below 1990 levels by 2030. Aggressive GHG pollution reduction has accompanied mandates such as the recycling of biomass (food waste and yard trimmings) by all commercial entities and requiring 50 percent of the state's electricity to come from renewable sources by 2030. Lawmakers are now eyeing mandatory composting for all Californians and increasing renewable energy production to 100 percent of in-state electricity by 2045 (following Hawaii's lead). Even if California's impact on global emissions is just over 1 percent (it's much higher nationally), eight of ten Californians think that it is either very important (58 percent) or somewhat important (23) that California leads on the issue of climate change; 72 percent favor laws mandating GHG emissions reductions.[13]

- *Poverty, Health, and Inequality*: The gap between rich and poor, or income inequality among the Five Californias, continues to widen, and about 17.3 million Californians are either Struggling or Disenfranchised Californians. Without CalWorks (temporary assistance for needy families); refundable tax credits; or CalFresh, a "food stamps" type program, a much larger number would slip below the federal poverty threshold of $24,600 for a family of four. Still, many taxpayers believe the state pays too much for safety net programs. When it comes to health care, California now boasts the largest insured population of all states, but continued success depends heavily on Medicare funding, which is threatened by proposed federal cuts that would disturb a large swath of retirees, who use the system more than other groups. Addressing poverty rates and human development gaps more broadly will require comprehensive political efforts to address "mutually reinforcing inequalities in health, education, environment, neighborhood conditions, wealth, and political power that have created an opportunity divide" among Californians.[14]

- *Business and Labor*: A large majority of California's 875,000 small and large business employers complain about the regulatory difficulties they face, and *Forbes* ranks California near the bottom of U.S. states: thirtieth as of 2016 in overall business climate, forty-fifth in regulatory environment, forty-third in business costs, but fourth in economic climate and growth prospects.[15] Driven by a Democratic-dominant state government, even more employee-friendly regulations—or "antibusiness" mandates, depending on your point of view—have been signed into law. Meanwhile, multibillion-dollar unfunded liabilities, existing mostly as health care insurance and pension obligations for teachers and other public employees, menace the state's long-term financial outlook. How will the state balance its books, protect 13.4 million private-industry workers with legal safeguards while enticing businesses to stay or expand in California and also make public service attractive to "the best and brightest" who can make government run effectively? How might a service economy accommodate massive numbers of low-skilled, unemployed, low-educated residents who require state services to fulfill basic needs, from food to housing to employment?

- *Water*: In April 2017, after a drenching winter, Governor Brown declared an end to the state's severe drought emergency that parched all parts of the state. Both the Sierra snowpack and the state's reservoirs were above normal for the first time in five years. However, the hydrologic effects of long-term drought persist in depleted groundwater aquifers all over the state. Drought prompted the state's first groundwater usage laws, but the new rules are taking shape slowly. In the meantime, vanishing underground reservoirs have caused substantial subsidence, or the sinking of the ground, which damages or destroys underground pipes, culverts, bridges, roads, and canals. Water scarcity has exposed the state's fissures over water, involving three separate rights-holders within the state: the *environment* (restoring or sustaining habitat, ensuring water quality, and so forth, which guzzles half of the state's water), *people*, including individual consumers and companies, and *agriculture*. Drought has pitted urban against agricultural users and farmers against fish as the state has tried to direct water flows to the Delta to sustain an endangered ecosystem. Between droughts and floods, policymakers have a hard time organizing storage and distribution systems that move water where it's needed, when it's needed, and ensuring quality when water is fouled by agricultural activity, reduced water flows, and urban runoff. A voter-approved $7.5 billion bond barely begins to address water management needs. Meanwhile, water users could eventually foot the bill for the "California WaterFix," key to which is the Twin Tunnels (or possibly single-tunnel) project, a massive infrastructure build that could cost an estimated $19 billion. Governor Brown has pushed this as a solution to moving water to thirsty Southern California, which houses about 75 percent of the state's residents who depend on the 75 percent of rainfall in the north. Prolonged disputes with neighboring states and Mexico over equitable distribution of Colorado River water continue to simmer. Degraded and vanishing wetlands are the norm, as are declining native tree and fish populations and inexplicable bird and fish die-offs. In many parts of the Delta region, where millions of people and animals reside and fertile lands are farmed, catastrophic levee failure due to earthquakes or flooding is a palpable risk. Drought forced residents to conserve water, but will California's leaders be able to craft strategic plans that comprehensively address the entire state's long-term water-related needs or come up with the money to cover them?
- *Housing*: Across virtually every demographic, housing eats up 30 percent or more of a household's income on average; for the poorest, more than half of a monthly paycheck. Housing is generally unaffordable: at a median price of over $565,000 in 2017, Californians pay over two-and-a-half-times what the rest of the country pays for a home.[16] Average monthly rents are also double that of other states. Shortages persist for a number of reasons; local zoning requirements and environmental regulations are among them. High housing costs force low-wage workers to commute further, and both worker retention and recruitment, especially for high-end jobs, becomes more difficult. State leaders intend to address housing issues through laws that streamline construction processes, tax incentives for builders, and bonds to stabilize markets. However, the success of state incentives for building affordable housing also depends on federal tax laws (such as those regarding mortgage interest deductions, being reconsidered under a Republican-driven tax overhaul in 2017).
- *Transportation*: The nation's highest number of cars (35.3 million registered vehicles) travel California's roadways, which are the most congested in the United States, and they cross more than 13,100 bridges that are maintained by CalTrans. About 40 percent of California's aging 50,000 miles of highway lanes require fixing. The backlog of state highway and road projects

MAP 11.1 Proposed High Speed Rail (HSR) Routes

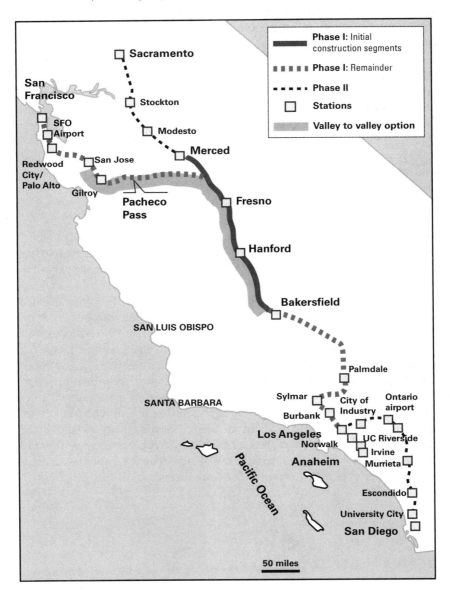

Source: California High Speed Rail Authority.

alone is currently estimated to be $85 billion, and this is on top of needed repairs to more than 300,000 miles of local streets and 12,000 bridges. Ironically, alternative fuel vehicles benefit air quality but have caused a shortfall in gas tax revenues to pay for roads. New systems are needed to move people more quickly around the state, and Governor Brown endorses high-speed rail that will connect San Francisco to Los Angeles by 2029, but the price tag is nearly $100 billion even as work gets underway in Fresno, and all funds are not in the bank. SB 1, the state's transportation funding bill, raises regular and diesel fuel taxes and imposes extra registration fees on low-emissions vehicles such as hybrids, and should provide $54 billion to address the state's current repair list (still $30 billion short of what's needed today). This is the first increase in fuel excise taxes since 1994, but these facts are likely to be lost on those who feel as if they are overtaxed already. Motorized vehicles, especially farm and construction equipment, also create dirty air that contributes to serious respiratory illnesses. California's airports, seaports, and railway systems pollute the air as well, an inevitable consequence of being a gateway to Asia and South America. Adding cleaner fuel burning vehicles and more electric cars will merely chip away at the problem. Can lawmakers improve California's air and travel systems by making them cleaner, safer, more navigable, and more efficient, and can they do so in cost-effective ways? Can they ensure the safety of residents as those systems expand; can they get more than 5 percent of the population to use public transit? Is high-speed rail worth it?

Although California is not a country, it often behaves like one.[17] The Golden State has a long history of standing apart, as seen in its unorthodox path to statehood after exploding onto the U.S. stage with the Gold Rush; in Progressive innovations in direct democracy; in political reform that transformed the legislature into a smaller version of the U.S. Congress; in a whirlwind recall effort that elevated an Austrian-born muscle man to the governor's office; and now in greenhouse gas regulations designed to combat global climate change. Sometimes the state is out in front, and sometimes it's just "out there"—its relative placement being a matter of perspective. Politics in the state are indeed exceptional in many ways, but more often than not, California keeps company with other states that have established kindred policy programs, are experimenting with new reforms, or follow similar electoral rules. Sometimes California is the follower who gets more credit because of the sheer size of the political failures, scale of the successes, or magnitude of their eccentricity. On balance, however, the state is a political juggernaut like no other, and as former Assembly Speaker (now state Senator) Robert Hertzberg phrased it, "There's a magic about California. There's a California brand. . . . We've got to stay ahead of the game."[18] With this in mind, it's hard to imagine a different title for the book penned by the late McWilliams, even though almost seventy years have passed since it was first published: *California: The Great Exception*.

Notes

Chapter 1

1. See World Bank, "Gross Domestic Product 2016," World Development Indicators Database, http://databank.worldbank.org/data/download/GDP.pdf; U.S. Department of Commerce, Bureau of Economic Analysis, "Interactive Data" (state GDP, TOTAL industries number, updated May 11, 2017), http://www.bea.gov.

2. The Department of Finance estimated the total population to be 38,715,000 on January 1, 2015. Source: State of California, Department of Finance, *E-1 Population Estimates for Cities, Counties and the State with Annual Percent Change—January 1, 2014 and 2015* (Sacramento, California, May 2015). Statistics Canada, "Population by year, province, and territory 2016," Government of Canada, http://www.statcan.gc.ca/tables-tableaux/sum-som/l01/cst01/demo02a-eng.htm.

3. Ryan Salchert, "Where the Wealthiest Live," *Forbes* (March 21, 2017), https://www.forbes.com/sites/ryansalchert/2017/03/21/where-the-wealthiest-live-cities-with-the-most-billionaires/#149e40113677.

4. Estimates vary widely. Based on American Community Survey (ACS) analysis by researchers at the Population Research Institute, the Policy Migration Center pegs the number at 3,019,000 in 2014. Using the same ACS, the Pew Research Center estimates the number at 2.35 million for the same year. See Migration Policy Institute, "Profile of the Unauthorized Population in California," http://www.migrationpolicy.org/data/unauthorized-immigrant-population/state/CA, and Pew Research Center, "U.S. unauthorized population estimates (by state, 2014)," http://www.pewhispanic.org/interactives/unauthorized-immigrants.

5. Demographics Research Unit, "California Population Facts," California Department of Finance, http://www.dof.ca.gov/Forecasting/Demographics.

6. Office of Communications, "New Arial Survey Identifies More Than 100 Million Dead Trees in California," Press Release No. 0246.16, U.S. Department of Agriculture (November 8, 2016) https://www.usda.gov/media/press-releases/2016/11/18/new-aerial-survey-identifies-more-100-million-dead-trees-california.

7. The contract awarded to fix the dam initially was $275 million, but twice as much concrete was needed to reach bedrock than originally estimated. See Paul Rogers, "Oroville Dam: Cost to repair spillways nearly doubles in price to $500 million," *The Mercury News* (October 19, 2017), http:\\www.mercurynews.com/2017/10/19/cost-of-repairing-oroville-dams-spillway-nearly-doubles-in-price-to-500-million/.

8. Ellen Knickmeyer, "Can California fish catch break with giant tunnels?" *SF Chronicle* (July 1, 2017), http://www.sfchronicle.com/news/science/article/Can-California-fish-catch-break-with-giant-11260885.php. See also California Water Fix, https://www.californiawaterfix.com.

9. Jose Cisneros, "California's Crumbling Infrastructure: An Urgent Priority," League of California Cities, *Western City Magazine* (February 2014), http://www.westerncity.com/Western-City/February-2014/PresMsg-CA-Crumbling-Infrastructure.

10. Mark Baldassare, Dean Bonner, David Kordus, and Lunna Lopes, "Californians and their government: Statewide Survey," *PPIC* (March 2017), http://www.ppic.org/content/pubs/survey/S_317MBS.pdf. The respondents were 1,706 California adult residents; interviews conducted in English and Spanish took place by landline and cellphone March 5-14, 2017. The poll's margin of error was ±3.3 percent.

11. Ibid. In the PPIC poll, 35% of residents said they paid much more taxes to state and local governments than they felt they should; 23% said somewhat more.

12. David Wasserman, "2016 Popular Vote Tracker," *The Cook Political Report* (updated 1/3/17), http://cookpolitical.com/story/10174.

13. A district judge issued the injunction in November 2017. Citing the separation of powers doctrine, he noted that Congress has the authority to place conditions on spending, not the president. Further, the Tenth Amendment requires that the conditions be timely and related to the funds at issue, and not be coercive. Source: Eli Rosenberg, "Federal Judge blocks Trump's executive order on denying funding to sanctuary cities," *The Washington Post* (November 21, 2017), https://www.washingtonpost.com/news/politics/wp/2017/11/21/federal-judge-blocks-trumps-executive-order-on-denying-funding-to-sanctuary-cities/?utm_term=.c001e66ec4ed.

14. Carey McWilliams, *California, the Great Exception* (Berkeley and Los Angeles: University of California Press, 1949; 1997).

Chapter 2

1. Andrew Rolle, *California: A History,* 6th ed. (Wheeling, IL: Harlan Davidson, 2003), 174.

2. Quote is attributed to Robert G. Cleland in Evelyn Hazen, *Cross-Filing in Primary Elections* (Berkeley: University of California, Bureau of Public Administration, 1951), 9.

3. Arthur Samish and Robert Thomas, *The Secret Boss of California* (New York: Crown Books, 1971), 10.

4. *Silver v. Jordan,* 241 Fed. S. 576 (1965), and *Reynolds v. Sims,* 377 US 533 (1964), following *Baker v. Carr,* 369 U.S. 186 (1962).

5. T. George Harris, "California's New Politics: Big Daddy's Big Drive," *Look Magazine* 26, 20 (September 25, 1962).

6. John Burns, The Sometime Governments: A Critical Study of the 50 American Legislatures, by the Citizens *Conference on State Legislatures* (New York: Bantam Books, 1971), 8.

7. Howard Jarvis and Paul Gann, "Arguments in Favor of Proposition 13," in *Primary Election Ballot Pamphlet* (Sacramento: California Secretary of State, 1978).

8. Proposition 13 limited property tax rates to 1 percent of a property's assessed value in 1975; for properties sold after 1975, the rate would be 1 percent of the property's sale price. These rates would not be allowed to increase more than 2 percent per year.

9. Dan Walters, "California Has by Far Nation's Largest Asian-American Population," *Sacramento Bee,* March 12, 2013, http://blogs.sacbee.com/capitolalertlatest/2012/03/california-has-by-far-nations-largest-asian-american-population.html, and "A Community of Contrasts: Asian Americans, Native Hawaiians and Pacific Islanders in Los Angeles County, 2013," *Asian Americans Advancing Justice,* 2013, http://advancingjustice-la.org/system/files/CommunityofContrasts_LACounty2013.pdf. See also, California Department of Finance Demographic Unit, "Report P-3: Total Population Projections by Race/Ethnicity and Age, 2010–2060," DOF, December 14, 2014, http://www.dof.ca.gov/research/demographic/reports/projections/P-3.

10. California Department of Finance Demographic Unit, "Report P-3: Total Population Projections by Race/Ethnicity and Age, 2010–2060," DOF, December 14, 2014, http://www.dof.ca.gov/research/demographic/reports/projections/P-3.

11. Pew Research Center, "U.S. unauthorized immigration population estimates (2014)," Pew, November 3, 2016, http://www.pewhispanic.org/interactives/unauthorized-immigrants.

12. National Immigration Law Center, "Driver's Licenses Map," NILC, May 2015, http://www.nilc.org/driverlicensemap.html.

13. Esther Yu-Hsi Lee, "200,000 Undocumented Immigrants Now Have a California Driver's License," *ThinkProgress.com*, April 7, 2015, http://thinkprogress.org/immigration/2015/04/07/3643779/ca-drivers-license. Jens Hainmueller, Duncan Lawrence, Hans Lueders, "Providing Driver's Licenses to Unauthorized Immigrants Improves Traffic Safety," Proceedings of the National Academy of Sciences, March 3, 2017, http://www.pnas.org/content/114/16/4111.

14. Sara Burd-Sharps and Kristen Lewis, "A Portrait of California 2014–15", *The Social Science Research Council* (2014), http://www.measureofamerica.org/california2014–15.

15. Edward "Ted" Costa, "Proponent's Statement of Reasons," and "Proponent's Recall Argument," California Statewide Special Election, Tuesday, October 7, 2003, Voter Information Guide for 2003, Special Election (2003), http://repository.uchastings.edu/ca_ballot_props/1215.

16. Proposition 23 in 2010 would have dismantled the law by suspending its implementation until unemployment dipped below 5.5 percent for four consecutive quarters, a phenomenon that last occurred in 2006–07.

17. Twenty-five same-party races in November 2014 included seven Congressional races (five featuring two Democrats and two featuring two Republicans); six state Senate races (five featuring two Democrats and one race featuring two Republicans); twelve Assembly races (seven featuring two Democrats and five featuring two Republicans). Among these, only nine were competitive as measured by the winner receiving less than 55 percent of the vote. Twenty-eight total same-party races in November 2012 included eight Congressional races (six races featuring two Democrats and two races featuring two Republicans); two state Senate races (both races involved Democrats only); and eighteen Assembly races (eleven featuring two Democrats and seven featuring two Republicans). Among these, only nine were competitive as measured by the winner receiving less than 55 percent of the vote. See the final official election results compiled by the Secretary of State (http://www.sos.ca.gov).

18. John Sides, "Can California's New Primary Reduce Polarization? Maybe Not," *The Monkey Cage*, March 27, 2013, http://themonkeycage.org/2013/03/27/can-californias-new-primary-reduce-polarization-maybe-not. See also Lucas Eaves, "Recent Study Misses Big Picture in Evaluation of Top-Two Primary," *Independent Voter Network*, May 22, 2013, http://ivn.us/2013/05/22/how-to-define-success-the-impact-of-the-top-two-primary-in-california.

19. Eaves points to the election of Democratic candidates who were not supported by Democratic leadership as evidence that the system is inducing intended change and, if only by implication, more moderation. He cites Eric Swalwell's victory over incumbent Pete Stark. Eaves, "Recent Study Misses Big Picture." In addition, the author has obtained data from the convener of the moderate caucus, a loosely affiliated group that assembles an agenda that tends to be probusiness. In 2015, there were over thirty Democratic members who could be counted on fairly regularly to cast what is considered to be the "moderate" vote on specific measures the caucus identified as priorities, in contrast to ten years ago when only six members associated with the "moderate caucus." A "mixed bag" of results was also described by Eric McGhee and Boris Shor, "Has the Top Two Primary Elected More Moderates?" Democracy, Development, and the Rule of Law, Stanford University (CDDRL Working Papers), http://cddrl.fsi.stanford.edu/sites/default/files/amdem-_1.pdf.

20. Of all adults, 63 percent reported it was "mostly a good thing," 23 percent said mostly a bad thing, and 13 percent didn't know. Mark Baldassare, Dean Bonner, Sonja Petek, and Jui Shresthra, "California and their government, statewide survey," *PPIC* (November 13, 2012 – Nov. 20, 2012), http://webapp.ppic.org/main/publication.asp? i=1042.

21. In 2008, voters approved Proposition 1A, which provides $9.95 billion in funding for high-speed rail. After a report in 2011 that revised the costs upward to nearly $98 billion, Governor Brown ordered redesigns that would bring costs down. In 2012, high-speed rail authorities reported new cost estimates to be closer

to $68 billion, a figure that the state's General Accounting Office found to be "reasonable." "GAO: Calif. High-Speed Rail Estimates Reasonable," *CBS Sacramento Local* (March 28, 2013), http://sacramento.cbslocal.com/2013/03/28/gao-calif-high-speed-rail-estimates-reasonable. See also Ralph Vartabedian, Dan Weikel, and Richard Simon, "Bullet Train's $98-Billion Cost Could Be Its Biggest Obstacle," *Los Angeles Times* (November 2, 2011), http://articles.latimes.com/2011/nov/02/local/la-me-1102-bullet-train-20111102; and Mike Rosenberg, "High Speed Rail Chief: Bullet Train Won't Cost $100 Billion," *San Jose Mercury News* (March 14, 2012), http://www.mercurynews.com/california-high-speed-rail/ci_20168582/high-speed-rail-chief-bullet-train-wont-cost.

22. Justin Worland, "Gov. Jerry Brown Vows to Fight Donald Trump on Climate Change: 'California Will Launch Its Own Damn Satellite,'" *Time* (December 15, 2016), http://time.com/4603482/jerry-brown-donald-trump-climate-change.

23. Edmund G. Brown, Jr., "California State Budget 2017-18: Introduction," California Office of the Governor, http://www.ebudget.ca.gov/2017–18/pdf/Enacted/BudgetSummary/Introduction.pdf.

24. Patrick McGreevy, "With strong message against creating new crimes, Gov. Brown vetoes drone bills," *Los Angeles Times* (October 3, 2015), http://www.latimes.com/politics/la-me-pc-gov-brown-vetoes-bills-restricting-hobbyist-drones-at-fires-schools-prisons-20151003-story.html.

25. Jessica Calefati, "Bill action deadline: Jerry Brown uses raft of veto messages to draw attention to his agenda," *San Jose Mercury News* (October 11, 2015), http://www.mercurynews.com/2015/10/11/bill-action-deadline-gov-jerry-brown-uses-raft-of-veto-messages-to-draw-attention-to-his-agenda.

26. Edmund G. Brown, Jr., "Veto message regarding Assembly Bill 902," California Office of the Governor, September 9, 2013.

27. The rate of implementation differs by $1 per hour depending on whether the employer has 25 or fewer employees, or 26-plus. Scheduled increases may be delayed by the governor based on certain conditions. There is also an exception for learners, defined as those who are new to a job in which they have no similar or previous experience; they may be paid not less than 85 percent of the minimum wage, rounded to the nearest nickel, for the first 160 hours of work. Department of Industrial Relations, "Minimum Wage," Labor Commissioner's Office, State of California (December 2016), https://www.dir.ca.gov/dlse/faq/minimumwage.htm. Information about the federal minimum wage can be found at http://www.dol.gov/whd/minimumwage.htm.

Chapter 3

1. Ballot Argument in Favor of California Proposition 7, the Initiative and Referendum Amendment, October 10, 1911, http://repository.uchastings.edu/cgi/viewcontent.cgi?article=1023&context=ca_ballot_props.

2. The quote is by Secretary of State Alex Padilla. Quoted in John Myers, "California's record-setting 224-page voter guide is costing taxpayers nearly $15 million," *Los Angeles Times* (September 9, 2016), http://www.latimes.com/politics/la-pol-ca-california-voter-guide-november-ballot-20160909-snap-story.html.

3. *Arizona State Legislature v. Arizona Independent Redistricting Commission*, 135 S. Ct. 2652 (2015).

4. The term *hybrid democracy* is attributed to Elizabeth Garrett, "Hybrid Democracy," *George Washington Law Review* 73 (2005): 1096–1130.

5. California Legislative Analyst's Office, "1974 to Present: Ballot Measures by Type," accessed July 1, 2017, http://www.lao.ca.gov/BallotAnalysis/BallotByType; Oregon Blue Book, "Initiative, Referendum, and Recall," accessed June 14, 2017, http://bluebook.state.or.us/state/elections/elections06.htm; Colorado State Legislature, "Ballot History by Year," accessed July 1, 2017, http://www.leg.state.co.us/lcs/ballothistory.nsf.

6. According to the California Legislative Analyst's Office, 521 measures were on ballots between 1979 and 2016. During the same period in Oregon, voters considered 301 measures, and between 1904 and 2016 approved 127 propositions, 23 referenda, and 257 of 434 legislatively referred measures (see Oregon Secretary of State, "Oregon Blue Book: Initiative, Recall, and Referendum Introduction," accessed July 1, 2017, http://bluebook.state.or.us/state/elections/elections06.htm). Colorado ballots have included 115 propositions and 65 referenda since 1979. These states represent the top three most active users of the initiative process.

7. Alex Padilla, "Summary of Data (Initiatives)," Office of the Secretary of State (2016), http://elections .cdn.sos.ca.gov/ballot-measures/pdf/summary-data.pdf.

8. The exact figure is 75.26 percent, or 1,469 out of 1,952 that were titled and summarized for circulation between 1912 and 2016. Source: Alex Padilla, "Summary of Data," Secretary of State, http://elections.cdn.sos .ca.gov/ballot-measures/pdf/summary-data.pdf.

9. "California Ballot Initiative Petition Signature Costs," Ballotpedia, accessed July 1, 2017, http:// ballotpedia.org/wiki/index.php/California_ballot_initiative_petition_signature_costs.

10. Elisabeth R. Gerber, Arthur Lupia, Mathew D. McCubbins, and D. Roderick Kiewiet, *Stealing the Initiative: How State Government Responds to Direct Democracy* (Upper Saddle River, NJ: Prentice Hall, 2001), 12.

11. Unadjusted dollars. The rest came from donations averaging over $10,000. The 48 big donors include nine labor groups, 15 businesses (led by PG&E), eight individuals, nine Native American tribes, the major political parties, two of Schwarzenegger's political committees, the League of Cities, one advocacy group, and one PAC. See: Mike Polyakov, Peter Counts, Kevin Yin, "California's Initiative System: The Voice of the People Co-opted," *California Common Sense* (November 6, 2013), cacs.org/pdf/22.pdf.

12. A filing fee of $200 was last set in 1943. Governor Brown agreed with arguments in favor of AB 1100 that the fee should be raised to reflect long-term inflation and to discourage the frivolous filing of initiatives. The increase took effect January 1, 2016. A public review period was also added in 2014 (AB 1253) to increase transparency in the process.

13. Signature invalidation rates vary by county. Center for Governmental Studies (CGS) reports that Los Angeles and Oakland have much higher invalidation rates (around 30 to 35 percent) due to duplicate signatures, signatures of unregistered voters, or names submitted in counties where they are not registered to vote. CGS estimates the average invalidation rate to be as high as 40 percent. See Center for Governmental Studies, *Democracy by Initiative: Shaping California's Fourth Branch of Government,* 2nd ed. (Los Angeles, CA: Center for Governmental Studies, 2008), http://policyarchive.org/handle/10207/bitstreams/5800.pdf.

14. Ballotpedia calculates the average cost per required signature (CPRS) based on the amounts paid to the signature collection firms (publicly reported information) and the actual numbers of signatures needed. In 2016, it was $6.20 for 15 initiatives. In 2014, the highest average cost per signature was $5.22 (for a referendum on a gaming compact); the remaining three were closer to $3.48 on average. Higher amounts were paid in 2012 with $10.86 (Prop 30) and $9.81 (Prop 38) CPRS. For all measures in 2012, the average cost per signature was $3.82. "California Ballot Initiative Petition Signature Costs," Ballotpedia, accessed July 1, 2017, http:// ballotpedia.org/wiki/index.php/California_ballot_initiative_petition_signature_costs.

15. California Secretary of State, "Power Search," http://powersearch.sos.ca.gov. A *Los Angeles Times* analysis puts the figure at $488.89 million. See: John Myers, "Political Road Map," *Los Angeles Times* (February 19, 2017), http://www.latimes.com/politics/la-pol-ca-road-map-california-2018-campaign-spending-20170219-story.html.

16. Governor Brown was aware that many voters only vote for measures appearing at the top of a ballot. The "roll-off," or reduction in number of votes for down-ticket measures, in this case was about 1 percent, meaning that 12,667,751 people cast their votes for Brown's "top of the ticket" Prop 30, whereas 12,331,091 voted for Prop 38, a difference of 336,660 votes (or 0.97 percent). Ultimately, however, Brown's measure won by such a large margin that the roll-off did not matter to the election outcome.

17. Center for Governmental Studies, *Democracy by Initiative,* 14. See also Polyakov et al., 2013.

18. Mark Baldassare, Dean Bonner, Sonja Petek, and Jui Shrestha, "Reforming California's Initiative Process," Public Policy Institute of California (October 2013), http://www.ppic.org/content/pubs/atissue/AI_1013MBAI .pdf. Results of polls conducted in 2000, 2006, May and September 2011, and 2013 were consistent.

19. Ibid. Of those surveyed in May 2011, 54 percent said that the initiative process in California today is controlled by special interests "a lot," 34 percent said "some," 6 percent said "not at all," and 6 percent responded that they didn't know.

20. For a complete list of referenda that were circulated or qualified for the ballot, see "Referendum," California Secretary of State, http://www.sos.ca.gov/elections/ballot-measures/referendum.

21. According to the National Conference of State Legislatures, "at least 29 states" permit recall elections to be held in local jurisdictions, and "some sources place this number at 36." See NCSL, "Recall of State Officials," last modified March 8, 2016, http://www.ncsl.org/research/elections-and-campaigns/recall-of-state-officials.aspx.

22. The last person to be impeached and convicted was Judge James Hardy in 1862. Judge Carols Hardy (no relation) was impeached and then acquitted in 1929.

23. For more details, see "Procedure for Recalling State and Local Officials," California Secretary of State, http://www.sos.ca.gov/elections/recalls/procedure-recalling-state-and-local-officials.

24. Source: "Recall History in California, 1913-Present," California Secretary of State, accessed July 1, 2017, http://www.sos.ca.gov/elections/recalls/recall-history-california-1913-present.

25. This figure represents 687 out of 872 total local ballot measures. California Elections Data Archive, "Table B, Summary of Outcomes for All County, City, and School District Ballot Measures by Topic of Measure and County, 2016," Institute for Social Research (Sacramento, CA) and Office of the California Secretary of State (Sacramento, CA), n.d., http://www.csus.edu/isr/projects/ceda%20reports/2016/table-b-2016.pdf. Note that some cities fail to report by the deadline, but they are the most accurate available.

26. For a more comprehensive report, see Tracy M. Gordon, *The Local Initiative in California* (San Francisco: Public Policy Institute of California, 2004), http://www.ppic.org/content/pubs/report/R_904TGR.pdf.

27. See San Francisco Ethics Commission website for 2016 campaign contributions: https://sfethics.org/ethics/2016/06/campaign-finance-dashboards-june-7-2016-and-november-8-2016-elections.html.

28. Emily Green, Joaquin Palomino, and Jessica Floum, "Big bucks donors wield their influence on SF ballot measures," *San Francisco Chronicle* (November 2, 2016), http://www.sfchronicle.com/bayarea/article/Big-bucks-donors-wield-their-influence-on-SF-10535247.

29. These were 2016 thresholds. See: Department of Elections, "Guide to Qualifying Initiative Charter Amendments, Ordinances, and Declarations of Policy," San Francisco, https://sfgov.org/elections/sites/default/files/Documents/candidates/Nov2016_Overall%20Guide%20for%20Ballot%20Initiatives.pdf and San Diego County Clerk, "Initiative Process," February 10, 2017, https://www.sandiego.gov/sites/default/files/sig.reqs2-10 2017.pdf.

30. Steve Boilard, David Barker, Valory Messier, and Mark Johnson, "California County, City, and School District Election Outcomes: Candidates and Ballot Measures, 2016 Elections," Institute for Social Research; Center for California Studies, http://www.csus.edu/isr/projects/ceda%20reports/2016/city-report-2016.pdf.

31. The other states that have the direct and/or indirect initiative, popular referendum for statutes and/or constitutional amendments and the recall are Arizona, Colorado, Idaho, Michigan, Montana, Nevada, North Dakota, Oregon, and Washington. See: NCSL, "Initiative and Referendum States" and "Recall of State Officials."

32. Mark Baldassare, Dean Bonner, Sonja Petek, and Jui Shrestha, "The Initiative Process in California," Public Policy Institute of California (October 2013), www.ppic.org/main/publication_show.asp?i=1072.

Chapter 4

1. The U.S. Census 2010 apportionment population in congressional districts is 710,767; California contains fifty-three U.S. House districts. National Atlas of the United States, "Congressional Apportionment," accessed June 20, 2015, http://www.nationalatlas.gov/articles/boundaries/a_conApport.html#one.

2. The six legislatures that *approach* the professionalized status are Alaska, Hawaii, Illinois, Massachusetts, Ohio, and Wisconsin. Most are in "mixed" categories (legislators maintain an outside job to support themselves, meet in longer or shorter sessions, etc.); and four—North and South Dakota, Montana, and Wyoming—operate as purely part-time, "citizen" bodies (very low pay, short sessions, a few institutional staff). Brian Weberg, "Full- and Part-Time Legislatures," NCSL, updated June 14, 2017, http://www.ncsl.org/research/about-state-legislatures/full-and-part-time-legislatures.aspx.

3. It should be noted that although high turnover in 2012 was also prompted by redistricting, term limits have provided the impetus for high turnover in non-redistricting years since 1990. In 2012, turnover reached 47.5 percent.

4. Five other states have advisory commissions to assist the legislature with state legislative redistricting, and five more have backup commissions that will spring into action if the legislature fails to agree. Yet more variety exists (December 7, 2015) http://www.ncsl.org/research/redistricting/2009-redistricting-commissions-table.aspx.

5. Proposition 11, Section 2(d).

6. Angelo Ancheta, "Redistricting Reform and the California Citizens Redistricting Commission," *Harvard Law and Policy Review*, 2014, (8) 1: 109–140.

7. State of California Citizens Redistricting Commission, "Final Report on 2011 Redistricting," August 15, 2011, http://wedrawthelines.ca.gov/downloads/meeting_handouts_082011/crc_20110815_2final_report.pdf.

8. Vladimir Kogan and Eric McGhee, "Redistricting California: An Evaluation of the Citizens Commission Final Plans," 4, 1 (2004): DOI: https://doi.org/10.5070/P23K5Q.

9. *Arizona State Legislature v. Arizona Independent Redistricting Commission*, 576 U.S. (2015).

10. Of the 120 legislators in office in July 2017, twenty-six were women (a loss of five from 2014–15 to 2016-17). In terms of race and ethnicity, sixty-seven were White, ten were African American, twenty-seven were Hispanic/Latino, thirteen were Asian American or Pacific Islander, two were of Middle Eastern descent (Jordanian and Armenian), and one was "multi-racial." In all, 52 of 120 (43 percent) were "nonwhite." California Research Bureau, "Demographics in the California Legislature," California State Library, December 15, 2016, www.library.ca.gov/crb/16/LegDemographicsNov16.txt, and author's data.

11. Quoted in Hannah Pitkin, *The Concept of Representation* (Berkeley: University of California Press, 1967), 60.

12. AB 1262, authored by Assembly Member Eduardo Garcia, introduced February 17, 2017.

13. California Natural Resources Agency, "Frequently Asked Questions About CEQA," http://resources.ca.gov/ceqa/more/faq.html.

14. This is the conclusion of the Legislative Analyst's office in their 2015 report, "California's High Housing Costs: Causes and Consequences," March 17, 2015, http://www.lao.ca.gov/reports/2015/finance/housing-costs/housing-costs.aspx.

15. LAO, 2015.

16. Senators Lindsay Graham and Bill Cassidy's bill to "repeal and replace" was the third of its type to fall short of passage in September 2017, and in November 2017, House Republicans inserted a provision in a tax overhaul bill to eliminate the Affordable Care Act's "individual mandate" (the requirement that individuals must buy health insurance). At this writing, the bill had not been voted on by the U.S. Senate. Source for current count of Medi-Cal enrollees: California Department of Health Care Services, "Medi-Cal Fast Facts," April 2017, http://www.dhcs.ca.gov/dataandstats/statistics/Pages/Medi-Cal-Certified-EligiblesRecentTrends.aspx

17. This statement assumes that trends have held steady since the numbers were reported in 2015. See Brian Weberg, "Size of State Legislative Staff," NCSL, 2015, http://www.ncsl.org/research/about-state-legislatures/staff-change-chart-1979-1988-1996-2003-2009.aspx.

18. The Republican Party achieved supermajority status in both chambers at least a dozen times between 1891 and 1933.

19. James Fallows, "Jerry Brown's Political Reboot," *The Atlantic* (May 22, 2013), http://www.theatlantic.com/magazine/archive/2013/06/the-fixer/309324/?single_page=true.

20. Donald Lathbury, "Two-Thirds Majority Battle Still on Radar," California Majority Report, September 22, 2008, http://www.camajorityreport.com/index.php? module=articles&func=display&ptid=9&aid=3581.

21. Author's interview with freshman assembly member in Sacramento, California, in March 1999.

Chapter 5

1. Headline is from the *New York Times*, https://www.nytimes.com/2017/06/06/world/asia/xi-jinping-china-jerry-brown-california-climate.html?_r=1; Jessica Meyers, "China is Now Looking to California—Not Trump to help lead the fight against climate change," *Los Angeles Times* (June 6, 2017), http://www.latimes.com/world/asia/la-fg-china-global-climate-20170606-story.html.

2. Headline is from the New York Times, https://www.nytimes.com/2017/06/06/world/asia/xi-jinping-china-jerry-brown-california-climate.html?_r=1. Alex Padilla, "Secretary of State Alex Padilla Responds to Presidential Election Commission Request for Personal Data of California Voters," California Secretary of State's Office, June 29, 2017.

3. Headline is from The Hill, http://thehill.com/homenews/state-watch/322081-california-attorney-general-opens-dc-office. Patrick McGreevy, "California Atty. Gen. Becerra to set up a Washington office as he prepares to fight Trump administration," *Los Angeles Times* (March 1, 2017), http://www.latimes.com/politics/essential/la-pol-ca-essential-politics-updates-cal-a-g-becerra-tells-sessions-that-1488395437-htmlstory.html.

4. Most state workers are members of the powerful union known as the California State Employees Association.

5. According to the Assembly Clerk's Office (personal correspondence with author, June 2013), there was a series of veto overrides in 1979 to 1980, but the last occurred when the Senate overrode a gubernatorial budget line-item veto on September 5, 1979 (Senate Journal, p. 7174). The Assembly overrode this line-item veto on February 4, 1980 (by a vote of fifty-five to twelve), but a motion to reconsider was noticed. The motion to reconsider lapsed on February 5, 1980, so the override took effect on that day (Assembly Journal, p. 11086).

6. According to the Human Resources Department at the Department of Finance, the actual number of employees in June 2015 was 467.

7. Brown typically grants pardons on the eve of Christmas and Easter. State of California, "Governor Brown Grants Pardons," press release, April 5, 2015, http://www.gov.ca.gov/news.php? id=18914. For the reasons behind Brown's decisions, see *Executive Report on Pardons, Commutations of Sentence, and Reprieves,* issued annually by the governor's office under statutory order.

8. According to the Secretary of State, final campaign finance filings, the National Institute on Money in State Politics reports that $4,371,501 was raised in support, and $56,961,711 was spent in opposition (see: powersearch.sos.ca.gov/advanced.php).

9. Governor Edmund G. Brown, "Government Reorganization Plan," March 30, 2012, http://gov.ca.gov/docs/Cover_Letter_and_Summary.pdf.

10. The total number was 208,714 as of July 2017, including full-time and part-time workers and excluding 20,448 intermittent employees and employees of the California State University system. In June 2009, the comparable state employee workforce numbered 244,061. California State Controller's Office, "State Employee Demographics," May 2015, http://www.sco.ca.gov/ppsd_empinfo_demo.html.

Chapter 6

1. James Queally, "ICE agents make arrests at courthouse…," *Los Angeles Times* (March 16, 2017), http://www.latimes.com/local/lanow/la-me-ln-ice-courthouse-arrests-20170315-story.html.

2. California Courts Newsroom, "Chief Justice Cantil-Sakauye Objects to Immigration Enforcement Tactics at California Courthouses" (March 16, 2017), http://newsroom.courts.ca.gov/news/chief-justice-cantil-sakauye-objects-to-immigration-enforcement-tactics-at-california-courthouses.

3. Mark Hensch, "DHS: Immigration agents cause courthouse arrests," *The Hill* (April 4, 2017), http://thehill.com/policy/national-security/department-of-homeland-security/327332-dhs-immigration-arrests-fair-at.

4. Judicial Council of California, "Court Statistics Report" (2016), http://www.courts.ca.gov/documents/2016-Court-Statistics-Report-Preface.pdf.

5. Mac Taylor, *California's Criminal Justice System: A Primer* (Sacramento: California Legislative Analyst's Office, January 2013), http://www.lao.ca.gov/reports/2013/crim/criminal-justice-primer/criminal-justice-primer-011713.pdf.

6. Judicial Council of California, Administrative Office of the Courts, *2016 Court Statistics Report: Statewide Caseload Trends, 2003–2004 through 2014–2015* (San Francisco: Judicial Council of California, 2016), http://www.courts.ca.gov/documents/2016-Court-Statistics-Report.pdf.

7. Proposition 66 passed by a tiny margin (51.1% to 48.9%) in November 2016. The case is *Briggs* v *Brown*, S238309, decided August 24, 2017 by a 5-2 margin.

8. Governors' Gallery, "George Deukmejian," http://governors.library.ca.gov/35-deukmejian.html.

9. Julie Patel, "Forum Sheds Light on How Judges Are Screened, Chosen," *San Jose Mercury News* (June 4, 2006); Howard Mintz, "Gov. Jerry Brown Puts Deep Imprint on California Judiciary," *San Jose Mercury News* (February 16, 2014).

10. State of California, "Governor Brown Releases 2016 Judicial Appointment Data," Governor Jerry Brown (February 28, 2017), https://www.gov.ca.gov/news.php? id=19698.

11. Scott Greytak, Adam Skaggs, Alicia Bannon, Allyse Falce, and Linda Casey, *The New Politics of Judicial Elections 2013–2014: Bankrolling the Bench* (Washington, DC: National Institute for Money in State Politics and Brennan Center for Justice at NYU School of Law, 2015), http://newpoliticsreport.org/report/2013–14.

12. See California Judicial Council, *2016 Court Statistics Report*.

13. Approximately 8 million persons were summoned for jury service in 2014–15; the number was 8.67 million in 2010–11 (see "About California Courts," 2017; 2012). "Completed service" means the individual appeared at the court on the appointed day, although he or she may not have been assigned to a trial and was dismissed at the end of the day.

14. According to data compiled by the author, in 2017, 36 states paid an average of $23.00 for the first day of service, plus mileage. According to data collected by the National Center for State Courts in 2007, the average compensation rate was $18.75 (plus mileage) for the first day of service and $25.30 for the second day (assuming the juror was sworn in by day two). Data for some states were incomplete. See Gregory E. Mize, Paula Hannaford-Agor, and Nicole L. Waters, *The State-of-the-States Survey of Jury Improvement Efforts: A Compendium Report* (Williamsburg, VA: National Center for State Courts, April 2007), http://cdm16501.contentdm.oclc.org/cdm/ ref/collection/juries/id/112.

15. See: 2014–15 Court Statistics Report, p. 73. The felony criminal filings, dispositions, and caseload clearance rate in FY2014 was 272,548 (slightly higher than the previous two years) and declined to 214,088 in 2015. The nontraffic misdemeanor rate was 402,188 in 2014 (about average for the previous two years) and 445,564 for 2015.

16. Magnus Lofstrom and Brandon Martin, "Just the Facts: California's County Jails," PPIC (April 2015), http://www.ppic.org/main/publication_show.asp? i=1061.

17. PPIC, "Corrections: California's Future" (January 2017), http://www.ppic.org/content/pubs/report/R_117MLR.pdf.

18. Magnus Lofstrum and Steven Raphael, "Public Safety Realignment and Crime Rates in California," PPIC, (December 2013), http://www.ppic.org/content/pubs/report/R_1213MLR.pdf; Magnus Lofstrom and Brandon Martin, "Realignment, Incarceration, and Crime Trends in California," PPIC (May 2015), http://www.ppic.org/main/publication_quick.asp? i=1151; Magnus Loftstrom, Steven Raphael, and Ryken Grattet, "Is Public Safety Realignment Reducing Recidivism in California?" PPIC (June 2014).

19. Jody Sundt, Emily Salisbury, and Mark Harmon, "Is Downsizing Prisons Dangerous?" *Criminology and Public Policy* (March 9, 2016), doi: 10.1111/1745-9133.12199, and Lofstrum and Raphael, 2013.

20. PPIC reports that 62 percent of adult respondents supported this choice, consistent with previous poll results. Mark Baldassare, Dean Bonner, Sonja Petek, and Jui Shrestha, "Californians and Their Government" (San Francisco: Public Policy Institute of California, May 2011).

21. In a January 2015 PPIC poll, 42 percent of adults and 42 percent of likely voters (incorrectly) named prisons and corrections as the largest area for spending in the state budget. See Mark Baldassare, Dean Bonner,

Renatta DeFever, Lunna Lopes, and Jui Shrestha, "Statewide Survey: Californians and Their Government," PPIC (January 2015).

22. According to Taylor: "The federal court stipulated that the transition from the receivership back to state control will begin when the administration can demonstrate both (1) the ability to maintain an inmate medical care system that provides care as good as or better than that being delivered under the Receiver and (2) that any outstanding construction or information technology projects initiated by the Receiver would not be jeopardized. Likewise, the federal court overseeing inmate mental health care recently expressed satisfaction with progress made to date by the department towards a constitutional level of mental health care." Taylor, *California's Criminal Justice System*, 66. Costs cited in governor's budget summary (June 2015), http://www.ebudget.ca.gov/FullBudgetSummary.pdf.

23. Data provided by the Legislative Analyst's Office, June 2017. Actual per capita expenditures were $51,889 in 2011–12, $60,723 per inmate in 2013–14, and $69,488 in 2015–16.

24. Cost estimates vary. According to the Legislative Analyst's Office (LAO; communication with author, September 2015) the average cost to house nonlegal inmates would be calculated on a "marginal cost" basis, which excludes fixed costs and includes marginal costs such as food. Using that formula, the cost is about $28,000 per inmate per year per contract bed. The precise number of nonlegal inmates is also elusive, because many of them lack a social security number. Current estimates of the nonlegal U.S. felon population are between 18,000 and 20,000 (source: LAO, communication with author, September 2015). Other reports that include fixed costs place the total closer to $1 billion per year. Numbers reported in the text include inmates who are targeted by Immigration and Customs Enforcement; these specific figures were supplied by the LAO in August 2017.

25. State of California, "The 2017-18 State Budget." See also Division of Juvenile Justice, "Average Daily Population (Month of June 2017)," California Department of Corrections and Rehabilitation, http://www.cdcr.ca.gov/Juvenile_Justice/docs/DJJ_ADP_Monthly_Report_2017/ADP_MONTHLY_REPORT_2017.06.pdf.

26. California Courts, "Chief Justice Releases Statement in Response to 2017–18 Budget," press release (June 27, 2017) http://newsroom.courts.ca.gov/news/chief-justice-releases-statement-on-judicial-branch-budget-for-fiscal-year-2017-18.

27. Education Unit, Legislative Analyst's Office (direct communication). Figures calculated based on 2015-16 funding and enrollment.

Chapter 7

1. U.S. Census Bureau, "Individual State Descriptions, 2012: 2012 Census of Governments," U.S. Dept. of Commerce (September 2013), https://www2.census.gov/govs/cog/2012isd.pdf.

2. The *Los Angeles Times* broke the story in 2010 (for which they won two Pulitzer Prizes). Archives of their investigative stories can be found on their website: http://www.latimes.com/local/bell.

3. California State Controller's Office, "Government Compensation in California, California Cities 2016," http://publicpay.ca.gov/Reports/Cities/Cities.aspx. The posting includes reported information for 473 cities.

4. Kevin Crowe and Joanne Faryon, "Do You Pay Extra Property Taxes? Mello-Roos: Who's Paying What," KPBS News, inewsource (May 29, 2013), http://www.kpbs.org/news/2013/may/29/mello-roos-taxes-vary-dramatically-whos-paying-wha.

5. Mac Taylor, "Common Claims about Prop 13," LAO (September 19, 2016), http://www.lao.ca.gov/Publications/Report/3497#Introduction.

6. California State Treasurer's Office, http://debtwatch.treasurer.ca.gov. This figure only includes principal amounts sold and excludes interest payments and projected bond sales. In September 2017, cities carried $222 billion in bond debt, including redevelopment agencies' and their successors' debts. Counties carried $199 billion, including bonds sold jointly with cities, transportation agencies, and (former) redevelopment

agencies. K-12 school districts had sold $201 billion in bonds; $48 billion were sold by community college districts; another $59.7 billion were sold to fund community facilities.

7. The case is *Cal Fire Local 2881 v. California Public Employees' Retirement System*, S239958.

8. These statistics are for the 2015–16 school year, published by the California Department of Education on their data website, http://www.cde.ca.gov/ds/sd/cb/ceffingertipfacts.asp.

9. CalEdFacts (2016–17 school year), https://www.cde.ca.gov/ds/sd/cb/ceffingertipfacts.asp. Note that 602,837 students were enrolled in California public charter schools in 2016-17.

10. The exact number of COGs is difficult to calculate because a number of transportation planning commissions, planning councils, and other more localized (but intergovernmental) organizations qualify as COGs. The California Association of Councils of Government listed forty-six member organizations in 2017, including major transportation authorities or commissions. CALCOG, https://www.calcog.org/index.php? submenu=OurOrganization&src=gendocs&ref=OurOrganization&category=AboutUs.

11. LAO, "How much money does the federal government spend in California?" Legislative Analyst's Office (January 18, 2017), http://lao.ca.gov/Publications/Report/3531/1.

12. The U.S. House passed HR 3004 in June 2017, also dubbed "Kate's Law," whereupon it moved to the Senate.

13. The 2015 SCAAP per capita reimbursement rate was $41.26 (only for eligible inmates), based on correctional officer salary costs; food, housing, medical care, administrative costs (etc.) are not reimbursable. U.S. Department of Justice, Bureau of Justice Statistics, https://www.bja.gov/ProgramDetails.aspx? Program_ID=86.

14. Office of the Attorney General, "In New Filing, Attorney General Becerra Says Trump's Threat to Defund 'Sanctuary Jurisdictions' Jeopardizes Safety of CA Communities," State of California Department of Justice (June 28, 2017) https://oag.ca.gov/news/press-releases/new-filing-attorney-general-becerra-says-trump%E2%80%99s-threat-defund-%E2%80%9Csanctuary.

15. Vote results supplied by California Secretary of State. Data from ballot measure summaries for Propositions 94–97 are from Follow the Money, "Ballot Measures," accessed September 17, 2013, http://www.followthemoney.org/database/StateGlance/ballot.phtml? m=493.

16. Legislative Analyst's Office, "Overview of Gambling in California" (May 20, 2015), http://www.lao.ca.gov/handouts/crimjust/2015/Gambling-Overview-052015.pdf. For campaign contributions, see Opensecrets.org, "Indian Gaming," Accessed July 24, 2017, https://www.opensecrets.org/industries/contrib.php? cycle=2016&ind=G6550.

17. Kent Cooper, "Indian Tribes Gave Record Amount," *Roll Call,* Political MoneyLine blog (March 1, 2013), http://blogs.rollcall.com/moneyline/indian-tribes-gave-record-amount. See also, Opensecrets, "Indian Gaming," accessed June 25, 2015, http://www.opensecrets.org/industries/summary.php? cycle=2010&ind=G6550.

18. Author's calculations based on lobbying reports for 2013–14, California secretary of state's campaign finance database, http://cal-access.sos.ca.gov. See also, California Fair Political Practices Commission, "Top Contributors to State Ballot Measure Committees Raising at Least $1 Million: November 2014 Election," http://fppc.ca.gov/topcontributors/past_elections/nov2014/index.html.

Chapter 8

1. Press Release, "California Controller Reports Revenues $2.68 billion Short of 2015-16 Budget Act," State of California Controller's Office, Press Release (July 10, 2017), http://www.sco.ca.gov/eo_pressrel_18596.html.

2. In 2017–18, taxes plus special funds (including excise taxes and motor vehicle fees) brought the total revenues to $178.441 billion, of which $1.773 billion was set aside for the state's Rainy Day Fund/Budget Stabilization Account, bringing the total reserves to $8.486 billion. See the full budget summary for 2017–18, http://www.ebudget.ca.gov/budget/2017-18EN/#/BudgetSummary.

3. The rate of inflation was 2.1 percent in FY 2016–17. The inflation rate was 1.3 percent the previous fiscal year.

4. Franchise Tax Board, "Table B-9.1, Personal Income Tax: Statistics for Resident Tax Returns, High Income Returns, Tax Year 2015," In 2016 Annual Report, FTB, Accessed September 29, 2017, https://www.ftb .ca.gov/AboutFTB/Tax Statistics/Reports/2016/B-9-1.pdf.

5. State Treasurer's Office, "General Obligation and Revenue Bonds, Summary of Debt Service Requirements" (July 1, 2017), http://www.treasurer.ca.gov/bonds/debt/07/summary.pdf.

6. State Controller's Office, "News Release: Treasurer Sells $2.79 Billion in Bonds" (March 9, 2017), http:// www.treasurer.ca.gov/news/releases/2017/20170309/14.asp.

7. Press Release (July 10, 2017), and Press Release, "CA Controller's June Cash Report Shows Another Surge to End 2014-15 Fiscal Year" (July 14, 2015), http://www.sco.ca.gov/eo_pressrel_16350.html.

8. Shane Goldmacher and Anthony York, "Governor Vetoes 'Unbalanced' State Budget," *Los Angeles Times* (June 17, 2011), http://articles.latimes.com/2011/jun/17/local/la-me-0617-state-budget-20110617.

9. Final figure from 2013–14 and estimate from 2017–18 provided by the LAO.

10. Educational Finance Branch, "Public Education Finances: 2017," U.S. Census Bureau, GS15-ASPEF (June 2017), https://www.census.gov/content/dam/Census/library/publications/2017/econ/g15-aspef.pdf. Amounts quoted in text have been supplied by the Legislative Analyst's Office and are calculated differently from those listed in the U.S. Census Bureau's report.

11. Covered California, "Report to the Governor and the Legislature, Fiscal Year 2015-16" (January 2017), http://hbex.coveredca.com/data-research/library/CoveredCA_Leg_Report_2015–2016.pdf.

12. Senate Rules Committee, Floor Analysis of SB-1 (April 5, 2017).

13. This is formally known as Budget Stabilization Account and is different from the Special Fund for Economic Uncertainty, a fund that helps bridge temporary gaps between revenues and expenditures. Governor Jerry Brown, 2017–18 California State Budget, State of California (June 20, 2017), http://www.ebudget .ca.gov/2017-18/pdf/Enacted/BudgetSummary/Introduction.pdf.

14. Figures are from the California Franchise Tax Board for the most recent tax year available (2015). See Franchise Tax Board, "Annual Report, 2016," https://www.ftb.ca.gov/Archive/AboutFTB/Tax_Statistics/ Reports/2016/Annual-Report.pdf.

15. The only exception involves the risky move of including one or more fee hikes in the budget itself, which requires just a simple majority vote for approval, such as when the majority Democrats raised vehicle license fees an additional $12 through the 2011–12 budget without the approval of Republicans.

16. Tracy Gordon, "California Budget," Public Policy Institute of California (July 2009).

17. Based on the most recent figures available, 2009–10, in Taylor, *Cal Facts 2013,* 11.

18. Jared Walczak and Scott Drenkard, "State and Local Sales Tax Rates, Mid-Year 2017" (July 2017), https://files.taxfoundation.org/20170705160031/Tax-Foundation-FF553.pdf.

19. As of July 1, 2017, the American Petroleum Institute pegged California's total state taxes on motor vehicle fuel at 40.58 cents per gallon, compared to 44.26 cents in Hawaii, 43.50 cents in New York, and 59.30 cents in Pennsylvania (the highest); the two lowest were Alaska at 12.25 and Oklahoma at 17 cents per gallon. American Petroleum Institute, "State Motor Fuel Taxes, Rates Effective 07/01/2017," API, http://www .api.org/~/media/Files/Statistics/ StateMotorFuel-OnePagers-July-2017.pdf.

20. Federation of Tax Administrators, "Tax Rates/Surveys," accessed September 27, 2017, https://www .taxadmin.org/current-tax-rates.

21. In response to a January 2014 telephone survey by the Public Policy Institute of California, 72 percent of California adults opposed increasing spending on "prisons and corrections" (23 percent favored, 5 percent didn't know in response to the question, "Next, please tell me if you favor or oppose increasing state spending in the following areas. [rotate questions 20 to 23] How about increasing state spending on prisons and corrections?"). These figures are virtually identical to survey results in recent years, including during lean economic times when budget cuts were imminent. Questions about prisons are periodically included in California Statewide

Surveys conducted by PPIC; survey samples generally include a minimum of 1,700 adults, yielding results that are reliable within +/− 3.3 percentage points. See Mark Baldassare, Dean Bonner, Sonja Petek, and Jui Shrestha, "Californians and Their Government" (San Francisco: Public Policy Institute of California, January 2014).

22. Two different questions about gas taxes were posed in each of two recent surveys; majorities were opposed in both. See Mark Baldassare, Dean Bonner, Renatta DeFever, Lunna Lopes, and Jui Shrestha, "Californians and Their Government" (San Francisco: Public Policy Institute of California, January 2017 and May 2016).

Chapter 9

1. E. E. Schattschneider, *Party Government: American Government in Action* (New York, NY: Holt, Rinehart & Winston, 1942), 1.

2. Mark Baldassare, Dean Bonner, David Kordus, and Lunna Lopes, "Californians and Their Government," PPIC (May 2016).

3. The Public Policy Institute of California (PPIC) reports that 72 percent of Californians feel they make better decisions. See Public Policy Institute of California, "California Statewide Survey" (May 2015), http://www.ppic.org/content/pubs/survey/S_515MBS.pdf. A 2010 PPIC survey found that 44 percent have little trust in their fellow initiative voters. See Mark Baldassare, Dean Bonner, Sonja Petek, and Nicole Willcoxon, "Californians and Their Government" (San Francisco: Public Policy Institute of California, December 2010), http://www.ppic.org/content/pubs/survey/S_1210MBS.pdf.

4. Cross-filing—the practice of allowing candidates to file nomination papers with any party, appear on multiple ballots, and gain the nomination of more than one party—was finally eliminated through legislative action in 1959, and a ban on preprimary endorsements was found to be unconstitutional in 1989.

5. Mark Baldassare, Dean Bonner, David Kordus, and Lunna Lopes, "California Statewide Survey," Public Policy Institute of California (October 2016), http://www.ppic.org/content/pubs/survey/S_1016MBS.pdf. Note that 1,704 adults were surveyed October 14–23, 2016 (sampling error +/− 3.4 percent; 58 percent said a third party was needed in response to the question, "In your view, do the Republican and Democratic Parties do an adequate job representing the American people, or do they do such a poor job that a third major party is needed?")

6. California Secretary of State, "Odd-Numbered Year Report of Registration (February 10), 2017," http://elections.cdn.sos.ca.gov/ror/ror-pages/ror-odd-year-2017/hist-reg-stats.pdf.

7. Mark Baldassare, Dean Bonner, David Kordus, and Lunna Lopes, "Just the Facts: California's Independent Voters," Public Policy Institute of California (September 2016), http://www.ppic.org/content/pubs/jtf/JTF_IndependentVotersJTF.pdf.

8. Baldassare et al., "California's Independent Voters"; National Election Pool poll results reported on CNN Campaign 2016, "Presidential Results," http://www.cnn.com/election/results/states/california; CBS Campaign 2014, "Exit Poll for Governor Race," http://www.cbsnews.com/elections/2014/governor/california/exit.

9. Baldassare et al., "California's Independent Voters."

10. Baldassare et al., "California's Independent Voters."

11. Mark Baldassare, Dean Bonner, David Kordus, and Lunna Lopes, "California Voter and Party Profiles," Public Policy Institute of California (September 2016).

12. Baldassare et al., "California Voter and Party Profiles."

13. Baldassare et al., "California Voter and Party Profiles"; "California Statewide Survey" (May 2017) (64 percent of Republicans and 18 percent of Democrats said government goes too far in restricting gun rights). See also Mark Baldassare, Dean Bonner, Renatta DeFever, Lunna Lopes, and Jui Shrestha, "Californians and Their Future," PPIC (December 2014), http://www.ppic.org/content/pubs/survey/S_1214MBS.pdf; Public Policy Institute of California, "Statewide Survey Interactive Tools," accessed June 26, 2015.

14. Baldassare et al., "California Statewide Survey," May 2017.

15. Baldassare et al., "Californians and Their Government," May 2017 and January 2017. On abortion, 60 percent of Republicans favor restrictions, whereas 87 percent of Democrats say the government should not interfere with a woman's right to access abortion.

16. Public Policy Institute of California, "California Statewide Survey, May 2017."

17. Baldassare et al., "California's Independent Voters." See also PPIC, "Statewide Survey Interactive Tools."

18. Mark Baldassare, Dean Bonner, Lunna Lopez, and David Kordus, "Californians and the Environment," *PPIC* (July 2017), http://www.ppic.org/publication/ppic-statewide-survey-californians-and-the-environment-july-2017.

19. See the special journal devoted to research on the topic, beginning with Betsy Sinclair, "The California Top-Two Primary," *California Journal of Politics and Policy* 7, no. 1 (2015), http://escholarship.org/uc/item/4qk24589.

20. See Seth E. Masket, *No Middle Ground: How Informal Party Organizations Control Nominations and Polarize Legislatures* (Ann Arbor: University of Michigan Press, 2009). See also Seth Masket, "Polarization Interrupted? California's Experiment with the Top-Two Primary," in *Governing California: Politics, Government, and Public Policy in the Golden State,* 3rd ed., ed. Ethan Rarick (Berkeley, CA: Berkeley Public Policy Press, 2013).

21. Eric McGhee, "The Top-Two System and Election 2016," PPIC (November 10, 2016), http://www.ppic.org/blog/the-top-two-system-and-election-2016.

22. See Masket, No Middle Ground.

23. Quoted in Lou Cannon, *Ronnie and Jesse: A Political Odyssey* (New York, NY: Doubleday, 1969), 99.

24. Marisa Lagos, "The Cost of a Seat," KQED (June 24, 2015). These amounts are in line with author's calculations for 2010 races, in which the winning Senate candidates spent over $1 million, and Assembly races cost an average of $750,000.

25. Figures obtained from Fair Political Practices Commission, California State Contribution Limits, Effective January 1, 2017 through December 31, 2018, http://www.fppc.ca.gov/learn/campaign-rules/state-contribution-limits.html.

Chapter 10

1. John Dobard, Kim Engle, Karthick Ramakrishnan, Sono Shah, and Lisa Garcia Bedolla, "Unequal Voices: Who Speaks for California? Part II," American Majority Project Research Institute (Advancement Project), University of California Riverside (February 2017).

2. Raymond E. Wolfinger and Steven J. Rosenstone, *Who Votes?* (New Haven, CT: Yale University Press, 1980).

3. Public Policy Institute of California, California Statewide Surveys, 2015 aggregate file.

4. Mark Baldassare, "Californians and the Environment," Public Policy Institute of California (July 2017).

5. Dobard et al. (2017).

6. Ibid., 27.

7. Ibid.

8. Ibid.

9. Kristin Lewis and Sarah Burd-Sharps, "A Portrait of California, 2014–2015," California Human Development Report, Measure of America (2014). "A Portrait of California brings together data, innovative analysis, and the American HD Index methodology to enable 'apples-to-apples' comparisons of California's counties, major cities, 265 Census Bureau–defined areas, women and men, and racial and ethnic groups. It provides a gauge of how different groups of Californians are doing in comparison to one another and a benchmark for tracking progress over time" (p. 7).

10. Ibid., 66.

11. Mark Baldassare, Dean Bonner, Lunna Lopes, and Jui Shrestha, "Californians' News and Information Sources," PPIC (October 2014), http://www.ppic.org/main/publication_show.asp? i=770. Respondents were 2,003 registered voters statewide, surveyed October 2014; margin of error ±3.5 percent.

12. Michael Barthel and Amy Mitchell, "Americans' Attitudes About the News Media Deeply Divided Along Partisan Lines," Pew Research Center (May 10, 2017), http://www.journalism.org/2017/05/10/americans-attitudes-about-the-news-media-deeply-divided-along-partisan-lines.

13. Barthel and Mitchell reported the online user rate by youth as 50 percent in 2017; a 2014 poll placed the figure at 51 percent. "Californians' News and Information Sources," (October 2014).

14. Barthel and Mitchell (2017) report that among those who prefer to watch (rather than listen to or read) the news, 80 percent watch it on television. Also, 70 percent of all viewers who watch televised news broadcasts are over age 49, according to the USC Annenberg–Los Angeles Times Poll on Politics and the Press (August 2012). Respondents were 1,009 registered voters nationwide, surveyed August 13–19; margin of error ±3.1 percent.

15. "Californians' News and Information Sources" (October 2014).

16. USC Annenberg–Los Angeles Times Poll on Politics and the Press (August 2012).

17. Barthel and Mitchell (2017), (infographic), http://www.journalism.org/2017/05/10/americans-attitudes-about-the-news-media-deeply-divided-along-partisan-lines/pj_2017-05-10_media-attitudes_a-06/.

18. Dobard et al. (2017) reported that 36 percent of Californians have worked to solve community problems.

19. Dobard et al. (2017).

20. Ibid.

21. Ibid.

22. Dobard et al. (2017); James Prieger and Kelly Faltis, "Non-Electoral Civic Engagement in California: Why Does the State Lag the Nation?" *California Journal of Politics and Policy*, 5,4 (2013), 671–710. (Note that the data were collected in 2009.)

23. Dobard et al. (2017).

24. Ibid.

25. John Myers, "California's 2014 Voter Turnout Was Even Worse Than You Thought," *KQED News* (February 11, 2015), http://ww2.kqed.org/news/2015/02/11/california-2014-voter-turnout-was-even-worse-than-you-thought. Note that the figure is 8.2 percent of all Californians, regardless of eligibility.

26. California Civic Engagement Project, "California's Youth Vote: June 2016 Primary Election," University of California Davis (October 2016); and California Secretary of State, "Historical Voter Registration and Participation in General Elections 1910–2016," Statement of Vote (November 8, 2016), http://elections.cdn.sos.ca.gov/sov/2016-general/sov/04-historical-voter-reg-participation.pdf.

27. Richard Fry, "Millennials and Gen Xers Outvoted Boomers and Older Generations in 2016 Election," Pew Research Center (July 31, 2017), http://www.pewresearch.org/fact-tank/2017/07/31/millennials-and-gen-xers-outvoted-boomers-and-older-generations-in-2016-election.

28. Richard Fry, "Millennials and Gen X voters edged out older generations in 2016 vote," Pew Research Center (July 31, 2017).

29. The number of undocumented immigrants is estimated to be between 2.35 and 2.6 million in California. See Joseph Hayes and Laura Hill, "Undocumented Immigrants in California" (San Francisco: Public Policy Institute of California, March 2017), http://www.ppic.org/content/pubs/jtf/JTF_UndocumentedImmigrantsJTF.pdf. Legal permanent resident statistics (2014 estimates) found in James Lee and Bryan Baker, "Estimates of the Lawful Permanent Resident Population of the United States: January 2014," U.S. Department of Homeland Security, updated June 2017, https://www.dhs.gov/sites/default/files/publications/LPR%20Population%20Estimates%20January%202014.pdf; and California Department of Corrections, Office of Research, "Weekly Report of Population as of August 2, 2017," http://www.cdcr.ca.gov/Reports_Research/Offender_Information_Services_Branch/WeeklyWed/TPOP1A/TPOP1Ad170802.pdf; the exact number was 182,865.

30. Mark Baldassare, "California's Exclusive Electorate," Public Policy Institute of California (March 2016), and Mark Baldassare, "Improving California's Democracy," PPIC (October 2012).

31. Ibid., (2016). See also: Mark Baldassare, Dean Bonner, Sonja Petek, and Jui Shrestha, "California's Likely Voters," PPIC (August, 2014).

32. Eric McGhee, "California's Missing Voters," PPIC (June 2017).

33. See Jan E. Leighley and Jonathan Nagler, *Who Votes Now? Demographics, Issues, Inequality, and Turnout in the United States* (Princeton and Oxford: Princeton University Press, 2014).

34. The differences reported here are between registered and nonregistered voters, but the responses of likely voters are within one or two percentage points of likely voters. Mark Baldassare, Dean Bonner, David Kordus, and Lunna Lopes, "Californians and Their Government," PPIC (May 2017), http://www.ppic.org/publication/ppic-statewide-survey-californians-and-their-government-may-2017. Respondents included 1,707 California residents, including 1,107 interviewed on cell phones, and 600 on land lines, May 12–22, 2017, and results had a sampling error of +/–3.2 percent for the unweighted sample.

35. Ibid.

36. The Planning Report, "California Legislature's 2016 Session Accomplishments Assessed by State Senator Hertzberg" (September 2016), http://www.planningreport.com/2016/09/22/california-legislature-s-2016-session-accomplishments-assessed-state-senator-hertzberg.

37. John Myers, "Political Road Map: There are more than 15 lobbyists for each lawmaker in Sacramento," *Los Angeles Times* (December 4, 2016).

38. Patrick McGreevy, "Spending on lobbying in California tops $309 million, the second-highest amount ever recorded in the state," *Los Angeles Times* (February 1, 2017).

Chapter 11

1. Carey McWilliams, *California, the Great Exception* (Berkeley and Los Angeles: University of California Press, 1949; 1997).

2. Matthew A. Winkler, "California Leads U.S. Economy, Away from Trump," *Bloomberg* (May 10, 2017), https://www.bloomberg.com/view/articles/2017-05-10/california-leads-u-s-economy-away-from-trump, and Mike McPhate, "California Today: How California Helps the U.S. Economy," *New York Times* (June 5, 2017), https://www.nytimes.com/2017/06/05/us/california-today-how-california-helps-the-us-economy.html.

3. Jens Manuel Krogstad, "Unauthorized Immigrants Covered by DACA Face Uncertain Future," Pew Research Center (January 5, 2017), http://www.pewresearch.org/fact-tank/2017/01/05/unauthorized-immigrants-covered-by-daca-face-uncertain-future.

4. Mark Baldassare, Dean Bonner, David Kordus, and Lunna Lopes, "Californians and Their Government," *PPIC* (May, 2015). A total of 1,706 adults were surveyed; sampling error was +/–3.6 percent.

5. For a study of these tendencies among Californians, see Kevin Wallsten and Gene Park, "Confidence, Perception, and Politics in California: The Determinants of Attitudes toward Taxes by Level of Government," *California Journal of Politics and Policy* 7, no. 2 (2015).

6. California Department of Finance, Demographic Research Unit, "Report P-1: State and County Population Projections by Race/Ethnicity, July 1, 2010–60 (by Decade)" (December 15, 2014), http://www.dof.ca.gov/research/demographic/reports/projections.

7. Ibid.

8. Ellen Hanak, "Paying for Infrastructure: California's Choices" (San Francisco: Public Policy Institute of California, January 2009), 1, http://www.ppic.org/content/pubs/atissue/AI_109EHAI.pdf.

9. This ranking can be calculated using a variety of costs. California ranks 42nd as a ratio of public money spent to personal income. This ranking reflects the U.S. Census Bureau's formula; state rankings found in Table 11 of Educational Finance Branch, "Public Education Finances: 2013," GS13-ASPEF (June 2015), http://www2.census.gov/govs/school/13f33pub.pdf.

10.   Kristin Lewis and Sarah Burd-Sharps, "A Portrait of California, 2014-2015," California Human Development Report, Measure of America (December 9, 2014), http://www.measureofamerica.org/california2014-15.

11.   Mark Baldassare, Dean Bonner, David Kordus, and Lunna Lopes, "Californians and their Government," *PPIC* (May 2016 and May 2015).

12.   "The ShakeOut Scenario," California Geological Survey (CGS) Preliminary Report 25; U.S. Geological Survey Open File Report 2008-1150 Version 1, 2008, page 11, http://pubs.usgs.gov/of/2008/1150; "HAZUS Scenario and Annualized Earthquake Loss Estimation for California," CGS Special Report 222, 2011, page 36, ftp://ftp.consrv.ca.gov/pub/dmg/rgmp/2011%20Annualized%20Losses/CGS_SR222_%20Losses_Final.pdf.

13.   Mark Baldassare, Dean Bonner, Lunna Lopes, and David Kordus, "Californians and the Environment," *PPIC* (July 2017), http://www.ppic.org/publication/ppic-statewide-survey-californians-and-the-environment-july-2017; 1,708 adult Californians were interviewed; sampling error was +/−3.4 percent.

14.   Lewis and Burd-Sharps, 7.

15.   Forbes, "Best States for Business: California," Forbes.com (November 2016), https://www.forbes.com/places/ca.

16.   California Association of Realtors, "CA Median Price Continues to Grow Year to Year," California Association of Realtors, (August 2017) http://www.car.org/marketdata/data/countysalesactivity. The LAO estimated that the average (mean) price of a home was $440,000 in 2015: LAO, "California's High Housing Costs" (March 17, 2015), http://www.lao.ca.gov/reports/2015/finance/housing-costs/housing-costs.aspx.

17.   Dan Kammen noted recently that "California is not a nation, but it's behaving as one" in an article on climate change: Rachel Uranga, "California Governor's Green Swing through China," *Long Beach Press Telegram* (June 10, 2017).

18.   The Planning Report, "California Legislature's 2016 Session Accomplishments Assessed by State Senator Hertzberg" (September 2016), http://www.planningreport.com/2016/09/22/california-legislature-s-2016-session-accomplishments-assessed-state-senator-hertzberg.

Index

variable conditions of, 128–129
See also Debt; Tax(es)
Budget Stabilization Account, 22, 183 (note) 12,
    184 (note) 13
See also Rainy Day Fund
Bureau of Indian Affairs, 110
Bush, George W., 108 (box), 141
Business, challenges concerning, 169

Cabinet secretary, 76
Cabrillo, Juan, 9
CalFresh, 169
Cal Grants, 19
California Army National Guard, 69
California Association of Realtors, 159
California Chamber of Commerce, 159, 162 (box)
California Coastal Commission, 58
California Correctional Peace Officers Association
    (CCPOA), 159
California Environmental Quality Act (CEQA), 52
"California Rule" (for pensions), 102
California State Employees Association,
    180 (note) 4
California State University system, 90, 120,
    122 (figure), 180 (note) 10
California Teachers Association (CTA),
    161 (box)
California WaterFix, 2–3, 170
    See also Twin Tunnels project
CalPERS (California Public Employees' Retirement
    System), 122
CalTrans, 170
CalWorks, 169
Campaign finance, 71, 142, 143
Campaigns
    contributors to, 143–144, 146 (table)
    description of, 142–144
Cantil-Sakauye, Tani, 79, 81, 82
Cap-and-trade system, 21, 51, 76, 107 (box)–108 (box),
    165, 168, 169
    See also AB 32, Global Warming Solutions Act,
    SB 32
Carillo, Wendy, 143
Casinos, 34, 108–111
Caucus, 51
Charter city, 97
Charter county, 96
Charter schools, 103

Chiang, John, 66, 118
Chief of security (governor), 69–70
China, 3 (figure), 70
Chinese immigrants, 11, 15
Choices
    implicit and explicit, 4
    importance of, 4, 6
    rules and, 6–7
Cities
    charter, 97
    contract, 97
    employee salary ranges, 99
    fast facts, 95 (box)
    initiatives (local ballot measures), 37, 39
    municipal governments, 97–99
    property taxes for financing of operations in,
        99–100
    public services offered by, 97
    revenues and expenses of, 99–102, 101 (figure)
Citizen legislature, 44
Citizens Redistricting Commission, 137, 166
    See also Proposition 11, Redistricting, Voters
    FIRST Act
Citizens United v. Federal Election Commission, 144
City council, 97
City manager, 98–99
Civil lawsuits, 80–81
Civil service exams, 15
Clemency, 69
Climate change, 22, 51, 63, 70, 107 (box)–108 (box),
    135, 168, 169
Clinton, Hillary, 7, 141
Closed primary, 139
Collaborative courts, 81
Collective action, 6
Colorado
    driver's licenses for undocumented immigrants, 19
    gun control in, 36
    number of initiatives in, 26, 176 (note) 6
Commander in chief, 69
Commission on Judicial Nominees, 84
Commission on Judicial Performance, 84
Commissions, advisory, 179 (note) 4
Committees (in the legislature)
    Assembly, 50–51
    Budget (legislative), 56, 114
    Rules (in Senate), 59
    Senate, 50–51

Director of finance, 69
Direct primary, 12
Discretionary funds, 114
Disenfranchised Californians, 153, 169
District attorney, 80
Districts. *See* Political districts
Districts/wards, 98
Diversity, 18–20
    of justices and judges, 83–84, 85 (table)
    See also Race/ethnicity
DREAM Act, 19
Dreamers, 7
Driver's licenses for undocumented immigrants, 19
Drought, 2, 170

Earthquakes, 168–169
East-west divide, 131–133, 132 (map)
Education
    boards of education, 103
    budget for, 18, 103, 120
    budgeting for, 56, 120
    challenges, 167–168
    charter schools, 103
    governor's oversight of, 65
    K-12, 100, 183 (note) 6
    superintendent of public instruction,
        72–73
    Trump and, 161 (box)
    tuition, 122 (figure)
    unions, 161 (box)
El Camino Real, 9
Election(s)
    all-mail ballot elections, 156
    general, 139
    nonpartisan, 84, 96, 98, 133, 139–140
    open-seat, 49 (box), 142–143
    primary (*see* Primary elections)
    recall, 20–21, 36, 37, 67
    reforms affecting, 139–141
    same-party races, 21, 175 (note) 17
    special, 34, 36, 39, 68, 140, 141, 156
    voter turnout, 21, 29, 37, 140, 155–156, 158
    voting technology for, 141
    See also Political parties; Term limits; Voters;
        Voting
Electoral laws, 12, 15
Elite Enclave Californians, 152
E-mail, 56, 154

Eminent domain, 102
"End Poverty in California" (EPIC) campaign, 16
Energy policy, 165
English, as official language, 19
Environment, 22, 51, 52
    challenges, 168–169
    energy policy, 165
    greenhouse gas emissions, 107 (box)–108 (box),
        168, 169
    See also Water resources
Environmental Protection Agency (EPA), 71, 76,
    108 (box)
Equal rights policy, 165–166
Ethnic makeup, 5 (box)
Exclusive electorate, 156
Executive branch
    administrators, 76
    organization chart of, 74 (figure)–75 (figure)
    oversight, 57–58
    plural executive, 64–67
    regulators, 76
Executive officers
    attorney general, 66, 71
    board of equalization, 66, 72
    controller, 71–72
    governor (*see* Governor)
    insurance commissioner, 66, 72
    lieutenant governor, 59, 66, 70–71
    musical chairs and, 66
    salary of, 65 (box)
    secretary of state, 66, 71
    superintendent of public instruction, 66,
        72–73
    term limits, 64, 66
    treasurer, 66, 72
Executive orders, 68, 73
Expenditures
    City, 96, 101–102
    County, 96, 98
    State, 118–123, 121 (figure)
Executive power, 67, 73
Extradition, 70

Facebook, 56, 154
Fair Political Practices Commission (FPPC), 144
Fast facts, comparative, on California, 5 (box)
Federal grants, 96, 105, 115, 116
Federalism, 105–106

Self-governance, 11, 17, 149
Senate
    committees of, 50–51
    demographics, 46
    description of, 43–44
    electoral changes and, 48 (box)–49 (box)
    fast facts, 44 (box)
    institutional changes and, 49 (box)
    president pro tem of, 59
    recall elections and, 36
    term limits and, 44, 48 (box), 53
Senate Rules Committee, 59
Separation of powers, 174 (note) 13
Servicing the debt, 35
Shrimpscam, 17
Signatures
    collection costs, 177 (note) 14
    for initiatives, 28, 29, 37, 39
    invalidation, 26, 29, 177 (note) 13
    for recall elections, 36
    registered voter requirement for, 29
Sinclair, Upton, 16
Sin (excise) taxes, 127, 127 (table)
Small claims cases, 80
Social capital, 51
Social networking, 149
Socioeconomic issues, 167, 169
Southern Pacific Railroad, 11–12
Speaker of the Assembly, 59, 60
Special districts, 102–103
Special elections, 34, 36, 39, 68, 140, 141, 156
Special Fund for Economic Uncertainty,
    184 (note) 13
Special interest, 159
Special interest groups
    budget process and, 124
    description of, 158–159
    initiative participation by, 15, 34, 161 (box)
    political power of, 15, 84, 159–160
    political weight of, 159
Stakeholders, 51, 124
Stanford, Leland, 11
State Board of Education, 65
State central committee, 138
State constitution, 11, 26, 27–28, 38 (box)
State Criminal Alien Assistance Program (SCAAP),
    106, 183 (note) 13
State of the judiciary address, 82

State Military Reserve, 69
State of the state address, 67
State Water Project (SWP), 16
Statutes, 50
Steinbeck, John, 15–16
Strong mayor government, 98
Structural budget deficits, 126
Struggling Californians, 153, 169
Subsidence, 2, 170
Substantive representation, 47
Superagency, 76
Superintendent of public instruction, 66,
    72–73
Superior court, 80–81, 84
    See also Trial court(s)
Supermajority status (of Democrats the legislature),
    17, 124
Supreme court
    description of, 81–82, 83 (figure)
    initiatives and, 82
    justices of, 81–82, 83–84, 85 (table)
    state of the judiciary address, 82
    See also Court(s)

Tax(es)
    corporate income, 118, 126, 127 (table)
    excise, 127 (table)
    gasoline, 7, 59, 121, 126, 127 (table), 128, 166,
        172, 184 (note) 19
    for local governments, 127 (table)
    parcel, 37, 100, 102–103, 127
    personal income, 116, 126–127 (table)
    progressive, 116
    property, 2, 17, 37, 99–100, 127 (table)
    requirements for raising, 6, 17, 26, 27, 54–55, 102,
        124, 166
    retail sales and use, 23, 116–117, 126,
        127 (table)
    upper income taxpayers, 166–167
Tax rate, 126–127
Technology, voting, 71, 141, 156
Television advertising, 31, 144
Term limits
    city council members, 98
    consequences of, 124, 140, 166, 179 (note) 3
    for county supervisors, 96
    description of, 45
    for executives, 64, 65 (box), 66 (figure)

Wall of debt, 119, 119 (table)
Warren, Earl, 16
Water resources, policy
  bond-funded projects, 35
  challenges, 170
  climate change's effect on, 168
  desalination plants, 104
  drought, 2, 170
  Oroville Dam spillway failure, 166,
      173 (note) 7
  Twin Tunnels project, 2–3, 170
  wetlands, 16, 170
  water wars, 16
Weber, Shirley, 57, 115
White flight, 19–20

Whites
  as Disenfranchised Californians, 153
  as Elite Enclave Californians, 152
  income inequality and, 157 (figure)
  as One-Percent Californians, 152
  percentage of schoolchildren, 167
  political participation by, 156
  as Struggling Californians, 153
Whitman, Meg, 144
Wholesale campaigning, 144
Women. *See* Gender

Xi Jinping, 70

Yee, Betty, 66